I0037547

Corporate Finance Terms

Financial Education Is Your Best Investment

Published February 07, 2020

Revision 2.2

Financial Terms Dictionary

Copyright And Trademark Notices

Limits of Liability and Disclaimer of Warranties

The materials in this book are provided "as is" and without warranties of any kind either express or implied. The Author disclaims all warranties, express or implied, including, but not limited to, implied warranties of merchantability and fitness for a particular purpose.

The Author does not warrant that defects will be corrected, or that that the site or the server that makes this eBook available are free of viruses or other harmful components. The Author does not warrant or make any representations regarding the use or the results of the use of the materials in this book in terms of their correctness, accuracy, reliability, or otherwise. Applicable law may not allow the exclusion of implied warranties, so the above exclusion may not apply to you.

Under no circumstances, including, but not limited to, negligence, shall the Author be liable for any special or consequential damages that result from the use of, or the inability to use this eBook, even if the Author or his authorized representative has been advised of the possibility of such damages.

Applicable law may not allow the limitation or exclusion of liability or incidental or consequential damages, so the above limitation or exclusion may not apply to you. In no event shall the Author's total liability to you for all damages, losses, and causes of action (whether in contract, tort, including but not limited to, negligence or otherwise) exceed the amount paid by you, if any, for this eBook.

Facts and information are believed to be accurate at the time they were placed in this book. All data provided in this book is to be used for information purposes only. The information contained within is not intended to provide specific legal, financial or tax advice, or any other advice whatsoever, for any individual or company and should not be relied upon in that regard. The services described are only offered in jurisdictions where they may be legally offered. Information provided is not all-inclusive and is limited to information that is made available and such information should not be relied upon as all-inclusive or accurate.

You are advised to do your own due diligence when it comes to making business decisions and should use caution and seek the advice of qualified professionals. You should check with your accountant, lawyer, or professional advisor, before acting on this or any information. You may not consider any examples, documents, or other content in this eBook or otherwise provided by the Author to be the equivalent of professional advice.

The Author assumes no responsibility for any losses or damages resulting from your use of any link, information, or opportunity contained in this book or within any other information disclosed by the author in any form whatsoever.

About the Author

Thomas Herold is a successful entrepreneur, mediator, author, and personal development coach. He published over 35 books with over 200,000 copies distributed worldwide and the founder of seven online businesses.

For over ten years Thomas Herold has studied the monetary system and has experienced some profound insights on how money and wealth are related. After three years of successful investing in silver, he released 'Building Wealth with Silver - How to Profit From The Biggest Wealth Transfer in History' in 2012. One of the first books that illustrate in a remarkable, simple way the monetary system and its consequences.

He is the founder and CEO of the 'Financial Terms Dictionary' book series and website, which explains in detail and comprehensive form over 1000 financial terms. In his financial book series, he informs in detail and with practical examples all aspects of the financial sector. His educational materials are designed to help people get started with financial education.

In his 2018 released book 'The Money Deception', Mr. Herold provides the most sophisticated insight and shocking details about the current monetary system. Never before has the massive manipulation of money caused so much economic inequality in the world. In spite of these frightening facts, 'The Money Deception' also provides remarkable and simple solutions to create abundance for all people, and it's a must-read if you want to survive the global monetary transformation that's underway right now.

In 2019 he released an entirely new financial book series explaining in detail and with practical examples over 1000 financial terms. The 'Herold Financial IQ Series' contains currently of 16 titles covering every category of the financial market.

His latest book "High Credit Score Secrets" offers the most effective strategies to boost the average credit score from as low as 450 points to over 810. It teaches the tactics to build excellent credit, repair credit, monitor credit and how to guard that good score for a lifetime. It reached bestseller status in 2020 in three categories.

For more information please visit the author's websites:

High Credit Score Secrets - The Smart Raise & Repair Guide to Excellent Credit
https://highcreditscoresecrets.com

The Money Deception - What Banks & Government Don't Want You to Know
https://www.moneydeception.com

The Herold Financial IQ Series - Financial Education Is Your Best Investment
https://www.financial-dictionary.com

The Online Financial Dictionary - Over 1000 Terms Explained
https://www.financial-dictionary.info

Please Leave Your Review on Amazon

This book and the Financial IQ Series are self-published and the author does not have a contract with one of the five largest publishers, which are able to support the author's work with advertising. If you like this book, please consider leaving a solid 4 or 5-star review on Amazon.

Herold Financial IQ Series on Amazon

Table Of Contents

AAA Rating

AAA Rating refers to the maximum potential credit rating that a credit ratings bureau can award to an issuing entity's bonds. Such a credit rating represents a superb level of creditworthiness. It means that the issuing entity is easily capable of meeting its various financial obligations. The three major ratings agencies of Moody's, Standard & Poor's, and Fitch Ratings all utilize the AAA as their top credit rating which designates those bonds and issuers which have the highest possible level of credit quality.

It is not possible to completely eliminate the potential risk of a credit default from a bond issuer. Yet those entities which possess AAA rated bonds are believed to have the least possible chance of defaulting on their interest payments or principal repayments. Because of this, such bonds provide their investors with the smallest possible yields of any bonds that possess the same dates of maturity.

Thanks to the Global Financial Crisis of 2008, many companies and countries lost their coveted AAA rating. In fact, by the middle of 2009, there were only four remaining firms out of the entire list of S&P 500 companies that still held their treasured AAA rated credit. The story was the same with the gold standard credit rated nations of the world as well.

Before the Great Recession, a number of nations enjoyed the highly coveted AAA credit rating from all three of the big three ratings agencies. Once the dust had settled, only the following nine nations still held it including Australia, Canada, Denmark, Germany, Luxembourg, Norway, Singapore, Sweden, and Switzerland. Countries that had lost it included Austria, Finland, France, the United Kingdom, and the United States. The U.S. still had the AAA rated credit from Moody's and Fitch, while the United Kingdom still held it from Standard & Poor's (who even removed it from negative watch).

High credit ratings like the AAA rating provide significant benefits to a company or nation which carries them. It allows the issuer to borrow at a reduced interest rate and ultimate cost. These companies and countries are also able to borrow greater amounts of money when they possess the highest ratings. Lower costs of borrowing allow for nations and corporations to access opportunities through cheap and easy credit. A company might be able to buy out a competitor as it is able to cheaply borrow the money for the transaction costs of the relevant merger and acquisition.

Where companies are concerned, it is possible for them to enjoy the highest AAA rating on bonds which they issue as secured while having a lower credit rating on those which are unsecured. This is simply because secured bonds provide a particular asset that has been put up as collateral in case the issuer defaults on the interest or principal payments of the bond in question. The creditor has the right to seize the asset if the issuer ends up defaulting. Such bonds could carry the collateral of real estate, machinery, or other forms of equipment. Conversely, unsecured bonds only carry the backing of the issuer's capability of repaying the obligation. This is why the credit ratings for unsecured forms of bonds only rely on the income source of the issuer in question.

Since the Global Financial Crisis destroyed the highest creditworthiness of many a long-standing AAA rated nation, neither the world's largest debtor nor creditor nations possess the all-important AAA rating. For example, S&P argues that it will only deliver the AAA rating in the cases where an "extremely strong capacity to meet financial commitments" exists.

The euro zone was long a shining example of many nations which possessed unanimous AAA rated credit. After the Great Recession and Sovereign Debt Crisis ravaged Europe, only the two nations of Luxembourg and Germany still retain this three ratings agency unanimous AAA status.

Acquisition

An acquisition refers to a corporate act where it purchases either controlling interest or complete interest in another company. Companies do this by buying out the stock shares in order to gain control of it. Technically, acquisitions happen as the buyer is able to acquire an over 50 percent ownership stake in the target firm. Typically the acquirer will buy all or many of the shares of the target's outstanding stock as well as assets. This allows them to make all decisions on the assets of the company they have taken over without needing any shareholder approval to proceed.

The buyer has several choices for how to pay for the acquisition. They can do it all in cash through buying out the target's shares, buy the company outright for cash, or use a combination of the two methods. The financial news is full of the mega merger and acquisition deals. As an example, Dow Chemical bought out DuPont in a $130 billion mega purchase back in 2015. Yet countless more medium sized to smaller businesses engage in merger and acquisition activity each and every year.

There are a number of reasons for why corporations engage in such acquisitions. It might be that they want to merge their enterprise with another for better economies of scale. This means that the costs of doing business, producing goods, and getting them to market decreases as a company becomes larger and does more volume in sales. They may desire to command a larger market share. It could be they foresee cost reductions and better synergy. Sometimes the acquirer wants a product, service, technology, research, or technical know-how that a target owns.

There are grander ambitions for acquisitions as well. Some domestic companies may want to grow their business into an international and eventually multinational corporate empire. Many times the only economically practical way (and the least expensive and simplest as well) to break into a foreign market is by simply buying out a company that is already operating successfully there.

This would be for the simple reasons that the target firm has a recognized brand name in the country, its own management and staff there, permission and licensing to operate there, and various intangible as well as physical assets in the country already. Besides this, the buyer will gain the solid customer base that the target has already established in the market.

Many times acquisitions will happen as a natural outgrowth of a firm's master strategy to increase its footprint in the business. The advantages to simply taking over already up and running operations versus starting new ones from scratch are considerable. Bigger corporations finally reach the stage where continuing to grow organically will cause them to decrease in operating efficiency. This can happen through too much bureaucracy as well as because of logistical or resource limitations. In such cases, the only viable means of gaining better growth and greater profits is through seizing hold of an aggressive young firm that it can simply fold into its own existing operations and revenue streams.

Another good reason for making acquisitions is because sometimes the competition in an industry becomes overcrowded. This can lead to overproduction of the goods in the company's line of business. Firms can utilize takeovers as a means of soaking up the overabundance of capacity through eliminating some competitors. It allows them to concentrate their operations on the greatest productivity providers as well.

A last good motivation for pursuing such acquisitions surrounds technology and know-how. Sometimes a new bit of technology becomes developed by a competitor. It may boost productivity yet cost a great amount of time and resources to develop internally. The most cost effective way of acquiring this technology is often in buying out the firm which already possesses or developed said technology. This saves the buyer the time, cost, and hassle of doing the research and development on their own.

Angel Investor

An Angel Investor refers to an accredited investor (with over a million dollars net worth) which invests funds into entrepreneurs and smaller startups. These special investors are commonly from the friends or family of the entrepreneur. This capital which they deliver is often in the form of a lump sum one-time payment to help get the business going or to keep it funded during the challenging early stages where they are still developing and beginning to market their products.

Another characteristic of such an Angel Investor is that they offer better terms to the startup than would a comparable bank or lender in the same scenario. This is principally because they believe in the entrepreneur they are backing more than the viability of the business itself. Such investors concentrate their efforts on assisting startups with successfully making their initial business steps. They are less concerned with the potential for profit they might make off of the fledgling company. This makes most Angel Investors the diametric opposite of the venture capitalists.

There are a variety of different names which such Angel Investors go by. These include angel funders, informal investors, private investors, business angels, and seed investors. Such wealthy individuals who choose to inject desperately needed startup capital into firms do so in exchange for either convertible debt or a stake in the company's equity. There are such investors who become involved through one of the various crowd funding platforms over the Internet, and others who join with networks of other Angel Investors in order to pool their resources to be more effective (as with an Angel Investor syndicate). Angel List is a popular and well respected site that puts together angels and entrepreneurs.

Using this phrase to describe noble investors originally came from Broadway Theater. It was here that wealthy patrons would contribute money in order to advance theatrical productions. This terminology Angel Investor was first utilized by William Wetzel of the University of New Hampshire. As founder of the Center for Venture Research, he backed an extensive study on the ways that entrepreneurs are able to bring in capital.

In order to be official Angel Investors, these individuals have to meet the definition set by the SEC Securities Exchange Commission for accredited investors. This means that the interested party must possess at least a million in net worth along with an annual income amounting to at least $200,000.

Most Angel Investors will actually deploy their own funds in their investments. This puts them in direct contrast with the venture capitalists which instead gather up a pool of money from many investors and then combine this into a fund which is strategically managed. In general the Angel Investors represent actual individuals. It is also possible for the entity offering the funding to be a limited liability company, trust, business or even an investment fund.

Those Angel Investors who actually seed the entrepreneurs' startups which ultimately fail will lose their entire investment. It helps to explain why angel investors who are professionals will always be on the hunt for a clearly defined exit strategy opportunity. This might be through an IPO Initial Public Offering or an acquisition.

In truth, successful angel investors boast of portfolios with an average success rate of from 20 percent to 30 percent. This may sound costly for entrepreneurs who are involved in early stage business startups. Finding alternative cheaper sources of financing like banks are not often viable options for these fledging companies. It means that angels are often the ideal funder or backer for those entrepreneurs who find themselves still in the financially struggling days of the early startup stages in their company.

Asset Backed Security (ABS)

An Asset Backed Security is also known by its acronym ABS. This refers to a type of financial security. These are commonly backed up using either a lease, a loan, or receivables against company assets (which would not include either mortgage backed securities or real estate). With the world of investing, such ABS provide other choices for those who wish to invest in something other than common corporate debt issues.

It is interesting to note that these Asset Backed Securities are more or less identical to MBS Mortgage Backed Securities. The primary difference lies in the securities which back the two financial instruments. With the ABS, they can include credit card debt, leases, loans, royalties, and even the receivables of the company issuing the debt. Yet these mortgage based securities may never underlie the ABS.

Such an Asset Backed Security delivers to the issuer of the security a means of creating more cash for the business. It allows yield hungry investors the chance to sink their money into a great range of assets which generate income. It is worth noting that most of these underlying assets will not be liquid. This means that they can not be readily sold as stand alone assets. Yet in pooling such assets into a single conglomeration, a financial security may be created. This is done in the process referred to as securitization. This permits the asset owner to employ them in a marketable fashion.

Among the assets of such pools could be car loans, home equity loans, student loans, credit card receivables, or other anticipated cash flow items. The capacity of Asset Backed Security issuers to be creative should never be underestimated. There have even been ABS which were established utilizing the cash flow generated by movie release revenues, aircraft leases, creative works and other forms of royalty payments, and even solar energy photovoltaic revenue streams. Practically any scenario where cash is produced can be packaged up via securitization into an ABS.

It is often helpful to consider an example of this somewhat complicated Asset Backed Security topic. Consider the case of a fictitious firm Car Loans For Everybody. When individuals wish to borrow funds to purchase a car, Car Loans For Everybody will issue them the cash in a check. The individual will have to pay back the loan along with a specified interest amount at a certain time in monthly installments. It could be that Car Loans is so successful at making automobile loans that they deplete their cash reserves and can no longer issue additional loans. They have the ability to sell off their present book of loans to the fictitious investment firm Imperial Legends. Imperial Legends will then provide them with the cash they need to continue issuing new loans.

This is only where the securitization process begins. Imperial Legends investment firm would then arrange the bought out loans into a collection of parcels known in the business as tranches. A tranche effectively is a batch of loans that posses similar features. This would include interest rates, maturity dates, and anticipated rates of delinquency. After this, the Imperial Legends firm would offer new securities with features much like bonds in every tranche they created.

Finally, investors will buy such securities. They obtain the underlying cash flow out of the pool of car loans, less the administration fee, which Imperial Legends will keep to cover their costs and towards their profit.

There are three typical types of tranches in an Asset Backed Security. These are commonly referred to as Class A, Class B, and Class C. Senior most tranches belong to Class A. They are generally the biggest tranche. They will be structured in such a way as to obtain a decent investment rating so that they are easily marketable to investors.

With the Class B tranche, the credit quality will necessarily be lower. This inversely means that the yield will be higher than that of the senior tranche. Since the risk is greater, investors need to be compensated for their appropriate risk of defaults.

Class C tranche has the lowest credit rating of all. It could be the credit quality is so poor that investors will refuse to consider it altogether. In such cases, the ABS issuer then holds the Class C tranche, collects the incoming revenues every month, and absorbs any losses themselves.

Audit

An audit refers to a third party evaluation and review of a business or individual's financial statements. The goal is to ensure that the financial records are both accurate and reflective of the transactions for the entity they represent. Such a review can be carried out by an external auditing firm or by accounting employees within an organization itself.

There is also the possibility for the Internal Revenue Service itself to conduct audits in order to confirm the veracity of a business or individual's tax payer returns and transactions. As the IRS engages in such audits, this usually creates a dark cloud over the victim organization or individual. This is because such IRS audits come with a negative connotation. It is as if the government suspects the taxpayers in question have engaged in illegal activities with their taxes or income declarations.

For those audits which an external company performs on behalf of corporations, these are often very useful in taking away the tendency towards personal bias. It means that the final picture of the corporation should be more complete, unbiased, and accurate. Such audits are often seeking any inadvertent material error in the corporations' statements or activities. They reassure shareholders of the company that the financial statements are accurate. As third parties undertake audits, the bias of the internal accountant who would otherwise be engaging in the auditing tasks is eliminated.

This could be regarding a company subsidiary or division, the entire corporation or one system within it, or the financial books of the business. There is also no pressure that a member of management will think negatively of the employee for producing less than stellar outcomes from the audit when the corporation engages and retains an external accounting firm.

The majority of publicly traded firms become audited one time each year. Enormous corporations can be audited even every month. There are companies in industries where their oversight organization requires legally that the firm receive routine audits so as to eliminate any temptation to deliberately misrepresent financial information. Such misrepresentation is literally called fraud. Still other large corporations look at audits and auditors as a valuable tool to ascertain how effective their financial reports and associated internal controls of them actually are.

Two different types of auditors exist in the realm of external audits. These are statutory auditors and external cost auditors. The statutory varieties independently labor to consider the quality of the financial statements and reports. The external cost auditors consider and review the cost sheets and statements to make certain they do not contain any errors, misrepresentations, or fraudulent facts or figures. Each of the two different kinds of auditing personnel work with a range of varying standards that are different than those which the corporation hiring them would engage in otherwise.

Such internal auditors will be hired by the firm or other organization on whose behalf they are engaging in the audit in the first place. They do their fiduciary best to deliver reliable and accurate information and certification to the management of the company, the board of directors, and shareholders regarding the books and all internal operating systems and procedures of the company in question.

Other auditors will be consultants. They will still utilize the standards of the corporation which they are auditing instead of an independent set of standards, even though they are not internal employees of the organization. Such consultants are brought in when the corporation or other organization lacks the necessary resources to perform their own internal operational audits.

Auditors must meet certain specified standards which their jurisdictional governments lay out when they conduct these audits. The American Institute of Certified Public Accountants has its respected external audit standards which they call the GAAS Generally Accepted Auditing Standards. Internationally, the International Auditing and Assurance Board maintain their International Standards on Auditing. The U.S. also has a regulatory body dating back to 2002 called the PCAOB, or Public Company Accounting Oversight Board.

Balance Sheet

Balance Sheet refers to a corporate financial statement. The purpose of it is to thoroughly summarize the liabilities, assets, and shareholders' equity in the firm at a fixed moment in time. The statement provides a revealing glimpse into the things the corporation owns and the money it owes, along with the total amount which shareholders have invested in the going concern. Where these financial statements are concerned, the formula for assets is liabilities plus shareholders' equity.

Balance sheets ultimately derive their names from the equation which pits the assets on one side while the shareholders' equity and liabilities remain on the opposite site. They have to balance out, which provides the concept behind the name. It makes perfect sense that corporations have only two choices when paying for their assets. They might either borrow the money through assuming liabilities or obtain it off of investors, which happens when they issue shareholder equity.

Consider an example to better understand what is involved with this concept. If a corporation obtains a $40,000 bank loan to be repaid in five years, then its assets (cash account section) will rise by the $40,000. At the same time, the total liabilities (long term debt section) will also rise by the $40,000 amount. This restores balance to the equation. Should the firm then receive $80,000 from investors, the assets will also increase by that same amount. On the other side of the equation, the shareholder equity rises by the same $80,000. When the company earns revenues which are greater than the liabilities, these go into the so called shareholder equity account. It is that category that stands for all net assets the owners of the corporation hold. The offsetting revenues balance out on the assets side in the form of inventory, investments, or cash categories.

The three main categories of the balance sheet equation--- assets, liabilities, and shareholder equity each break down further into a few of their own sub accounts. These sub accounts actually reveal the particulars of the corporate finances. Every industry will have its own range of sub accounts. Many of the sub account terms will mean different things from one type of business to another. In general, there are always several sub account categories that different industries have in common.

As an example, under the assets category, such sub accounts are broken out from top down to bottom according to which is most liquid. This simply means the ease of selling them for cash. The divisions for all sub accounts will be by current assets and long term assets. The current ones may be changed to cash in under a year. Longer term ones obviously may not be converted so quickly. Current assets generally list top to bottom according to the following precedence: cash or cash equivalents, marketable securities, accounts receivable, inventory, and prepaid expenses. Longer term assets have the following general top down order: long term investments, fixed assets, and intangible assets such as goodwill, trademarks, and intellectual property.

Under the liabilities category will be the total amount firms owe to other entities. These include building rent, salaries, utilities, supplier invoices, and interest on loans or bonds. The current liabilities will be due in under a year, while the longer term ones are due after a year. Some sub accounts for current liabilities include: currently due part of longer term debt, interest payable, bank debts, wages payable, rents/utilities/taxes, dividend payments, and customer prepayments. Under longer term liabilities there are pension fund liabilities, long term debts, and deferred tax liabilities. There can also be off-balance sheet liabilities, like operating leases.

Shareholders' equity includes money from the owners of the business, the stake holding shareholders. This includes the net assets like treasury stock, retained earnings, preferred stock, and additionally paid in capital.

Balloon Loan

A balloon loan is a kind of loan that does not divide its payments up evenly throughout the life of the loan. These kinds of loans are not fully amortized over the loan's term. As a result of this, one time balloon payments are mandatory at the end of the loan's time frame in order to pay off the loan's remaining principal balance.

Balloon loans have their advantages. They are often appealing to you if you are a short term borrower. This is because balloon loans commonly come with an interest rate that is lower than the interest rate of a longer term loan. These lower interest rates provide a benefit of extremely low interest payments. This leads to not only lower payments throughout the loan, but also incredibly low outlays of capital in the life span of the loan. Because the majority of the loan repayment is put off until the loan payment period's conclusion, a borrower gains great flexibility in using the capital that is freed up for the term of the loan.

The downsides to these balloon loans only surface when the borrower lacks discipline or falls victim to higher interest rates later on. If a borrower does not possess focused and consistent discipline in getting ready for the large last payment, then the individual may run into trouble at the end of the loan. This is because substantial payments along the way are not being collected. Besides this, if a borrower will be forced to engage in refinancing towards the end, then the borrower may suffer from a higher interest rate on the balloon payment that is rolled forward.

Some balloon loans also include a higher interest rate reset feature later in the life of the loan. This further exposes a borrower to the risk of higher interest rates. This is common with five year types of balloon mortgages. When a reset of the interest rate feature is present at the conclusion of the five year period, then the interest rate will be adjusted to the current rates. The amortization schedule will then be recalculated dependent on a final term of the loan. Balloon options that do not include these reset options, and many that do reset, generally encourage the loan holder to sell the property in advance of the conclusion of the original term of the loan. Otherwise, many borrowers will simply choose to refinance the loan before this point arrives.

The reasons that you might choose to get a balloon loan are several. A person who does not plan to hold onto a house or property for a long period of time would benefit from such a loan arrangement. This individual would plan to resell the house in advance of the loan expiration. Another reason for taking a balloon loan is in a refinancing. Finally, if a person anticipates a significant cash settlement or lump sum award, then they might take on a balloon loan. Commercial property owners often like balloon loans for the purchase of commercial properties as well.

Balloon loans are sometimes called balloon notes or bullet loans.

Blanket Loans

Blanket loans are those which cover multiple properties or parcels of land. They handle the costs for or can be secured by more than a single piece of real estate. These are most typically employed by commercial land developers or investors. For individual consumers, they can be utilized as a type of bridge between new and old properties and mortgages. For these consumers, such a blanket loan will make it possible to pay for both mortgages until the owner reaches the point of selling the old property.

The feature that makes these mortgages most useful for developers is their release clause. These permit the borrowers to sell a single or even several pieces of real estate without the need of being forced to refinance the mortgage. This makes them significantly different from traditional mortgages. Normal mortgages make borrowers completely pay down their loan balance before they can sell the property which secures them.

For developers of residential properties, they find these blanket loans particularly helpful. They employ them to pay for large tracts of land on which they will build. When it is time for the loan to fund, it becomes secured by the full piece of property. The developer is allowed to subdivide his property and sell it in individual lots. For part of the security to be released, the developer must utilize some of the sale proceeds to pay down part of the loan.

This is helpful when builders are constructing subdivisions. Such a developer could put the blanket loan to use to buy the consecutive pieces of land while they are available. The developer would then be able to subdivide the total land into specific lots for building houses. With each home that he finishes and sells, the property becomes detached from the blanket loan without the financing having to be disrupted on the remainder of the development project.

Consumers also find these types of blanket loans helpful in making it possible to transition from the sale of their current home to the building or buying of the new house. This makes much more sense than having two concurrent mortgages or obtaining a more costly short term bridge loan. It can also help them so that they do not have to sell the property early and move into a rental while they look for a property to purchase.

These kinds of blanket loans are often governed by a contingency clause. These clauses detail that the newly purchased house and its mortgage will not close until the person is able to sell the existing home. The problem with such a contingency clause is that they have limited time frames on them. They may force a borrower into selling the home in a panic in order to meet the clause expiration date. This can lead to a lower selling price or disadvantageous terms on the sale.

Blanket loans get around such a dilemma by providing the borrowers with an extended period of time in the clause to sell their old house. Sometimes they are arranged as interest payment only loans for a full 12 months before amortizing starts. This gives the seller a sufficient time period to sell the house for a good price and reduces the overall burden of the mortgage at the same time.

The main downside to blanket loans for individuals is that they are significantly harder to find since the real estate crash and Great Recession of 2009. Their advantages include both flexibility and efficiency in financing. For an individual consumer, this means a single mortgage payment rather than two. Developers do not have to worry about constantly refinancing their property debt as they sell off parts of the property. Should a developer default on his loan, the bank simply assumes control of all remaining property which secures the loan.

Bond Market

A bond market is a financial market where investors buy and sell bonds. In practice this is mostly handled electronically over computers nowadays. There are two principal types of bond markets. These are primary markets where companies are able to sell new debt and secondary markets where investors are able to purchase and resell these debt securities. Companies generally issues such debt as bonds. These markets also trade bills, notes, and commercial paper.

The goal of the bond markets is to help private companies and public entities obtain funding of a long term nature. This market has generally been the domain of the United States that dominates it. The U.S. comprises as much as 44% of this bond market on a global basis.

There are five primary bond markets according to SIFMA the Securities Industry and Financial Markets Association. These include the municipal, corporate, mortgage or asset backed, funding, and government or agency markets. The government bond market comprises a significant component of this market thanks to its massive liquidity and enormous size. Because of the stability of U.S. and some international government bonds, other bonds are often contrasted with them to help determine the amount of credit risk.

This is because government bond yields from countries with little risk like the U.S., Britain, or Germany are traditionally considered to be free of default risk. Other bonds denominated in these various currencies provide greater yields as the borrowers are more likely to default than these central governments.

Bond markets often serve a useful secondary function to reveal interest rate changes. This is because the values of bonds are inversely related to the interest rates which they pay. This helps investors to measure what the true cost of obtaining funding really is. Companies which are perceived to be riskier will have to pay higher interest rates on their bonds than companies believed to have strong and stable credit and repayment abilities. When companies or government entities are unable to make a partial or full payment on their bonds, this becomes a default.

When a company or a government needs to raise money and does not want to issue stock, it can sell bonds. These are contracts the issuers who are the borrowers make with investors who function as lenders. When investors purchase such instruments, they lend money to the issuing organization (company or government). The issuer of the bond promises to repay the original investment back along with interest in the future.

Bonds traded on these markets have many elements in common, whichever type of market they represent. All bonds have a face value. This is the amount of money which a bond would be valued at when it matures and the amount on which interest payments are based. They also have coupon rates that represent the interest rate which the issuer of the bond pays in its interest payments.

The coupon dates turn out to be the times when the issuer will pay its interest payments. Issue prices are the amounts for which the issuer sells the bond in the first place. The maturity date proves to be the exact date when the bond would be repaid. At this time, the issuer of the bond would pay the bond's face value to the bond holder.

Though a holder of a bond might keep it until maturity, this is often not the case. Many investors buy and sell them on the bond markets as their needs dictate. It is possible to sell a bond at a premium when the market value becomes greater than the original face value. Investors could also sell them at a discount to their original face value as the market price declines.

C Corporation

C Corporations refers to the primary subchapter under which American businesses decide to incorporate themselves in order to restrict the total financial and legal liabilities of the owners. Such C Corporations prove to be the principle alternatives to S Corporations, whose profits are able to pass directly through to the owners and so only become taxable on the individual level. Limited liability companies are the other main choice to the C corporations. They deliver all of the legal safeties of corporations yet become tax treated as if they were sole proprietorships.

Unfortunately for C Corporations, they do suffer the effects of double taxation. Yet they do also permit the businesses to reinvest their profits back into the firm with a lower corporate tax rate penalty. The majority of incorporated companies within the United States turn out to be C Corporations.

Organizing a corporation starts with the new owners selecting the new entity's name (and in many states registering or reserving it with the secretary of state) of the new business enterprise. The owners must draft up the articles of incorporation and file them with the appropriate state business department. The first shareholders will then be issued their stock certificates once the business is established. Every C Corporation has to first file the Form SS-4 in order to get their EIN employer identification number. Every jurisdiction has its own varying requirements for these obligations, yet the corporations generally must file income, state, payroll, disability, and unemployment taxes for their employees.

Such C Corporations must hold minimally one meeting per year for the benefit of both the directors and the shareholders. These must have meeting minutes kept in order to transparently display the ways and means in which the business functions. There will have to be voting records maintained of the company directors as well as a full list of all owners' names and their ownership percentages in the firm. The company bylaws are required to be kept on the business headquarter premises at all times. Such enterprises also have to file all necessary financial disclosure reports, annual reports, and relevant financial statements with the SEC.

There are many benefits to such C Corporations. Most importantly for owners, they first limit the liability of all shareholders, directors, officers, and employees. It is not possible for the legal and debt obligations from the company to transfer over to one or more individuals under this type of corporate structuring. Even if each of the company owners become changed out, the corporation continues its existence. There is no limit to the numbers of shareholders and owners with this kind of corporation either as there would be with an S Corporation. Yet these must be registered properly with the SEC Securities and Exchange Commission once they reach a certain number of shareholders.

The primary downside to the C corporations centers on the idea of double taxation. As the firm generates its income, it will have to file a corporate tax return with the IRS Internal Revenue Service. Once the appropriate business expenses (including salaries) have been deducted from the gross income, the rest becomes subjected to corporate income taxes. Much of the remaining net income will then be distributed out to shareholders in what is called dividends. The income to the shareholders must be reported on the recipients' tax returns. This means that the C Corporation profits are being twice taxed, once at the corporate tax rate level and a second on the individuals' tax rate level. That income which is retained earnings will avoid double taxation only. It helps to explain why mega corporations like Apple hold on to billions of dollars in retained earnings routinely.

Cap Rate

Cap rate refers to the real estate property and its rate of return. Investors figure this out by utilizing the income which they anticipate the property will generate. The cap rate is also referred to as the capitalization rate. Realtors utilize it to gauge how much return investors will realize on their investments.

The way people determine this cap rate is by using an easy to understand formula. Investors take the property's NOI net operating income and divide it by the current fair market value of the property. This NOI turns out to be the annual return less all operating costs. The capitalization rate formula can be written as Capitalization Rate = Net Operating Income / Current Market Value. Investors and realtors express it as a percentage.

Investors consider the cap rate to be very helpful because it summarizes information regarding real estate investments. It is also simple to understand. This important rate discerns the profitability of a given piece of property. In order for it to remain consistent, the net operating income and current market value have to be constant compared to each other. If the NOI goes up when market value remains constant, the capitalization rate rises. If instead market value increases while NOI remains the same, then this rate will go down.

Real estate investments only stay profitable if the NOI goes up at the same rate as or a greater rate than the increase in the value of the property. This is another way that the capitalization rate is helpful. It can be employed to track the performance of real estate investments through time to learn if their performance is increasing. When the rate declines instead, investors may decide to sell the property so that they can reinvest the capital in some other place.

The cap rate is especially practical because it allows individuals to measure different investments in property. It permits them to compare and contrast a number of different investment possibilities against each other. Sometimes it is not easy to compare operating income or market values of radically different properties. Comparing percentages to one another is simple and intuitive. The rate is at its most useful when either the current market value or NOI are similar. This is because investments where the cost is vastly different can create a variety of other considerations that interfere with effective comparison.

Many times investors will come up with a minimum capitalization rate which they are willing to take so that the investment is practical. They might set 12% as their minimum rate. This helps them to sift through the various possibilities to rule out the ones that do not measure up to their desired minimum.

Investors may also employ the capitalization rate to figure out the amount of time it will take for the investment to reach its payback point. They can find the payback period by taking 100 and dividing it by the capitalization rate. This will provide an estimate of the payback period and not a fixed number. Most investments will see their capitalization rate change during significant amounts of time.

Another useful way of determining the value for a real estate investment is to utilize direct capitalization. To find this number, investors simply divide their NOI by the cap rate. This provides them with the capital cost of the real estate investment in question.

Investors should realize that the capitalization rate is not so helpful for shorter time frame investments as it is for longer ones. Figuring up NOI requires some time to determine a cash flow number that is reliable.

Capital Account

Capital Account demonstrates the net changes in the financial asset ownership for any country. When added in with the national current account, this makes up the given country's balance of payments. This capital account will always include such things as portfolio investment and FDI foreign direct investment as well as any changes in the reserve account. It is also possible for the capital account to refer to any account which displays a company's net worth at a particular moment and snapshot in time.

On a macro-economic scale, what the capital account actually figures up is the total economic production for a region or entire nation. With corporations it is different. Here the capital account is actually a general ledger account that the firm will utilize to record the sums of money which any investor provides the company with in exchange for a stake. It also shows the accumulative amount of the earnings of the firm less the accumulative distributions to the various stakeholders in the firm. These balances become reportable in the owner's equity section, the stockholder's equity section, or the partner's equity section on balance sheets.

Where nations are concerned, the capital accounts total up all of the economic affairs of the nation as a whole. Markets are particularly concerned with this figure as it reveals the total picture and general direction of the nation economically. It also delivers a range of sell and buy signals for a number of different portfolio strategies and particular industries.

The balance of trade for a nation is a component of the national balance of payments. Take the United States as an example. The balance of payments within the U.S. is comprised of three subaccounts. These are the capital account, the current account, and the financial account. Each of these possesses its own special outflows and inflows.

Analysts and economists like to use the balance of trade. It helps them to more effectively grasp the national economic strength as measured against other competing nations. Take another example. Nations that possess huge trade deficits like the United States and Great Britain will generally borrow money in order to purchase foreign-produced goods and services. Those countries like Germany with enormous trade surpluses usually engage in the opposite activity. Such a balance of trade often corresponds to the political situation in a nation as it reveals how much foreign investment occurs in the receiving nation.

With corporations, it is once again different. They will have a great number of capital accounts. Those capital accounts which are for paid-in capital include preferred stock, common stock, and paid-in capital that stands in excess of par. These sums report in the money which the firm receives in as they float their share of capital stock to various investors. Retained earnings represent the accumulative earnings less accumulative dividends which they have paid out to stake holders. The account for treasury stock reports the sum of money the firm pays out to buy back shares of its stock (which are not retired).

Where sole proprietorships are concerned, there will be a capital account that shows the initial investment of the owner. This will grow every year by the amount of the annual earnings less the yearly withdrawals. There will also be a drawing account, many times referred to as a contra account. Its debit balance will equate to the amount of assets of the firm that the owner draws down in a given accounting year for his or her personal use. When the conclusion of the accounting year arrives, this drawing account becomes closed through transferring over any debit balance to the company capital account. It is a requirement that the balances in the various capital accounts have to equal the as-reported sum of all assets less liabilities of the firm.

Capital Expenditures

Capital expenditure refers to money that a firm employs to purchase physical assets. This can also be used to upgrade existing assets. These can include items such as equipment, industrial buildings, and property. It is also known as CapEx. Companies often use this CapEx to make new investments or to begin a new project.

Other corporations utilize capital expenditures to build up their operations' size and scale. Such expenditures can cover many different items like buying a new piece of equipment, fixing the roof on a company building, or constructing a new factory for the company.

Accounting procedures utilize this capital expenditure concept regularly. Expenses will be labeled as CapEx if the item the company buys is a new purchase of a capital asset. They also fall under this category when the purchase is some type of investment that extends the practical life of an already owned capital asset.

When a purchase falls under the capital expenditure's category, the accounting department will be required to capitalize it. They do this when the fixed cost of the purchase is spread out over the asset's useful life. In other cases, the money they spend will only keep the capital item in its present condition. For these scenarios the company and accountants may simply deduct the entire expense for the year in which they spend the money.

Different industries will employ varying levels of capital expenditures. Some use very little, while others are more capital intensive. Among the most intensive capital industries in the world are the exploration and production of energy such as oil or natural gas, manufacturing businesses, telecommunications, and electricity, gas, and water utilities.

It is important to not confuse capital expenditures with other ideas like operating expenses, known as OPEX, or revenue expenditures. Operating and revenue expenses are money that companies pay to cover the daily cost of running the business. Revenue expenses are different from CapEx in another significant way. The former can be completely deducted from taxes in the year in which the company spends them.

Capital expenditures can be used to help come up with the relative value of a company also. Cash flow to capital expenditure ratio is one such measure. It is commonly referred to as CF/CapEx. This explains the ability of a company to purchase assets for long term use by utilizing its free cash flow. This ratio commonly goes up and down for businesses as they engage in cycles of small capital versus large capital expenses.

Ideally a business wants to have a higher multiple in this ratio. Higher numbers signify that the company is in a position of solid financial health and strength. This is because firms that possess the financial capabilities to invest in their future with capital expenditures can expand with greater ease and flexibility.

Cash flows to capital expenditures are ratios that are specific to every industry. Each segment's ratio will be different. This means that the ratio of one company in one business should not be compared to a second company in another industry. Instead, the ratio is only useful for comparison when two companies that possess comparable CapEx requirements are examined. Comparing various CapEx ratios from two oil firms or utility companies makes sense. Holding up the CapEx ratios of an oil company or telecom firm against a consulting business or advertising agency does not.

The higher a company's capital expenditure is, the lower its other measures of financial health may be. As an example, firms with high CapEx will often show less free cash flow to equity.

Capital Flows

Capital Flows relate to the general movements of money and investments so that they can be invested in securities, business, or trade production. This also takes into consideration flows of such capital that occur naturally within a multinational corporation. This might result from capital spending in other divisions, investment capital allocation, acquisitions of rival companies, or R&D research and development spending.

Governments can also engage in capital flow direction by steering money they collect in tax levies into particular policies and programs as well as with their trade policies and financial policies on currency management and bilateral trade with other countries. Even individual investors can be involved in capital flow through their saving and investing personal capital into mutual funds, bonds, and stocks as well as other types of financial securities.

The United States corporate, not for profit, and government organizations direct capital flows as a result of legislation, regulation, and analysis. Economists within the U.S. and other developed nations like to study these various categories of capital inflows and outflows. This includes specific types like mutual fund flows, venture capital, asset class balancing and reallocation, federal budgets, and capital spending budgets of corporations.

In fact there are many different categories of capital flow. Within the movements in asset classes, these can be sufficiently measured as they move back and forth between stocks, cash, bonds, mutual funds, and other forms of financial securities. Venture capital can measure the shifts of investments moving around startup businesses and industries. Mutual funds will actively track the net withdrawals and additional cash deposits from and to a wide range of fund classes. With capital spending budgets, these can be studied on a companywide level. This way firms can monitor their various growth plans. Governments utilize their capital flow studies to match their budgets appropriately up with government spending plans.

Another insight that such capital flow studies provide pertains to the capital markets. They can prove the weaknesses or strengths of the various markets as economists examine the direction and pace of capital inflows and outflows. This is particularly useful for investors who can know the growth rates in specific capital flows which provide them with ideas of trends and possible opportunities. Capital spending flows will help them to know which industries and specific corporations are on the move and might be good investment opportunities. Venture capital flows reveal risks involved with venture financing of different startup industries and even specific startup operations.

Real Estate is another investment arena where capital flow direction can be most illuminating for investors. For example, during the devastating global financial crisis of 2007-2009, the capital inflows to Real Estate markets drastically slowed down. Sales did not again reach the pre-crash levels until the year 2013. By 2015, such capital flows grew as much as 45 percent compared to the levels in 2014 with regards to commercial property investment inflows.

The study of capital flows can also reveal big pictures for emerging market economies as well. As these more volatile economies often undergo rapid growth spurts and sharp contractions, the capital flow can correspondingly rise and fall steeply. Higher capital inflows often create credit booms. This leads to hot money asset price inflation. Sometimes it is offset by currency depreciation losses as exchange rates shift or equities' prices drop.

India is a classic example to consider among the developing nations of the world. The huge nation has experienced significant fluctuation periods which started back in the decade of the 1990s. Capital inflows occurred throughout the 1990s to the first years of the 2000s. This coincided with steady and positive growth. From the first years of the 2000s through 2007, capital inflows shifted into overdrive. The rapidly accompanying growth stalled out suddenly because of the peak of the global financial crisis in 2008/2009. Capital outflows became highly volatile during these several years.

Capital Inflow

Capital Inflow refers to money (in the form of investments) moving into a certain benefitting nation. The country which is the recipient of the inflow is best known as the host country. The source countries are the ones sending or investing the initial funds. Host nations often have a range of causes for attracting such capital inflows.

Direct foreign investment occurs when multinational corporations purchase literal tangible assets in the host country. This could come in the form of purchasing a local company outright or building a manufacturing plant locally. There could also be portfolio investment in the host nation's financial securities. This might include bonds and stocks which may be bought by international banks, foreign residents, insurance companies, pension funds, hedge funds, or other cross-border groups.

A third way that this occurs is when host governments are forced to borrow money off of international governments or foreign banks in order to pay their deficit on the balance of payments. It also occurs when domestic corporations or citizens elect to borrow from foreign banks. Finally inter-company transfers can finance investment and consumption in this category of capital inflow.

A last form of capital inflow happens when the host country has higher interest rates than the source nations' own corresponding rates. In this scenario, shorter term deposits will often flock to the banks' and money market instruments of the host nation. This could be straight up investment or speculation that the host national exchange rate will increase and so lead to a capital gain. This is the opposite of capital outflows. Outflows occur as funds move out of the host nation into other competing countries for the same reasons detailed above.

There are many beneficial effects to a country which receives capital inflows. As money comes into the host country via a business or stock purchase on the nation's stock market exchange, the recipient firm will deploy the funds either for startup purposes or to expand their existing business products and lines. This is really good for the companies which receive the funds. Such expansion of the companies in question then leads both job creation and employment growth in the host nation. Businesses will finally realize profits utilizing the original capital investment and the projects they subsequently fund with it. With these profits, the company is able to pay for additional expansion or investment in other projects and/or financial investments.

In the last few decades, foreigners have invested literally hundreds of billions worth of foreign capital into the United States economy. This has massively advantaged the American economy and workers (besides just creating countless jobs) as it boosted the international value of the dollar, lowered interest rates for American individuals and businesses, and grew the capital supply for loans which banks could make to residents and companies alike. With the onset of the catastrophic Global Financial Crisis from 2007-2009, the capital inflows to the United States dropped considerably. The subsequent Sovereign Debt Crisis in Europe dramatically decreased the capital inflow to Europe as well.

Years later by 2012, China finally surpassed the U.S. to capture the spot as the globe's greatest host of direct foreign investment . At the conclusion of 2012, the United States managed to recapture this coveted top spot. China had several reasons to steal the American thunder this way. The Chinese economy grew quicker than the United States as well as the other developed nations. Besides this, China has finally matured into a country that does not appear to be a high risk investment any longer. This has helped to draw in direct foreign investment by the hundreds of billions over the decades.

Capital Markets

Capital markets refer to those marketplaces for the sales and purchase of both debt and equity financial issues. These markets move investments and savings back and forth between capital suppliers like institutional and retail investors to capital users. These are individual entrepreneurs, businesses and corporations, and governmental agencies. Economies do not function efficiently or successfully without such liquid markets of capital. This is because capital is a crucial component for producing economic output.

There are two types of such capital markets. These include the primary markets and secondary markets. In the primary markets, investors buy and sell new bond and stock instruments. Secondary markets are the ones that trade already existing securities. The two financial instruments categories are equities and debt securities. The equities are typically called stocks. The debt securities are usually called bonds. Such markets revolve around the selling of bonds and stocks for longer and medium term durations, typically of at least a year.

These capital markets in the United States function under the auspices of the Securities and Exchange Commission. In other nations, they operate under different financial regulators. In general, such markets tend to cluster in the several important financial centers of the globe. The greatest of these are London, New York City, Hong Kong, and Singapore. Despite the fact that the markets lie in these principal city centers, the majority of their trades happen via sophisticated electronic and computer trading systems. While members of the public can access some such capital centers in person, the other ones remain highly secured and regulated.

Primary markets are where these investments first appear. The companies which need to raise capital issue bonds and stocks directly to the financial institutions, businesses, and investors here. They typically buy these in a process called underwriting. Another advantage offered by companies which require capital is that they can do it there without having to hold initial public offerings (IPOs) so that the profit remains theirs. When companies do opt for IPOs, they typically sell all of their stock shares off to several underwriting investment banks through a lead investment bank and other financial firms which choose to participate.

From this stage, the new shares become a part of the secondary market. Here the investment banks, financial firms, and private investors are allowed to resell their debt and equity instruments to retail investors.

There are many entities which participate in capital markets. These include institutional investors like mutual funds and pension funds, retail investors, corporations and other organizations, governments and municipalities, and financial institutions and banks. Governments may be allowed to issue bonds on these markets, but they can never sell equity via stocks.

These markets are where supply and demand between capital suppliers and users meet and adjust. While capital users desire to raise their capital for the lowest cost they possibly can, the suppliers wish to obtain the highest return they possibly can for the least amount of risk possible.

A country's capital markets' size will be directly proportional to the economic size of the nation in question. As the biggest economy on the planet, the U.S. boasts the deepest and biggest capital markets. These markets are still interdependent on other such capital centers in the global economy of today. Small ripples in another center such as London or Hong Kong can lead to substantial waves in Singapore and/or New York City.

The downside to the interconnectedness of the financial and capital centers is illustrated by the financial and credit crisis of 2007 to 2009. It was actually the failure of the mortgage-backed securities markets in the United States that triggered the crisis and collapse. This de facto meltdown in the U.S. became transmitted around the world by the global capital markets as financial institutions, investment banks, and commercial banks throughout both Europe and Asia were holding literally trillions of U.S. dollars worth of such securities.

Capital Outflow

Capital Outflow is a phenomenon where financial assets and money move away from a given nation. All countries of the world consider this to be a negative action. It typically occurs as a result of economic and/or political instability or at least the perception of it. Such asset flight results from domestically and especially foreign-based investors choosing to sell their stakes within a certain nation. They do this as they see potential weakness in the economy or political establishment of a country. They begin to feel that greater and safer opportunities for investment lie overseas.

When such Capital Outflows become too fast and great, it is a serious indicator that economic and political turmoil is present and a primary cause of the asset and capital flight. Many governments will begin to set limitations for capital choosing to exit. The connotation of such actions tends to warn still other investors who have not left that the condition of the host nation and economy is rapidly deteriorating.

Abnormal capital outflow creates increasingly severe pressure on the macroeconomics of a country and its economy. It tends to dissuade domestic and foreign investors alike from investing in the state and its companies. There are a range of valid explanations for why such capital flight actually occurs. Among them are unnaturally low national interest rates and growing political unrest.

It often helps to look at a real world example to better understand a difficult concept. Japan chose to decrease its interest rates to actual negative levels back in 2016. This applied to all government bonds and securities. They simultaneously began unprecedented aggressive stimulatory measures to boost the growth of the GDP Gross Domestic Product at the same time. The economic problems in Japan started after massive capital outflows from the island nation throughout the decade of the 1990s kicked off two long decades of sub-par stagnated growth in the country which formerly boasted the position of second greatest economy in the world.

Often times, governments impose severe restrictions on capital flight in a valiant effort to stop the fleeing money and financial assets. This is in an endeavor to shore up the capital markets and especially domestic banking institutions and system which can fail if all the money is simultaneously withdrawn. Too few bank deposits often cause banks to crater into insolvency when a great number of assets depart all at once. Subsequently, many banks find it difficult if not outright impossible to call back in existing issued loans in order to make good on customer withdrawal demands.

Consider the sad case study of Greece. Back in 2015, the government of the world's first democracy had no other choice than to instate a week long bank holiday. Wire transfers became restricted only to those recipients with Greek bank accounts. When such events occur in developing (or sometimes third world) countries, the weakness it institutes can create a vicious downward spiral that leads to domestic public panic and foreign investment fear and resistance.

There are also dramatic effects on exchange rates. The supply of a given country's currency rises dramatically as investors cash out of the state. Investors in China have periodically sold off the Yuan in order to obtain American dollars. This drives down the value of the Chinese Yuan, which has the additional side benefit of reducing the costs of Chinese exports while simultaneously boosting the costs to import foreign goods. It unfortunately also leads to inflation since import demand will fall while exported goods demand increases. During the second half of the year 2015, Chinese assets to the tune of $550 billion departed China looking for a higher ROI return on investment. This caused not only Chinese government fears but ensuing worldwide government worries.

Similarly Argentina suffered from sudden, unexpected, and runaway capital outflows back in the decade of the 1990s following a dramatic currency realignment. Their new fixed exchange rate created a resulting recession. The nation has now become the popular example and poster country for fledgling economies and the difficulties they all too often encounter in boosting their economic development.

Capital Stock

A business' capital stock is the up front capital that the founders of the firm invest in or put into the company. This capital stock also proves useful as security for a business' creditors. This is because capital stock may not be taken out of the business to disadvantage the creditors in question. Such stock is separate from a business' assets or property that can rise and fall in value and amount.

A company's capital stock is segregated into shares. The complete number of such shares have to be detailed when the business is founded. Based on the entire sum of money that is put into the company when it is started up, each share will possess a particular face value that must be declared.

This value is referred to as par value of the individual shares. These par values are the minimum sums of money that may be issued and sold in stock shares by the business. It is similarly the capital value representation in the business' own accounting. In some countries, these shares do not contain any par value period. In this case, the capital stock shares would be termed non par value stock. Such shares literally represent a portion of an ownership in the business in question. These businesses may then declare various classes of shares. All of these could have their own privileges, rules, and share values.

The owning of such capital stock shares is proven by the possession of a certificate of stock. These stock certificates prove to be legal documents that detail the numbers of shares each shareholder owns. Other particular data of the capital stock shares, including class of shares and par value, is similarly detailed on these certificates.

These owners of the firm in question may decide that they need more capital in order to invest in additional projects that the company has in mind. Besides this, they might decide that they want to cash out some of their own holdings in order to release a portion of capital for their own private needs. They can do this by selling all or some of their capital stock to many partial owners. The ownership of one such share gives the share owner an ownership stake in the company. This includes such privileges as a tiny portion of any profits that may be paid out as dividends, as well as a small part of any decision making powers.

These shares sold from the capital stock each represent a single vote. The owners could decide to offer various classes of shares that could then have differing rights of voting. By owning a majority of the shares, the owners can out vote all of the little shareholders combined. This permits the original owners to maintain effective control of their company even after issuing shares of their capital stock to investors.

Cash Flow Statement (CFS)

The Cash Flow Statement (CFS) proves to be one of three critical components in any corporation's financial reports. The other two are income statements and balance sheets. From 1987, the SEC Securities Exchange Commission has mandated that such cash flow statements be included with all corporate financial reports. This statement details the quantities of cash and cash equivalents that come into and flow out of a firm. Such a CFS permits the stake holders and potential investors alike to comprehend the way corporations' operations are functioning, how they are effectively spending the money, and from where their money originates in the first place.

There are differences that separate these Cash Flow Statements from the balance sheets and income statements. The principal one is that CFSs do not cover the future anticipated outgoing and incoming cash amounts which have already been recorded under the credit sales category. It explains why the component cash is never identical to net income. Both balance sheets and income statements cover not only cash sales, but also sales that happen on credit. In the end, a firm's cash flow is derived from three separate means of money coming in and leaving a corporation. These are cash from operations, cash from financing, and cash from investing.

Cash from Operations comprise both the cash inflow and outflow which result from the mainstay operation of the business. This means that they show the quantity of cash that the firms' services and products actually accrue to the business. Cash from operations would usually include changes to cash, depreciation, accounts receivable, accounts payable, and inventory.

The Cash from Financing component includes loans, changes in debt, and dividends. As capital becomes raised, this is a cash-in accounting item. As dividends pay out, it becomes marked as a cash-out event. As an example, when firms sell bonds on the markets, the firm obtains cash financing. As the corporation pays the associated interest out to the holders of the bonds, then the firm reduces its cash by the corresponding amount.

The final category of Cash from Investing covers all changes in assets, equipment, or company investments. These are commonly considered to be cash out events. This is because cash will be utilized to purchase new buildings, buy factory or other production equipment, and acquire other types of assets which are short term (like securities which are easily marketable). It is not always the case that these are cash negative events though. As any firms choose to sell off one or more of their assets, this creates a cash-in transaction. It would then be notated as a positive accounting item under the cash from investing category. When companies sell shares they hold in another firm, the revenue this generates becomes accounted for under the Cash from Investing.

Cash flow becomes calculated by adjustments that accountants make to net income. They simply add in (or alternatively subtract out) any differences in expenses, revenue, and credit types of transactions that appear on the income statements and balance sheets since the last accounting period. Such transactions happen every accounting period. These adjustments will be reviewed and amended as non-cash items go into the income statement under net income while liabilities and total assets go on to the balance sheet. Since not every type of financial transaction of a firm relates to real cash items, a great number of items must be reconsidered when the accountants are figuring up the cash flow from operations.

Company accountants deduce the cash flow statement calculations and compile them into official corporate report documents every reportable quarter. The SEC requires that they make this a part of every quarterly report and also each annual report which they must divulge to analysts and members of the investing public by law.

Cash Management

Cash management refers to the corporate functions of gathering, handling, and short term investing cash. This represents a critical part of making certain a firm is financially viable and stays solvent. In many cases, the business managers of a company or corporate treasurers of a large corporation will handle the aggregate cash management responsibilities. This means they will be responsible for ensuring the firm continues to be financially viable and solvent on a week to week basis.

There is more to successfully handled cash management than simply sidestepping financial problems or even bankruptcy. This job also involves bringing in invoice payments and account receivables, boosting the rates and speed of collection, improving the level of available cash at hand, and picking out relevant short term investment instruments which will all contribute to better profits and a stronger cash position for the firm in question.

Those small business managers and developers must learn to manage cash flow well since they do not enjoy low cost access to easy credit. They also encounter many ongoing running costs that they have to stay on top of while they are waiting for their customers to pay their receivables. By properly and prudently managing their cash flow, firms are able to cover unanticipated costs and to effectively cover their routine financial events like payroll on a bi-weekly or semi-monthly basis. The point of cash management is to effectively balance out two main corporate counteracting forces. These are the receivables for incoming cash and the outflows of payables.

Part of the dilemma for many companies struggling to effectively run their cash management operations is that invoices and receivables are positive cash flow on the books, yet in practice they are not always received immediately. Some invoice terms allow for the customer to wait from 30 to 60 to even 90 days to settle their invoices. This is how businesses can actually find themselves in the uncomfortable position of their sales growing even rapidly and still have cash flow problems because their receivables come in slowly or even unfortunately late.

Businesses have a variety of tools and means to speed up their receivables so that their payment float becomes reduced. Some of these are to deploy an auto billing service that immediately invoices the customers electronically, to make clear the billing and payment terms to the clients, to keep on top of all collections with an aging receivables spreadsheet, to offer incentives for same as cash 10 day invoice payments, and to collect payments via electronic payment processing at a bank.

Businesses which are successful in controlling their payables will be better capable of maintaining positive cash flows. Through streamlining the efficiency of the payables operations, firms are able to lower their costs all the while holding on to more cash which they can put to work in the company operations. There are a wide variety of effective payable management solutions available today. Some of these include direct payroll deposits, payment processing which is handled electronically, and closely and carefully controlled cash disbursements. Each of these processes will help to both automate and make efficient all of the payout operations.

Thanks to the variety of digital age offerings, the vast majority of payable management and receivable operations may be simply automated through current day solutions in business banking. Smaller companies are now able to operate with the same big scale technologies for cash management as the mega corporations. This is in no small part due to the rapid march of technological advances across business solutions and banking. Such cost savings created by these cutting-edged cash management techniques effectively more than offset the costs of utilizing them. The best part of the process nowadays is that a firm's management is capable of allocating critical resources to expanding the core business better than ever before possible.

Cash Operating Cost

Cash Operating Cost refers to a cash flow statement which effectively follows all cash types of business expenditures. It is in the first section of a cash flow statement, the operating activities, that keeps all relevant and pertinent information regarding the cash operating costs. Such expenses are derived from the firm's information on financial accounting. It does not matter if the expense items are variable or fixed.

The cash flow statement merely details the quantity of such cash operating costs as well as if the firm had a cash outflow or inflow over a particular time frame. This section covers a variety of cash expenditures. Among these are payables, assets, and various other current liabilities.

Payables are those things that corporations buy on account. They promise to pay the vendor later on in the arrangement. There are a wide variety of items which will be detailed in this section. Among them are wages, notes, interest, payroll, and any taxes due. Cash utilization happens as a company pays off the prior balance on any such items in the current month period. There will be a single line that refers to the repayment of these types of liabilities in the cash operating costs. Payables accounts increasing mean that cash flow for the firm is decreasing to match. This is because these are money the company has spent.

Assets prove to be among the most significant category of these cash operating costs. This is particularly the case with retail and manufacturing businesses that will be heavy on assets especially. Such assets detailed out here would include inventory, prepaid assets, supplies, accounts receivable, and other forms of current assets. Such items are typically utilized in the day to day business operations. The anticipation is that the various individual groups will not last for over 12 months. For these, the statement of cash flows shows real money which the firm pays for such items. Each particular category will have its own line on the statement along with the aggregate amount the category spend in a particular time frame.

The categories of other current liabilities will be a last section of the cash operating costs. Such items can be revenue that is unearned or various other current liabilities which firms incur in the normal course of business operations. Every item which does not adhere to the above two criterion will be listed out by the accountants in this category section. This includes special and one time items. It allows for the company accountant to make shareholders aware of substantial types of expenses which the normal business operations are costing. Sometime special disclosures will be required to be made to the various stock holders when major cash position reductions occur as a result of them.

Such statements of cash flow are useful for external and internal stake holders in a given corporation alike. The company accountants can also put together various other types of reports to show the cash operating costs for the firm. Such reports would be less formal yet still official. They explain the relevant cost items for the internal stakeholders such as upper level management and the board of directors. So long as the accountant utilize standard accounting processes, any range of statistics and figures could be included in the informational reports. In these cases, they may use whatever format they wish to produce the additional illuminating report.

Cash Reserves

Cash reserves refer to money which an individual person, a company, or a corporation saves in order to be ready to cover any emergency funding or short term requirements. They can also be utilized to refer to a kind of extremely liquid, short term investment which usually garners a poor rate of return (under three percent in a year).

An example of this would be Fidelity Cash Reserves, one of the Fidelity mutual families of funds particular investments. Sometimes individuals will hold money they need rapid access to in such a fund which can be instantly liquidated on the same day they issue the order. Possessing a major amount in a cash reserve fund provides corporations, companies, individuals, families, or communities with the necessary capability to engage in a significant purchase right away.

There are various reasons why firms wish to maintain some cash reserves. They need to have sufficient money on hand in order to cover all of their costs which may be anticipated or even unanticipated over the short term time-frame. Besides this, they often prefer to have enough cash readily available for such interesting possible investments which could arise with little to no warning.

Though cash is always considered to be the most liquid type of wealth and assets, there are also short term kinds of assets like three month U.S. Treasury bills which investors also deem to be a type of a cash reserve because of the ease and frequency with which they can exchange them and their close proximity to maturity date. Major corporations like Alphabet (Google), General Electric, IBM, and Apple keep enormous cash reserves available. These typically range from fifty billion dollars to one hundred and fifty billion dollars.

At the beginning of 2016, Apple boasted such cash reserve ranging from fifty billion to one hundred fifty billion dollars. At the same time, Alphabet (Google) counted $75.3 billion in their immediate cash on hand reserves. This permitted Google to buy out major corporate purchases like their acquisition of Nest, which they bought for a hefty $3 billion price tag back in 2014.

With banks, governmental oversight agencies require that they maintain a minimum quantity of cash reserves on hand. This is because their operations are critical for the functioning of any economy. In the United States, it is the American Federal Reserve that determines these cash reserve amounts for the banks. In other countries, it is often the national central bank or some other governmental oversight regulator who makes the call.

Banking cash reserves will typically be set as a certain percentage of the banks' liabilities or net transaction accounts. With those banks which contain in excess of $110.2 million in their net transaction accounts, this amount within the U.S. proves to be 10 percent of such liabilities. This amount became effective on January 1st of 2016. Such bank reserves have to be kept in either deposits at a Federal Reserve Bank or in their own vaults as cash on hand. With euro currency liabilities or time deposits of a non-personal nature, these liabilities are not subjected to such a cash reserve requirement.

Economists and personal finance gurus generally state that individuals are wise to keep minimally sufficient cash on hand to cover from three to six months of expenses in the event they suffer a family emergency. Such an emergency fund is a form of a cash reserve. These reserves would be kept in either their local bank accounts or otherwise in a stable and short term time frame investment which will maintain its value regardless of what happens in the markets. In this way, individuals are able to draw on their own emergency funds or alternatively to sell such investments at a moment's notice without taking a financial loss. This needs to be the case no matter how the financial investment markets are performing.

Other forms of personal cash reserves could be held in a savings account, checking account, money market account, money market fund, or even CDs and Treasury Bills. For those businesses or individuals who do not plan ahead with enough cash reserves, they may have to instead to fall back on credit, loans, or in some drastic cases, declaring bankruptcy.

Chapter 11 Bankruptcy

Chapter 11 Bankruptcy proves to be a specific type of bankruptcy. This kind has to do with the business assets, debts, and affairs being reorganized. The business reorganization filing was named for the Section 11 of the United States' Bankruptcy Code. Corporations commonly file it that need some time to rearrange the terms of their debts and their business operations. It gives them a fresh start on repaying their debt obligations. Naturally the indebted company will have to stick to the terms of the reorganization plan. This proves to be the most highly complex type of bankruptcy filing possible. Companies have been advised to only entertain it once they have contemplated their other options and analyzed the repercussions of such a filing.

This Chapter 11 bankruptcy rarely makes the news unless it is a nationally known or famous corporation which is filing. Among the major corporations that have filed such a Chapter 11 bankruptcy are United Airlines, General Motors, K-Mart, and Lehman Brothers. The first three successfully emerged from it and became as great or stronger than they were before falling into hard times financially. In reality, the vast majority of these cases are unknown to the general public. As an example, in the year 2010, nearly 14,000 separate corporations filed for Chapter 11.

The point of this Chapter 11 Bankruptcy is to assist a corporation in restructuring both obligations and debts. The goal is not to close down the business. In fact it rarely leads to the corporation closing. Instead, corporations like K-mart, General Motors, and tens of thousands of others were able to survive and once again thrive thanks to the useful process of protection from creditors and reorganization of business debts.

It is typically LLCs Limited Liability Companies, partnerships, and corporations that make application for Chapter 11 Bankruptcy. There are cases where individuals who are positively saddled with debt and who are not able to be approved for a Chapter 13 or Chapter 7 filing can be qualified for Chapter 11 instead. The time table for successfully completing Chapter 11 bankruptcy ranges from several months to as long as two years.

Businesses that are in the middle of their Chapter 11 cases are encouraged to keep operating. The debtor in possession will typically run the business normally. Where there are cases that have gross incompetence, dishonest dealings, or even fraud involved, typically trustees come in to take over the business and its daily operations while the bankruptcy proceedings are ongoing.

Corporations in the midst of these filings will not be permitted to engage in specific decisions without first having to consult with the courts to proceed. They may not terminate or sign rental agreements, sell any assets beyond regular inventory, or expand existing business operations or alternatively cease them. The bankruptcy court retains full control regarding any hiring and paying of lawyers as well as signing contracts with either unions or vendors. Lastly, such indebted organizations and entities may not sign for a loan that will pay once the bankruptcy process finishes.

After the business or person files their chapter 11 bankruptcy, it gains the right to offer a first reorganization plan. Such plans often include renegotiating owed debts and reducing the company size in order to slash expenses. There are some scenarios where the plan will require every asset to be liquidated in order to pay off the creditors, as with Lehman Brothers.

When plans are fair and workable, courts will approve them. This moves the reorganization process ahead. For plans to be accepted, they also have to maintain the creditors' best interests for the future repayment of debts owed to them. When the debtor can not or will not put forward a plan of their own for reorganization, then the creditors are invited to offer one in the indebted company or person's place.

Charge Off

A charge off refers to an expense item found on a corporation's income statement. This could be one of two things. It might be connected with a debt that the reporting firm has decided is not realistically collectable. They would then write this off from the corporate balance sheet. It might also be a likely one time only expense which is called an extraordinary event. The company incurs this, and it impacts the earnings negatively. This then leads to a portion of the corporate assets' becoming written down in value. Because the assets have become impaired, the write down occurs.

Where bad debt costs crop up, this is related to a company not being able to collects bills owed for at least a portion of its accounts receivable, also called AR. These events unfortunately happen sometimes, and firms can do little about them. They might attempt to sell off the likely bad debts to an interested collection agency. The company would then record a sale on the books, yet it would not be marked down as an expense item. Otherwise, they might simply charge off the amount which is uncollectable on the income statement by calling it an expense.

In order for debts to be considered to be bad debts, they have to be run up in the typical operations of the business. Such a debt could be incurred by either a person or another company. These charge offs for the bad debts more typically happen as companies extend credit (to other entities) that is unsecured. Examples of this would be signature-only loans or credit cards.

One time expenses which are charged off are another story altogether. Sometimes a firm will consent to an extraordinary charge off in a given period of accounting. This would impact the current period earnings, yet they feel it will not likely happen again in the near future. The end result is ultimately that the company will commonly offer its EPS earnings per share numbers both without and with the charge off in question reflected. This allows them to show the company shareholders that the expense is unusual and uncommon. They might also call this a one off charge.

Such charge offs could involve the buying of a major asset. This could be a significant piece of equipment or a brand new production facility. These expenses would not be repeated too often. There might also be charges that are associated with an unusual event. Examples of this are paying deductibles for insured items that became damaged in a natural disaster. There could also be a flood or a fire for which the firm has to pay the costs to cover the damage.

There might also be maintenance types of expenses that are not normal. These might include replacing a roof. It is true that maintenance issues like these can be predicted to a degree. Because the exact date of service and amount of charge can not easily be quantified. Since such maintenance issues are only necessary every few decades, they are extraordinary items indeed.

Charge offs could also pertain to individuals who have seen one of their personal debts charged off. Such an event does not mean that a creditor has specifically cancelled the debt. Borrowers will still have to pay off the balance in theory. When credit card payments become late, they go into late payment status. After a payment is 180 days late, the creditor companies will at last charge off the debt. They might then send it out for collection agencies or file lawsuits if the laws of the state where the debtor resides allow.

Conversion Discount

Conversion Discount refers to a special option applied to conversion investments. Understanding what a conversion is first becomes necessary in order to make sense of the discount clause. Conversions are the abilities to exchange some from of a convertible debt instrument into another kind of asset such as company stock. This conversion will be contractually spelled out at a prearranged price for a pre-set date deadline. The feature of a conversion itself proves to be a financial derivative type of instrument which has a separate and distinct value from the security itself. This is why including a conversion option in a security will only increase its all around value to the potential buyers.

Convertible bonds are excellent examples of assets that go through conversions and may end up with these discounts. Such a bond provides the holders with the ability to trade in the bond for a previously arranged quantity of stock in the company which issued the bond. This would usually be attractive to the holders of the bonds when the stock shares' value is greater than that of the bond itself. This is the point when most bond holders choose to exercise their conversion clause.

Looking at a tangible example helps to clarify the issue. Consider that Paul has a convertible bond from Astra Zeneca the Anglo-Swedish pharmaceutical company. The bond has a value of $1,000. Should Paul have the option to convert this bond into 10 shares of Astra Zeneca stock, then he will probably choose to do so only if the stock is worth more than $100 per share. This would give him equity holdings greater than the $1,000 original value of the company bond.

The idea becomes interesting with discounts. The interest rates on such bonds is often very low, even less than five to six percent. This does not fairly compensate investors for the risks they often take on with companies that have non-established track records, insecure income streams, or shaky credit. Because of this, investors can be additionally compensated with the option to convert the note into equity. Once upon a time in the early years of the 2000's, companies used to set this up as a stock warrant. In the last ten plus years they have been using conversion discounts with these notes instead.

Conversions discounts are quite attractive for investors. They do not simply deliver an options to buy a stock at a given time in the future as warrants do. Instead, they provide the right (but usually not the obligation) to convert into the stock at a lower price for every share (compared to other buyers) in a certain Qualified Financing event of the convertible notes. Naturally the investors' benefits in this are far more instantaneous than with warrants. They are not required to wait for a company sale in order to buy more shares. They also receive these shares instead of having to buy them all over again, as with warrants. This means that no exercise price applies. This conversion discounted price for shares actually pays the cost of the additional shares which they are provided in the round of Qualified Financing.

As a result, they are getting more shares for their money. This is because the conversion discount is commonly 20 percent to 40 percent or even higher. As a concrete example, if the holder of a conversion note in the Cancer Cure Company offers the conversion discount at 30 percent, then for every seventy cents of the note the bond holder owns, he will receive a dollar face value share of stock.

Convertible Bond

A convertible bond is like a hybrid between a stock and a bond. Corporations issue these bonds which the bondholders may choose to convert into shares of the underlying company stock whenever they decide. Such a bond usually pays better yields than do shares of common stocks. Their yields are also typically less than regular corporate bonds pay.

Convertible bonds provide income to their investors just as traditional corporate bonds do. These convertibles also possess the unique ability to gain in price if the stock of the issuing company does well. The reasoning behind this is straightforward. Because the bond has the ability to be directly converted into stock shares, the security's value will only gain as the stock shares themselves actually rise on the market.

When the stock performs poorly, the investors do not have the ability to convert the convertible bond into shares. They only gain the yield as a return on the investment in this case. The advantage these bonds have over the company stock in these deteriorating conditions is significant.

The value of the convertible instrument will only drop to its par value as long as the company that issues it does not go bankrupt. This is because on the specified maturity date, investors will obtain back their original principal. It is quite correct to say that these types of bonds typically have far less downside potential than do shares of common stocks.

There are disadvantages as well as advantages to these convertible bonds. Should the issuer of the bond file for bankruptcy, investors in these kinds of bonds possess a lower priority claim on the assets of the corporation than do those who invested in debt which was not convertible. Should the issuer default or not make an interest or principal payment according to schedule, the convertibles will likely suffer more than a regular corporate bond would. This is the flip side to the higher potential to appreciate which convertibles famously possess. It is a good reason that individuals who choose to invest in single convertible securities should engage in significant and extended research on the issuer's credit.

It is also important to note that the majority of these convertible bonds can be called. This gives the issuer the right to call away the bonds at a set share price. It limits the maximum gain an investor can realize even if the stock significantly outperforms. This means that a convertible security will rarely offer the identical unlimited gain possibilities which common stocks can.

If investors are determined to do the necessary research on an individual company, they can purchase a convertible bond from a broker. For better convertible diversification, there are numerous mutual funds which invest in only convertible securities. These funds are provided by a variety of major mutual fund companies.

Some of the biggest are Franklin Convertible Securities, Vanguard Convertible Securities, Fidelity Convertible Securities, and Calamos Convertible A. Several ETF exchange traded funds provide a similar convertible diversification with lower service charges. Among these are the SPDR Barclays Capital Convertible Bond ETF and the PowerShares Convertible Securities Portfolio.

It is important to know that the bigger convertible securities portfolios such as the ETFs track have a tendency to match the performance of the stock market quite closely in time. This makes them similar to a high dividend equity fund. Such investments do offer possible upside and diversification when measured against typical holdings of bonds. They do not really offer much in the way of diversification for individuals who already keep most of their investment dollars in stocks.

Corporate Banking

Corporate Banking refers to the banking services for businesses. It relates specifically to those accounts that apply to corporate clients. The United States initially employed the term to separate it from the branch of banking activity known as investment banking following the congressionally passed Glass-Steagall Act of 1933. This act separated out the two different activities for more than half a century.

In the 1990s, Congress repealed this act and once again allowed for investment banking and corporate banking to be combined jointly under a single roof. Most banks jumped at the chance to become involved in both activities once again. Where the majority of banks are concerned, this banking for corporate customers proves to be a mainstay profit center. At the same time, this largest originator of customer loans also turns out to be the continuous source of routine write offs for loans that have not repaid. In fact, combing investment and retail banking again led to the root causes of the Global Financial Crisis.

The divisions of banks which handle corporate banking commonly help a large variety of customers. This might range from international multinational conglomerates with billions in revenues and offices around the world on down to medium-sized regional businesses that boast several million in income to small family run companies in only a single city. These commercial banks provide a significant range of services and products to companies and corporations, as well as other smaller financial institutions.

Treasury and cash management operations are a first key service. Corporations utilize these services to convert currency and manage their daily cash and working capital. There are also credit products and loans, often the largest segment of the corporate banking world. It is also among the greatest single sources of both risk and profit for the corporate banks. There will also be commercial real estate services offered involving portfolio evaluation, real asset analysis, equity and debt structuring.

Besides this, many such banks will provide trade finance such as bill collecting, letters of credit, and factoring. Equipment lending is another important arena as the commercial banks will structure specifically tailored loans as well as leases for a wide variety of different types of equipment which companies may need for various industries. Finally, employer services deliver group retirement plans and payroll services. They offer these through special subsidiaries of the bank.

The commercial banks will also offer to cross-provide a range of useful services through their investment banking divisions. These include securities underwriting and asset management.

Commercial banks prove to be crucially important to both national and global economies. Commercial institutions provide the loans which help businesses to expand and hire additional staff members. It is the fuel that allows the economy to grow larger. In the wake of the Global Financial Crisis of 2007 to 2009, banks suddenly stopped lending money to companies and corporations alike.

It led to an almost complete freeze in the worldwide lending and banking activities necessary to keep companies operating. This meant that the recession which ensued proved to be the most devastating and deep one since the Great Depression of the 1930s and early 1940s. The global economy suffered the total shock of a near-death experience. It woke up the global regulators and forced them to renew their regulatory focus on the biggest international banks which have since been considered to be "too big to fail" thanks to their critical importance to the global financial system.

The largest commercial banks in the United States (as of 2017) are JPMorgan Chase, Bank of America, Citigroup, Wells Fargo, and U.S. Bancorp. This contrasts with the largest American banks overall which include Bank of America, Wells Fargo, JPMorgan Chase, Citigroup, and U.S. Bancorp.

Corporate Bonds

Corporate bonds are debt securities that a company issues and sells to investors. Such corporate bonds are generally backed by the company's ability to repay the loan. This money is anticipated to result from successful operations in the future time periods. With some corporate bonds, the physical assets of a company can be offered as bond collateral to ease investors' minds and any concerns about repayment.

Corporate bonds are also known as debt financing. These bonds provide a significant capital source for a great number of businesses. Other sources of capital for the companies include lines of credit, bank loans, and equity issues like stock shares. For a business to be capable of achieving coupon rates that are favorable to them by issuing their debt to members of the public, a corporation will have to provide a series of consistent earnings reports and to show considerable earnings potential. As a general rule, the better a corporation's quality of credit is believed to be, the simpler it is for them to offer debt at lower rates and float greater amounts of such debt.

Such corporate bonds are always issued in $1,000 face value blocks. Practically all of them come with a standardized structure for coupon payments. Some corporate bonds include what is known as a call provision. These provisions permit the corporation that issues them to recall the bonds early if interest rates change significantly. Every call provision will be specific to the given bond.

These types of corporate bonds are deemed to be of greater risk than are government issued bonds. Because of this perceived additional risk, the interest rates almost always turn out to be higher with corporate bonds. This is true for companies whose credit is rated as among the best.

Regarding tax issues of corporate bonds, these are pretty straight forward. The majority of corporate bonds prove to be taxable, assuming that their terms are for longer than a single year. To avoid taxes until the end, some bonds come with zero coupons and redemption values that are high, meaning that taxes are deferred as capital gains until the end of the bond term. Such corporate debts that come due in under a year are generally referred to as commercial paper.

Corporate bonds are commonly listed on the major exchanges and ECN's like MarketAxess and Bonds.com. Even though these bonds are carried on the major exchanges, their trading does not mostly take place on them. Instead, the overwhelming majority of such bonds trading occurs in over the counter and dealer based markets.

Among the various types of corporate bonds are secured debt, unsecured debt, senior debt, and subordinated debt. Secured debts have assets underlying them. Senior debts provide the strongest claims on the corporation's assets if the venture defaults on its debt obligations. The higher up an investor's bond is in the firm's capital structure, the greater their claim will ultimately be in such an unfortunate scenario as default or bankruptcy.

Corporate Finance

Corporate Finance refers to any and all sundry activities that pertain to the business of operating a corporation. This is typically done in a department or a division that is established with the specific goals in mind of running the financial side of the business. The main concentration of such activities and oversight lies in optimizing the stakeholder value via shorter-term and longer-term financial planning. They also endeavor to affect financially advantageous strategies. There are many different activities that fall under the overall umbrella of such financing activities. Among these is everything from investment banking to making capital investments.

Capital investments are a critical area of concern for any company. They need to decide if they ought to make a certain potential investment or not. How will they pay for it, with debt, equity, or the two combined? Will they bring in shareholders via dividends on investments in the corporation? These and other difficult questions the financial officers must wrestle with continuously. There are also shorter-term headaches for them to deal with, such as financial management of current liabilities and current assets, investments, inventory control, and other shorter-term financial issues. Among the longer-term ones are the investments and new capital equipment purchases.

The corporate finance people will spend a huge amount of time deciding their capital investments. The company needs to develop its long term capital meaningfully. It is the department of corporate finance which will have to make such decisions. This starts with capital budgeting, one of the most important financial processes. The firm will need to decide on capital expenditures for the present year, and try to accurately guestimate the resulting cash flows that will come from potential capital projects. They also have to compare and contrast possible investments against the costs they will require so that they can choose the best, most advantageous projects to write into the capital budget.

It is no exaggeration to claim that such capital investments will likely be the most critical financial task which results in real-world business operational impacts. Under-investing or over-investing can result from poor capital budget choices. This can drastically weaken the financial position of any enterprise. Companies that have a resulting inadequate amount of operating capacity or which suffer from higher financing costs because of poorly made choices can be impacted for years, decades, or permanently over these choices.

Sourcing investing capital is another critical task of the corporate finance people. They must arrange the funding with which they will invest in operations and future expansion projects though either equity or debt (or a careful combination of the two means otherwise). They could issues stocks to investors, particularly when they are looking to generate longer-term funds to expand (whether organically or through acquisitions). Alternatively, they might issue bonds on the capital markets via investment banks or borrow money from corporate banking arms of financial institutions.

This represents a true balancing act when decisions are made on the right mix of equity and debt. An over-emphasis on debt can lead to higher risks of defaulting on bonds or loans. An over-emphasis on equity will massively dilute earnings and weaken the investment positions of the earliest stake holders in the firm. Yet whatever mix is pursued by the corporate finance team, the capital will have to be effectively sourced so that capital investments can be successfully implemented in a timely fashion.
The corporate finance department also has to micromanage the shorter-term financial management of the firm. The end-goal of this is to be certain that there is more than sufficient liquidity available to the company in order to maintain its critical daily operations. This involves current liabilities versus assets, also known as operating cash flows and working capital.

The firm will have to be able to cover all of its bills and debt obligations as they become due. This means that a sufficient quantity of the current assets has to be readily converted to cash so that there will not be an embarrassing cash crunch or liquidity crisis from the normal daily and weekly company operations. This is why shorter-term financial management can pursue issuing regular commercial paper for emergency liquidity or otherwise obtaining additional lines of credit for the firm to backstop its various expenses.

Corporate Taxes

Corporate Taxes refer to the United States' based taxes on corporations. These are not the same for every business structured entity. Corporations receive completely different tax treatment from other business entity structures. In fact such corporations are the only kinds of firms in the U.S. which have to pay in their own profit-based income taxes. With LLC limited liability companies, sole proprietorships, and partnerships, these business structures do not receive business profit tax assessment. Instead, all profits literally pass through on to the owners of the businesses in question. These individuals then report their own personal losses or income via their own individual tax returns.

The reasoning for singling out corporations for special (and some would say punitive) tax treatment like this results from their being a completely separate legal entity that has no connection with its owners. Taxable profits will be those that remain after all business expenses have been deducted. Those profits which remain in the firm accounts in order to pay for expansion or cover other ongoing expenses (sometimes called retained earnings) and profits parsed out to the stake holders (or shareholders) in the form of dividends will be the taxable profits.

Corporations employ all sorts of tactics in order to reduce their amounts of taxable profits. Among these will be a dizzying array of deductions for business expenses incurred throughout the course of the operating year. Besides operating expenses, startup expenses, advertising budgets, and product outlays, such corporations may also deduct out the salaries, payroll, and bonuses plus all expenses pertaining to retirement and health care plans for all of their staff and management.

Corporations do have to file their corporate tax return and pay their applicable corporate income taxes on any and all profits utilizing the Form 1120 from the IRS. When corporations know they will owe the government taxes, the Internal Revenue Service requires them to engage in good faith estimates for the tax dollars they will owe so that they can make quarterly payments. The IRS expects to receive these each April, June, September, and January, the months following the ends of the various four quarters.

When corporations pay out dividends to their various stake holding owners, these recipients will be required to report and then pay their own personal income taxes on such sums. Corporations will similarly have to pay taxes on all money they distribute as dividends as these are not deductible from corporate taxes. It causes dividends to be double taxed, once by the corporate income tax rate and a second time by the receiving stake holders. Smaller-sized corporations do not have such problems. Since their stake holders generally are employees of the corporation, they can receive their cuts of the profits in the form of bonuses and salaries which are in fact tax deductible instead of giving them out as dividends that are taxable.

A great number of corporations will decide that they should in fact keep some of their profits as retained earnings at the conclusion of the year. They will need this money to pay for potential future growth, expansion, or even acquisition targets. Such retained earnings become taxable at the company's corporate income tax rates.

This is a strategy for owners of a smaller corporation to reduce taxes. They can keep a portion of the profits within the corporation to avoid having to pay the higher personal income tax rates, as the first $75,000 in corporate profits assess at lower rates of from 15 percent to 25 percent. This accounting trick does now work for owners of the LLCs, partnerships, and sole proprietorships whose profits are all passed through to the individual personal level every year. This happens regardless of if they choose to take out profits from the business or instead leave them.

There is a limit to the largess of the Internal Revenue Service. They will permit the majority of such corporations to keep as much as $250,000 in the firm at any point before the government begins to assess tax penalties.

Cost of Goods Sold (COGS)

The Cost of Goods Sold refers to those costs which directly arise from the creation of a firm's goods or services. The phrase also sometimes is summarized by its acronym COGS or by an alternative name the "cost of sales." It will cover many expenses. Among these are all of the materials the company utilizes to physically produce the goods.

It also considers the labor expenses employed to create the items. It will not include expenses that are considered to be indirect. This means that sales force and distribution expenses will not be taken into account. COGS shows up on income statements. Accountants and economists can utilize it to subtract it out from the given company's revenues in order to establish the firm's gross margin.

Every business has the ultimate goal to earn profits at the heart of what it is doing. This is why a less expensive goods production for their product or service will lead to higher profits, all else being equal. A fuller explanation of what the Cost of Goods Sold includes involves inventory, materials, labor, factory equipment for production, and even overhead. All of these factors of production directly pertain to the goods or services the company produces. The calculation also takes into consideration the freight or shipping of inputs utilized. It would never include associated costs like rent for a facility or general payrolls of a company.

Looking at an example helps to clarify the Cost of Goods Sold concept. Where an automobile manufacturer is concerned, there will be a number of material costs. Chief among these would be those parts that actually combine to produce the car, as well as the cost of labor for assembling the car. The COGS would not include the cost of the sales force personnel which actually sell the car nor the price for getting the cars out to the dealership. Both of these last ideas are post-production costs, so they are not a part of the primary COGS.

There are a number of different ways for calculating the Cost of Goods Sold. It also varies from one certain kind of business to those in another industry. Among the most simple means of figuring this number out is to start with the costs of inventory over the production period. Next they would add in the aggregate purchase amounts in the same time frame. They would likely then subtract out the inventory at the end of production point. Such a calculation will provide the literal cost of the inventory which the company produced in a given time frame.

Another example helps to make the explanation clearer. Assume that a firm begins its production phase with $15 million worth of inventory. If they make $3 million in additional purchase in this time and end the production period with $14 million of inventory, then the firm's Cost of Goods Sold is calculated by taking the $15 million and adding in the $3 million in purchases and subtracting out the final $14 million in remaining inventory. This gives a final COGS of $15M plus $3M minus $14M for a final result of $4M.

The significance to this formula and Cost of Goods Sold figure is important. The COGS reveals how effectively the firm is able to convert its inventory into revenues and profits. This is why it is critical to compare the COGS against the revenue of the period under consideration. When the company above had a revenue exceeding $4 million, then it would boast a gross profit that was positive. If the revenue of the firm in question was less than the $4 million COGS, then there would be a negative gross profit. In other words, understanding and knowing the COGS figure for a company tells investors which companies are ultimately successful and which are in financial trouble, assuming that state of (negative profit) affairs continues for long.

Credit Analysis

Credit analysis refers to a kind of detailed consideration of a corporation or similar agency which issues debt. It is performed by managers of bond portfolios and investors. They seek to determine the ability of the borrower to cover their obligations of debt with this type of analysis. The ultimate goal is to discern the correct amount of default risk which investing in that specific agency or company will entail.

There are a number of different considerations in performing this credit analysis. Some of these are fixed expenses, operating margins, cash flows, and overhead costs. These are also considered in equity analysis, yet with a different emphasis. It is true that stronger credit ratings do not equate to any guarantee of impressive share price performance. Yet when investors grasp a company's credit ratings and the implications, they are able to better assess both the debt and equity results for a given corporation.

Financial elements of a particular company are extremely important in credit analysis. Analysts will consider incoming revenues as well as costs and expenses of the corporation. These will be assessed both as stand-alone values and versus the competitors in the industry. For a firm to be considered strong where credit is concerned, its overhead must permit it to attain better than average profit levels in all points of the business life cycle. Even in a downturn in the economy, stronger companies can deliver results which are higher than average for the industry. Stronger firms also can demonstrate pricing power. This represents the capability of passing on cost increases for inputs and raw materials to the customers via higher prices.

Competitive position is also important in a thorough credit analysis. Only companies which are strong competitively will be capable of maintaining their financial performances in the future. Companies which are highly competitive show long-running positive trends and abilities with quality of service, development of new products, and customer retention and satisfaction levels. It also helps a company's competitive position when there are effective barriers to competition. These can be in the form of protective regulations, substantial copyright and/or patent protections, or agreements on licensing, permits, and franchising.

The business environment is a third area of consideration for those performing credit analyses. This refers to three primary areas known as country risk, currency risk, and industry risk. Country risk relates to the ways in which the business activities of the enterprise can be negatively impacted by changes in the tax, regulatory, social, legal, and political regimes in those nations where they have a significant business presence.

Currency risk simply refers to the effects of drastic foreign exchange movements on both the corporate balance sheet and the company's capabilities of sourcing raw materials and other inputs or of selling their goods and products abroad. Industry risk pertains to the dynamics of the business, regulatory regime, and legal and market elements within the industry. These considerations can impact not only the industry but a particular company being evaluated by credit analysis.

Looking at some examples of this can help to better understand the concept. Where there are currency exposures throughout the supply chain, the company could hedge these appropriately in the futures markets. Another example is that the company may know its earnings will not change much even as their industry segment progresses along a change in technology.

There are many parallels between credit ratings of even different borrowing entities. This is why though the risk profile on an AAA-rated state government is less than that of an AAA-rated corporation, triple A rated borrowers in either scenario will always be far safer and less risky than the comparable B- and especially C-rated borrowers in each field. As an example, the A-rated S&P 500 companies boasted an average return of 10.74% in the period ending August 30th of 2013. For those same S&P companies with BB or lower credit ratings, their average return over the identical time period proved to be only 6.53%.

Credit Crunch

A Credit Crunch refers to an economic malaise caused by the inadequacy of freely flowing investment capital which becomes harder to get. Both investors and banks suddenly become more choosy in whom they will loan money to. This includes corporations which are worthy of and deserving of the credit. It ultimately leads to the cost of debt products going higher for issuing borrowers. Such crunches are commonly an outgrowth of a recession. They ensure that most firms cannot borrow enough funds since lenders are fearful of rising defaults and bankruptcies. This leads to higher interest rates in nearly all cases where it occurs.

A Credit Crunch can also be referred to as a credit crisis or even a credit squeeze. These crises often trip off when some external factor beyond a mere shift in the underlying interest rates occurs. Those businesses and people who previously were easily able to get financing and/or loans in order to pay for significant purchases or grow operations are suddenly left without recourse to such critical funds. It creates a devastating ripple effect throughout the whole economy. Home ownership percentages begin to decline while businesses begin to cut back their operations since they suffer from a devastating loss of readily and cheaply available capital supply.

Such credit crunches commonly occur as a natural reaction to a period where the lenders were too lenient with their standards for extending credit to businesses and individuals. Their previous loans they issued to various borrowers who were questionable in their capability of repaying the loans in the first place. It causes the default rates to skyrocket. This then leads to an appearance of toxic debt in direct consequence.

There have even been extreme scenarios like with the Global Financial Collapse and Great Recession of 2007-2009 where the levels of bad debt grow so high that a great number of financial institutions become insolvent. This forces them to either close their doors for good or to accept help from government bailouts in order to continue funding their daily operations.

These desperate crises can force the lending standard pendulum to swing to the complete opposite side of the spectrum. Since the lenders have grown fearful of being burned for a second time, they begin to pull back severely on their lending efforts to only engage with those borrowers who possess perfect credit and so represent the very lowest potential default risk possible. When this behavior occurs, it is called a flight to quality.

Such a credit crunch invariably leads to a lengthy and painful recession, or slowdowns in economic growth to negative levels. With the available supply of credit shrinking, it becomes a self-fulfilling prophecy. Besides tighter standards of available credit, the lenders often decide to raise their interest rates in the crunch to be sure that they can obtain higher revenues from their fewer numbers of loans and customers which they allow to borrow their money.

Higher borrowing costs also reduce individuals' capabilities of spending money to help the economy. This further reverberates into the businesses and their decisions as their sales can consequently slow down. Finally it all eats up limited and precious business capital which might have been utilized to hire workers and expand company operations.

There are consumers and companies for whom the credit crunch and its consequences will be greater than simply a higher cost to obtain capital. Such firms which cannot at all find a source of readily available capital will in the best cases be unable to expand; while in the worst cases will fail to remain a going concern. Such companies have no choice but to pull back on their various operations and to reduce the staff on their payroll. This leads to declines in productivity as well. The two conditions feed through into the leading indicators for a recession that is growing worse by the day.

Credit Derivatives

Credit derivatives refer to bilateral contracts which are privately held. These contracts permit the holders to manage their credit risk exposure. Such derivatives turn out to be financial assets. Examples of the better-known ones in the derivatives universe are swaps, forward contracts, and options. The price of these is necessarily based upon the credit risk of economic entities like governments, companies, or private investors. This means that banks which are worried about one of their customers not being capable of repaying their loan are able to purchase protection against such a potential loss in default. They do this by keeping the loan on their books at the same time as they transfer the credit risk off to a third party more commonly referred to as the "counter party."

Such credit derivatives are only one of numerous different kinds of financial instruments available to investors and financial institutions today. With these derivatives, they are merely instruments whose existence derives from underlying financial instruments. The value which underlies them comes from a stock or other asset.

Two different principal forms of derivatives exist. These are calls and puts. Calls provide the right but not obligation to purchase a stock for a pre-set price called the strike price. Puts deliver the right but not obligation to sell particular stocks for pre-arranged strike prices. With either calls or puts, investors are obtaining insurance in case a stock price rises or falls. This makes every form of derivative product an insurance vehicle and particularly these credit derivative examples.

Numerous credit derivatives exist on the markets today. Among these are CDO Collateralized Debt Obligations, CDS Credit Default Swamps, credit default swap options, total return swaps, and credit spread forwards. Banks are allowed to utilize these complicated instruments in order to completely take away their default risk from even an entire loan portfolio. The financial institutions or banks pay a premium, or upfront fee, for this accommodation.

Considering a concrete example helps to make the credit derivatives concept clearer. Plants R Us borrows $200,000 off of a bank with a ten year repayment term. Because Plants R Us shows a poor credit history, they are forced to buy the bank a credit derivative in order to be able to receive the loan. The bank accepts this product which will permit them to transfer all of the default risk to a third counter party. This means that the counter party would be forced to deliver all unpaid interest and principal on the loan in the event that Plants R Us defaults on the said loan. For this guarantee, Plants R Us pays an annual fee to the counter party for their assumed risk. Should the Plants R Us not default on the loan, then the counterparty firm keeps the entire fee. This makes it a win-win-win situation for all three parties. The bank is protected against a default by Plants R Us, which gets to have its loan. The counter party collects the yearly fee. All parties gain and benefit from the arrangement.

Credit derivatives' values vary widely depending on several factors. These include the borrower's credit quality as well as the counter party's credit quality. The biggest concern comes down to the credit quality of the third party - counter party. If the counter party defaults or is otherwise unable to honor their commitments specified in the derivatives contract, then the financial institution will not get its payment for the loan principal and interest. The counter party would naturally no longer receive its annual premium payments any longer either. This is why the quality of credit for the counter party is so much more critical than is the credit quality of the borrower (Plants R Us in the example).

Credit Ratings Agencies

Credit Ratings Agencies are those companies whose purpose is to consider and report on the financial strength which firms and government agencies demonstrate. They report on national as well as international corporations and agencies in this capacity. Their reports are most interested in the ability of the entities in question to fulfill their obligations for both principal and interest repayments of their bonds and other kinds of debts. Besides this, the various ratings agencies carefully examine and review the conditions and terms on every debt issue.

The end result of the agencies' work is to release a credit rating on both the debt issues in particular and the debt issuers more generally. When they agencies have high confidence that the issuer will be able to meet their debt servicing of principal and interest as promised, they will issue a high credit rating. When the opposite is true, the credit rating will be lower. It is entirely possible for a particular issue of debt to receive a differing credit rating from the issuer. This heavily depends on the particular terms of the issuer.

The impacts of these debt issue ratings are enormous in the industry and for the specific issuers in question. Those debt issues that obtain the best credit ratings will receive the most attractive interest rates from the credit markets. This is because the confidence of investors in an entity's capability of making their various payment obligations comes down to the credit ratings agencies review, analyses and especially ratings. Since the interest rates which investors demand for a specific debt issue will be inversely correlated to the borrower's particular creditworthiness, weaker borrowers will have to pay more while the stronger ones will enjoy paying less.

In this way, the credit ratings agencies act on behalf of businesses in much the same capacity as the consumer credit bureaus do for individual consumers. Such credit scores which the credit bureaus develop for individual people will greatly impact the interest rates at which individuals are able to borrow money.

The downside to these credit ratings agencies and their work is that they have been made the scapegoat for company and government defaults in recent years. Their research quality in particular has been the target of heavy criticism from observers and analysts who point out companies which they rated highly suddenly collapsed. Governments in Europe on which they provided high credit ratings defaulted or almost defaulted on their debts, as with Greece in particular.

This caused third party observers to argue that the various credit ratings agencies are actually poor at financial forecasting, at uncovering growing and negative trends for the debt issuers they follow, and also are overly late in revising down their ratings. Besides this, critics point to the many conflicts of interest of the ratings agencies. This is because the debt issuers are able to pick out and pay the ratings agencies for the reviews of their bonds. In a survey conducted in 2008, 11 percent of the various investment professionals surveyed by the CFA Institute responded that they had observed personally instances where the major ratings agencies had actually upgraded their given ratings on bonds when they were pressured by the debt issuers in question.

There are only three firms today which dominate the space, and this is part of the problem. The Wall Street Journal provided the ratings shares of the big 3 agencies in their 2011 report. Of the 2.8 million ratings they issue collectively (with the other seven minor agencies), S&P 500 controls the greatest market share with 42.2 percent. Moody's holds 36.9 percent of the market. Fitch rounds out the top three with 17.9 percent.

The article claimed that fully 95 percent of all revenues in this industry were earned by the big three. Only 2.9 percent of the ratings issued came from the other seven firms. The other seven credit ratings agencies were A.M. Best, DBRS, Japan Credit Rating Agency, Rating and Investment Info., Egan-Jones Ratings, Morningstar Credit Ratings, and Kroll Bond Rating Agency.

Between the top two issuers Moody's and Standard & Poor's, they provide ratings for roughly 80 percent of all municipal and corporate bond issues. They are typically regarded as a level higher than Fitch. One particular example speaks volumes. While Egan-Jones had downgraded the U.S. Federal government debt to the second highest rating years earlier, it was ignored largely by the markets and world. When Standard & Poor's took the same action by downgrading the Federal government of the United States debt to AA+ on August 5th of 2011, this shook the world bond, currency, and stock markets. It demonstrates the clout S&P and Moody's especially enjoy over all of their various credit ratings agencies rivals.

Debenture

A Debenture refers to a form of debt instrument. The differentiating factor of such instruments is that they do not have the physical backing of either collateral or assets securing them. Instead, they are only guaranteed by the overall reputation and creditworthiness of the issuing corporation or municipality. Governments and corporations alike commonly issue such bonds in order to obtain much needed fresh capital. As with other forms of bonds, these are recorded in indentures.

Since such Debentures come without any collateral, the buyers of bonds purchase them on the hopes that the issuer will not default on interest and principal repayments. Government examples of these kinds of bonds abound in the marketplace. T-bills and T-bonds are both classic debentures. They have always been deemed to be completely risk free as the government can always raise taxes to pay its debt obligations or resort to printing money in order to cover them.

Corporations most often resort to issuing Debentures as their longer term loan vehicles. They typically come with a maturity date that is fixed at an interest level that is similarly fixed. Corporations will most often make such interest payments ahead of giving any dividends to the stock shareholders, as with other types of senior debt obligations. This makes debentures beneficial with their lower interest rate and farther away repayment date as compared to other forms of debt bonds and loans corporations and governments can take out.

Two forms of Debentures exist. These are either non-convertible or convertible ones. The convertible ones represent bonds that the holders can convert into stock shares from the issuer once a pre-set time period has elapsed. Investors like these kinds of bonds more than others since they gain the ability to convert to more lucrative and price appreciative stock. Issuers appreciate them best since they come with the lowest of interest rates.

Alternatively, the non-convertible types are more regular Debentures which cannot be exchanged for stock in the issuer. The compensation for this lack of flexibility in the instrument is that they come with a higher interest rate than their non-convertible debenture cousins.

Every debenture on the market comes with particular characteristics. The trust indenture must be drafted. This agreement is set up between the managing trust and the issuing corporation. The coupon rate must subsequently be determined, as it is the critical interest rate which the firm will pay the investors and debt holders. While the rate is often fixed, it may also be floating. This comes down to how high the firm's credit rating or the credit rating of the bond issue itself proves to be.

With non-convertible debentures, the maturity date turns out to be among the key features of the issue. Maturity date is the point when the issuer has to return the principal to the investors. Yet the firms possess several options for how they will repay this money. It is most common for companies to do a redemption from their capital. This means that the issuers will simply offer a lump sum one-time payment on the maturity date. The second choice is known as the debenture redemption reserve. In this form, the issuer is allowed to transfer a set quantity of funds every year up to the point where the debenture has been fully repaid into the fund by the maturity date.

With either way, the company or government agency still repays all funds due on the maturity or repayment date. The only difference lies in whether they set aside the funds in part ever year or have to front them all entirely in the year they are due to be repaid.

Debt Coverage Ratio (DCR)

Debt coverage ratio has different meanings dependent on what entity is using it. In the world of corporate finance, it is the amount of cash flow that a company has to service its current debts. This ratio utilizes the net operating income divided by the debt payments due in a year or less. This includes principal, interest, lease payments, and the sinking fund.

It has a different meaning with governments and individuals. For finances of a national government, debt coverage ratio refers to the export earnings required for the country to make its yearly principal and interest payments with the external debts of the nation. With individual finance, banks and their loan officers utilize this ratio to decide on income property loans.

Debt coverage ratios must be higher than one in order for the government, company, or individual to prove enough income to satisfy its present debt obligations. With a DCR under 1, it lacks the means to do so. This ratio is determined by dividing Net Operating Income by the Total Debt Service.

The net operating income turns out to be the revenue of a company less its operating expenses. This does not cover interest payments or taxes. The NOI can also equate to the EBIT Earnings Before Interest and Tax. Investors and lenders which are evaluating the creditworthiness of corporations and companies should use criteria that is consistent when they figure out the DCR.

Total debt service is the term that concerns the present debt obligations. This will include principal, interest, lease payments, and sinking fund all owed in the next year. Balance sheets also include both the long term debt current portion and the short term debt.

When a debt coverage ratio is lower than one, it says that the entity cash flow is negative. With a DCR of .90, the company would only possess sufficient NOI to handle 90% of their yearly debt payments. With personal finance this would mean that the borrower had to access some outside funds each month in order to cover the payments. Lenders usually discourage loans with negative cash flow. They may permit them when the borrower can show a strong outside income.

Lenders almost always consider the debt coverage ratio of borrowers before they extend loans to them. They do not want to loan money to entities with lower than one. Such groups will have to draw on sources outside of their traditional income or borrow more in order to make their debt payments. When the DCR is dangerously close to one, then the borrower is considered to be vulnerable to a slowdown in income. Only a minor setback to its cash flow would mean it would not be able to service the debts. Some lenders will actually insist that the borrowers keep minimum levels of debt coverage ratios while they have a loan balance. In these cases, borrowers whose ratios decline below this minimum level are in technical default.

Lenders can be more lenient on debt coverage ratios when the economy is booming. An expanding economy means that credit is available more easily. This often causes lenders to work with companies and individuals on their lower ratios. The problem is that borrowers which are under qualified can impact the stability of the economy.

In the 2008 financial crisis, subprime borrowers received credit in the form of mortgages without proper consideration of their finances. As such borrowers defaulted in large numbers, the lenders that had made loans to them failed. The largest savings and loan institution Washington Mutual turned out to be the most egregious example of this scenario.

Debt Ratio

Debt Ratio refers to a highly favored financial ratio. This one measures the consumer or company's debt leverage. This ratio is best explained as the ratio for all of the longer-term and shorter-term debt divided by all assets of the individual or enterprise. It is then expressed out in percentage or decimal format. Another way of stating it is the proportion of a firm's assets financed by outright debt. The debt ratio is sometimes called the debt to assets ratio as well.

All else being equal, as this debt ratio is higher it means that the firm has a higher degree of leverage. This generally implies a higher amount of financial risk. Yet simultaneously it is true that such leverage is a critical tool which many corporations employ to expand. Countless firms have discovered many sustainable uses of such debt.

Naturally, acceptable and average debt ratios will range drastically from one industry to the next. Utilities and pipelines are capital-intensive firms. They will necessarily possess far greater debt ratios than do companies in such industries as technology. Consider a clear example to help understand this term better. When corporations have assets of $200 million and aggregate debts of $50 million, then the debt ratio would amount to 25 percent or .25 alternatively. This company would therefore be in a stronger financial position than a comparable one with a 35 percent debt to asset ratio, but not always.

This is because 25 percent debt to asset ratios can be excessive in an industry that boasts unstable cash flows. These businesses simply cannot assume too much debt. Such a firm that possessed an overly high debt ratio as measured up against its rivals would discover how costly additional borrowing would become. This means that it might fall into a cash crunch in shifting circumstances. The fracking industry starting in summer 2014 found itself in dire straits thanks to its huge debt levels and plunging energy prices.

At the same time, debt levels that amount to 35 percent could be easy to manage for those firms which are in an industry like utilities. The cash flows in these businesses are far stronger and more stable. Higher debt to assets ratios are not only acceptable in this business, they are expected. For those firms that find themselves with an over 100 percent debt ratio, you know that its debt levels actually exceed its amount of assets. Conversely, when firms possess a ratio under 100 percent, the firm possesses more assets than debt. Alongside other metrics for determining financial soundness, this ratio will allow investors to ascertain how high the risk level is for a given business.

Debt ratios do not take into account all money that a firm owes necessarily. While they will always count longer- and shorter-term debts, they will leave out liabilities. Some of these liabilities that do not figure into the calculations are negative goodwill, accounts payable, and "other" items.

Consider a real-world example of how this works out in practice. Starbucks possesses a debt ratio of around 22.5 percent. Morningstar considers that the typical ratio for the industry is more like 40 percent on average. This means that the Starbucks Corporation can easily borrow money on the markets. Creditors understand that its finances are solid as a rock. They anticipate receiving full repayment on time. The non-callable and fixed rate Starbucks' bonds that mature in 2045 possess coupon rates of only 4.3 percent.

Contrast this with a basic materials firm like Arch Coal Incorporated. The industry of coal mining is regarded as highly capital intensive. This is why the industry forgives utilizing leverage to operate effectively. The average debt to assets ratio proves to be 47 percent. Yet Arch Coal Inc. has a 64 percent ratio. This makes it costly for them to borrow money. In fact their non-callable, fixed rate bonds that mature in 2023 come with a painful interest coupon rate amounting to 12 percent.

Debt Restructuring

Debt restructuring refers to a means which corporations or countries with overwhelming debt loads utilize to change the terms of their outstanding debt arrangements so they can gain advantage in repayment. Corporations will often utilize a form of debt restructuring so that they can sidestep defaulting on their already existing debt levels. They might also wish to gain the benefits of lower interest rates that may be available to them on the markets.

One way that companies accomplish this is by issuing a series of callable bonds. These permit them to easily and rapidly restructure their new debts at a given point in the future. In this case, the firms' existing debts will be called. They will then replace them with a newer issued debt for the lower, more advantageous interest rate. Another way that corporations are able to restructure their debt lies in changing the provisions and terms of the current debt issue.

With corporate debt restructuring, a company will typically reorganize its actual obligations by lowering the debt burdens on their firm. They can do this by reducing the payable rates on the debt or by extending the amount of time they have until they repay the debt obligations. By doing either of these, the company ensures it is able to service its relevant debt burdens. There are other cases where the creditors will opt to forgive a part of the debt in exchange for obtaining an equity stake in the firm.

A need for this type of corporate debt restructuring most often occurs when corporations or companies are experiencing financial difficulties. These make it most difficult to keep up with their full range of financial obligations. Sometimes such troubles can be sufficient to create a significant risk of the company declaring bankruptcy. In these cases, they have the ability to engage in a structured negotiation with the creditors to lower the burdens so that they can avoid entering bankruptcy-led defaults.

Within the United States, there is a provision of the corporate bankruptcy code known as Chapter 11. These protocols permit corporations to obtain effective protection from their creditors so that they are able to try to rearrange the debt terms to continue on as a reorganized, ongoing, viable concern. Thanks to federal bankruptcy courts becoming involved in this process, even when the creditors refuse to accept such a settlement and reorganization, the courts can mandate that the creditors accept the plan if they deem it to be reasonable and fair.

It is not only corporations and companies which can avail themselves of such debt restructuring. Governments also have needs for help with their debts when they finally become unsustainable. This is not a new phenomenon. It stretches back to the first historically recorded sovereign debt default of the fourth century B.C. At this time, ten different Greek city-states defaulted on loans they had taken from the sacred temple of Delos. Despite the fact that this has occurred for at least 2,300 years, today no clear and mutually understood rules exist to structure the process for what will occur if a sovereign state can not pay their debts.

The most recent classic example of this dates back to the huge default by Argentina. Their enormous debt default in 2001 was among the largest in modern history. The rules are unclear as to who has jurisdiction and who can set restructuring terms. For years Argentina refused to negotiate terms with the eight percent of its bondholders who would not agree to the terms the country set in 2001. Then a court ruling from the U.S. Supreme Court confused the issue by ordering Argentina to settle with the remaining holdouts at full value plus interest before they could pay the agreed-upon settled amount to the other 92 percent of debt holders.

Argentina then came back to the table for the eight percent of mostly opportunistic hedge funds which had bought their defaulted debt for pennies on the dollar. Grudgingly under duress they paid the hedge fund eight percent claimants. This was an unusual case study that only worked out because the debt had been issued under American debt law. In other cases and scenarios, it is only the IMF International Monetary Fund that is attempting to create some sort of rules on situations like these.

Yet in the end, no one can force a country to pay its debts back to creditors short of going to war with them to seize their physical assets or by freezing assets of the offending country in the banks or vaults of the debt holders' countries.

Debt to Equity

Debt to Equity refers to a ratio that is extremely important and often scrutinized in the world of business. It is the amount of longer term debt on the balance sheet of a corporation as related to and divided by the company equity. Long term debt for a company means money that it will not be expected to pay back in the coming 12 months. Both are critical factors in effective balance sheet analysis.

This ratio tells an analyst or investor a great deal about a company and the amount of debt it is carrying compared to its true net worth. This is accomplished by gathering together all of the company liabilities and then dividing this amount up by the shareholder equity. The end result which comes back in dividing the total debt by the equity proves to be the percentage of the firm which is leveraged (or more accurately stated--- indebted).

Over time, the acceptable and average amount of debt to equity has varied significantly in the corporate world. Today it heavily depends on both the state of the economy, the industry in which the company operates, and the all-around feelings of society concerning credit and debt. If all else is equal, any firm with a debt to equity ratio in excess of 40 percent to 50 percent should be more careful about the risk hidden within its balance sheet and books. These could lead to a liquidity crisis at some point in the future.

When analysts consider the working capital of the company and find that both it and the current ratios of the firm are dramatically low, then this is a glaring sign of significant financial weakness in a corporation. This is why an analyst or investor truly needs to adjust any current profitability numbers to the economic cycle at hand. Many investors have lost fortunes over the years because the plugged in peak earnings at the height of an economic boom as their base case scenario metric for a firm's ability to pay back its various debt obligations.

There is no good reason to fall for this age old trap after all. All that is required to avoid it is to predict that the economy may fall off a proverbial cliff at any point and time. Then consider if the cash flow would be sufficient to cover the liabilities without the corporation being hurt and hampered by a lack of money for critical daily, monthly, and yearly expenses on items such as plant, property, and equipment.

The truth is that debt and elevated debt to equity ratios is not necessarily a bad thing. Many businesses are quite adept at earning a greater return on their capital than the cost of the interest which they incur in borrowing the money. This would make it extremely profitable to borrow money in such cases. It allows such firms to boost their earnings and profitability for one thing. The real key element is that the company management clearly understands the level of debt which will represent a danger level for smart and forward thinking stewardship of their company. Leverage cuts both ways. It dramatically boosts returns when it is working well for a firm, and it similarly can even totally wipe out a company if things turn on the firm in an economic recession or even economic depression.

Investors especially need to be careful in buying corporate bonds in such environments. Bonds issued in the lower interest rate environments of today will suffer drastically when the interest rates invariably rise higher, especially if this is quick and unexpected. This will lead to less profitability for the firm when the bonds have to be financed again. If the management did not wisely prepare for such an issue well in advance, then the company will truly have been mismanaged during the golden boom days and will suffer needlessly during the inevitable bust economic times.

Deferred Maintenance

Deferred maintenance proves to be the action of putting off maintenance procedures that are needed and routine on both personal property, such as machinery, or real estate property, such as infrastructure. This is done to save on expenses, to reassign money that is available in the budget, or to achieve the available levels of budget funding.

The downside to this avoidance or delay of generally needed repairs is that it causes the deterioration of assets, and finally their total impairment, if continued for an extended period of time. Usually over time, the practice of constantly deferring your maintenance will end up with greater costs in the future, the eventual failure of assets, and from time to time with safety and health concerns resulting.

Maintenance is one of the budgetary items that is forced to battle along side other needs' and programs' funding. Since the money is simply not always available for the category of maintenance's use, it is often short changed. Other times, the money is available until it is directed by management to higher priority assignments and requirements later.

Maintenance that is deferred is most usually not reported to the necessary parties right away. Many times, it is never even reported at all. Such deferred maintenance that goes on over a lack of funds appropriated to the cause will finally lead to a greater number of incidences of inefficient service for the public, possible safety dangers, operations that are inefficient and ineffective, and greater costs overall at a future point in time.

Examples of personal deferred maintenance and business deferred maintenance cases abound. Deferred maintenance in a home would include delaying the car's recommended one year inspection or tune up, or not having those repairs done that the mechanic recommended. As a result of this, the car will likely not operate as effectively or efficiently. It could also suffer mechanical or electrical failures or even become involved in an unnecessary crash over safety issues.

This term of deferred maintenance is more commonly used with large corporations or governments though. A large corporation slashing its budget might result in the company's plants and equipment not undergoing their annual cleaning and refurbishing.

The firm might get away with this for a year or even two. In time though, problems will begin to show up in machinery break down, equipment misses and failure, and possible shut downs of the plant, if this practice of ignoring critical plant maintenance is put off much or for too long.

Deficit Financing

Deficit Financing refers to a particular emphasis in money management. In this unique angle on financing, companies or governments happily spend a greater amount of money than they take in over the comparable period. This is also called a budget deficit strategy. In fact governments on most levels, small businesses to corporations, and individuals with their household budgets all attempt to engage in this form of financing whenever they can. If it is used carefully and constructively, such a means of financing can create conditions which improve the financial condition of the entity along with the creation of debt that comes alongside it. Such debt might or might not ever be repaid.

Governments take the lead role in such Deficit Financing. Among the more commonplace examples of this is attempting to stimulate the national economy to end recessions. To do this, governments will borrow resources and use the funds to purchase things. This will directly boost the demand for output from businesses sectors, who will in turn hire workers to keep pace with growing government demand. It lowers unemployment and provides salaries to employees who will also increase their spending apace.

This creates a money multiplier effect within the economy. As the marketplace strengthens, consumer confidence will also typically rise, helping still other consumers to save less out of fear and purchase more out of increasing optimism about economic prospects. This leads to a greater quantity of goods and services being purchased by the consumer sector. When properly followed, such a deficit spending plan will actually increase the economic prosperity of a given national economy throughout a period from several months to even a few years in length.

Deficit Financing in the science of economics is not merely restricted to the government though. All sizes and types of businesses may attempt to spend more money than they can practically afford upfront in an effort to generate plenty of funds down the road to pay back the investment when it comes due.

Consider a concrete example. A manufacturing company might elect to buy new factory plants or machinery. They realize that the updated equipment and greater production line space will allow them to produce more goods in a shorter time frame and at a more advantageous cost per unit produced. Given enough time, such advantages of using the strategy will allow them to pay down the upfront debt and maintain a surplus to corporate cash flow and retained earnings.

Consumers similarly attempt to do this with their money management tools. Deficit financing for them means that the individuals will buy things now to improve their house in an effort to boost the value of their real estate. The debt would be then paid back and the owner would keep the higher fair market value home. When the homeowner sells the house, he or she will realize a greater price than before the improvements were made using the Deficit Financing. In the meanwhile, the occupants of the home have the pleasure of enjoying the upgraded facilities, appliances, and amenities that have improved the home value over the long run.

Economic theory and development has held with the idea of Deficit Financing for a long time now. John Maynard Keynes is credited with coming up with the full articulation of the idea in economics. Many economists since him have appreciated the strategy, its advantages, and the dangers if it is not carefully orchestrated. Deficit financing and spending is not necessarily the best means of righting a poor and deteriorating financial situation for an economy, business balance sheet, or household budget. Yet responsibly deploying it may boost the financial status of the country, business, and quality of life of the individuals involved.

Deficit Spending

Deficit spending is a generally unsustainable scenario where a greater number of resources are employed to secure purchases than are brought in to the organization through revenue generating means. When this is the case, the business or government outfit actually operates in a budget deficit.

This simply means that not enough financial resources are being created by the organization in order to effectively fund the operating budget. As this occurs, the additional expenses are paid for by utilizing deferred payment plans that permit the organization to buy now and pay later, or alternatively with credit accounts.

Even though such deficit spending can occur with consumers and businesses, it is generally discussed pertaining to governments and their operations. These days, governments are mostly incapable of running their operations without resorting to deficit spending. As the taxes that are collected generally are insufficient to cover all of the costs that are proposed by the annual budget, the shortfall is commonly covered by buying things with money that has been borrowed. In such a way, these governments run their activities in a deficit spending scenario.

Not every government runs its affairs from a negative budget scenario all of the time. There are periods where governments can look forward to the revenues that come in from taxes and any investments surpassing the money that is required to cover the costs of budgetary items. In these moments, governments have the opposite of deficit spending situations. They are running on budget surpluses. Surpluses are used for a variety of different needs, such as infrastructure improvements, repayment of debt from past deficit spending, or savings for future budget deficits.

Without a doubt, deficit spending proves to be all too common for governments. This does not make it a wise economic policy to pursue continuously over extended time frames. The reason for this is that deficit spending commonly requires borrowing funds that must be paid back with interest that accrues over time. In such a way, enormous amounts of government debt can be built up in short time frames.

Because of this, a number of responsible governments attempt to intelligently manage their deficit spending in such a way that they only engage in it to keep up critical operations and services that the citizens need for their well being. Other less important programs they try to cut back on whenever possible.

Companies may sometimes operate on a deficit spending basis. If they do this for long periods of time, then they are often unable to turn the failing trend around. The end result of this behavior leads to bankruptcy or being purchased by other, more fiscally responsible businesses. Consumers that engage in deficit spending for longer periods than only temporary time frames similarly discover that the scenario ends up in financial destruction. Outstanding assets may then be liquidated to satisfy the debts that result.

Demutualization

Demutualization is the decision undertaken by the members of a mutual corporation to convert their company into one which shareholders own instead. This means that the members and users of the mutual company give up their rights of use in exchange for stock shares in the new usually publically traded company.

Such mutual companies were originally established in order to offer specific services to their members. They are able to provide said services for the least expensive price possible to their members. This is because they are not forced to earn profits, as with publically traded or for profit corporations. Instead, their goals are to remain at least financially stable and solvent, to offer member benefits, and to return any profits that remain after they pay expenses to their member owners.

This has been a practice most common with insurance companies in recent years. A number of mutual insurers that could not earn sufficient returns on their investments, or which faced limited possibilities in acquisitions and mergers on their own, chose this path. They evolved into companies which were publically traded stock corporations. It has aided insurance companies in raising much-needed fresh capital. It also helped them to become more competitive in the domestic marketplace.

The question remains is this a good strategy for the mutual insurance company owners? They already enjoy the rights to elect the members of the board of directors. They also have some voice in the way the firms operate. All premiums which the owners pay go towards the insurance company's bottom line. If there is a profit, then a portion of those premiums are returned as dividends. This is not the case for those life insurance policy holders who own term life insurance only.

The insurance companies pay out these dividends once they determine what money remains after key expenses. Among these costs they look at are policy expenses, mortality payouts, and administration costs. Interestingly enough, mutual companies do not have to disclose to their owners how they come up with their dividends.

There are several important reasons why firms elect to pursue a demutualization. They are usually first and foremost interested in gaining greater access to additional capital. With this fresh infusion of substantial amounts of cash they can raise by selling shares, they are able to pursue mergers and acquisitions. The mutual insurance companies have found that laws which permit the mega banks and publically traded insurance companies to offer similar services have created huge amounts of pressure to compete effectively in the marketplace for financial services. At least on paper and on balance sheets, additional money a company obtains from its IPO initial public offering provides them with a healthier and more powerful firm.

The process of demutualization can require in the range of 18 to 24 months. Before the insurer can affect conversion, they will invest significant amounts of time to fashion a draft proposal. This has to first be approved by the board of directors of the firm. Next this proposal has to be turned in to the state's insurance department for review. The firm will also want to run meetings giving out information in the state where their head office is based. Policy holders must be informed with regards to their rights to vote yes or no on the final proposal.

Those policy holders which have a right to participate in the process are usually allowed to choose one of three benefits. They can request shares of stock in the publically traded company, a cash payout, or an enhancement to their existing policy. Finally, after the policy holders approve the demutualization process, it is up to the department insurance of the state to review the plan. They must give final approval to the decision for demutualization to commence.

Depository Bank

A Depository Bank refers to a facility like an office, building, or even warehouse that acts as a depository for safeguarding and storage purposes. This might be a bank, a vault, an organization, or even a financial institution which inventories and helps with the act of trading securities. The term also pertains to any depository institution which takes in financial deposits from their clients.

These depository institutions deliver financial services to both business and personal customers. These do not have to be cash-based only. They could be stocks and bonds certificates. The institution will inventory the securities. They often keep them in an electronic format called book-entry form. They might also hold physical paper certificates or dematerialized virtually-based certificates as well.

Depository banks carry the primary function in this regard of transferring stock shares ownership from the seller of an investment to the buyer as the trade becomes executed. They also assist with reducing paperwork needed to execute trades. They also increase the speed at which the transfer process will be completed. These depositories also get rid of any risk in maintaining physical format securities and keeping them from loss, theft, damage, fraud, or delay in actual delivery.

There are other depository services these institutions carry out for their clients. These include savings and checking accounts and also transferring funds electronically via debit cards and online banking. They also handle electronically submitted payments as part of these services. Customers surrender their cash to these banks and financial institutions under the core belief that the firm will simply hold on to them and then return them as the customer requests the money back upon demand.
In reality, the banks cheerfully take the clients' money and then pay them interest on this money slowly over time. As they hold the customers' money, they loan it out to other businesses and individuals as business loans and mortgages. They do this with the goal and hope of generating a higher amount of interest on the money than the amount which they pay out to their customers as interest.

In the field of depository institutions are three different types. These are commercial banks, savings institutions, and credit unions. All of them count on deposits from their clients in order to obtain their primary sources of funding. The Federal Deposit Insurance Corporation insures these consumer accounts up to a limit of $250,000 per account in case of bank failure.

Commercial banks prove to be for profit enterprises that represent the biggest of the depository institutions. These often times mega-banks provide a vast array of services to businesses and consumers in the form of commercial and consumer lending, checking and savings accounts, certificates of deposit, investment products, and credit cards. Their goals in accepting inbound deposits are to offer them back out to still other clients in the form of real estate loans, commercial loans, and mortgage loans.

With savings institutions, these are also for profit ventures called savings and loan institutions. They concentrate their efforts mostly on consumer mortgage lending although they do also provide commercial loans and consumer credit cards. The customers deposit their money in an account. This purchases shares within the firm. In one fiscal year, savings institutions might approve 710 real estate loans, 250,000 personal and automobile loans, and 75,000 mortgage loans. They then collect interest on all of these various loans, a portion of which pays the interest on their clients' deposits.

Credit Unions are quite different from the above two previous types. They are not for profit groups which instead concentrate their efforts on customer service. The customers bring in their deposits to the account. This is much like purchasing shares within the credit union in question. The earnings of the credit union become distributed back to the customers as dividends on a regular basis.

Discretionary Expenses

A discretionary expense refers to those business or home costs that are not considered to be critical for the entity to function or operate effectively. This is important, since both businesses and individuals often are required to pay for discretionary expenses using discretionary income.

As an example, businesses might permit their staff to charge specific kinds of entertainment and meal expenses to the firm when they engage in these activities to build up business ties with clients, vendors, or potential customers. They might also cover meals and entertainment simply to foster better relations with their staff. A home would refer to discretionary expenses as those that they do not need, but instead want to have.

Discretionary income refers to any funds which remain after businesses or individuals pay their taxes and mandatory costs. On an individual level, those persons who do not have any money left once they pay the bills do not have any discretionary income. In order for them to pay for a discretionary expenses, they will be forced to take on debt by obtaining a loan or utilizing credit cards. An example of using debt to pay for a discretionary expense is utilizing credit cards to pay for a family vacation.

There are two kinds of expenses which consumer households incur. Some they are required to pay according to the law. This includes income and other taxes as well as health insurance (at least in tax years 2014 and 2015). Costs they have to pay out in order to make sure the family and household functions are also non-discretionary in nature. These include transportation costs, food, utilities, and rent or mortgage.

The people making the money do not have a choice of whether or not to pay these costs every month without suffering sometimes-severe consequences. The other kind of cost qualifies as a discretionary expense. This would be luxury items such as fine clothing, watches, or expensive liquor and vacation related costs. These are simply those services and goods costs which an earner may choose to pay for according to their personal discretion.

When economic conditions warrant, both businesses and households may find that they have to reduce their outlays as revenues and incomes go down. This is why it is important to have a thorough understanding of discretionary expenses before hand. When these are separately broken out on paper or a spreadsheet, then businesses and consumer decision makers can quickly and easily ascertain what expenses can be lowered or cut altogether.

A helpful technique for budgeting lies in ranking those discretionary expenses by their order of relative importance. This could be done by putting the least important at the top of the list and continuing on down to most important. When business income reduction or a cut back in hours on the job occurs causing businesses or households to slash expenses, then it is easy for the spending decision makers to choose which expenses can and should be cut first.

It is also to keep in mind that there are differences between what businesses and consumers consider to be discretionary in nature. Families which have two cars will likely have two car payments. They may think that the two cars are necessities and not discretionary. The truth is different. In an emergency, they could manage with only the one car in many cases. When times become hard and a job is lost, the family can decide the second car is actually discretionary and not essential. This way, they can sell the second vehicle to remove the second payment overhead from the family or household budget.

Distressed Assets

Distressed assets are assets that a company or individual has been forced to place for sale at a significant discount to the acquired or actual value. This usually happens as the owner has no choice but to sell the asset to raise cash. Several different reasons might exist for why this is the case. These include excessive debt levels, bankruptcy, and regulatory requirements. Even debt can be put on sale at an amount that is lower than its face value. When this happens, it is known as distressed debt.

Although there are various types of distressed assets offered for sale, among the most common in the wake of 2007-2010's financial crisis and Great Recession are non performing loans on houses or foreclosures on mortgaged properties. Investors of all sizes are able to take advantage of such distressed assets in property by availing themselves of a homeowner's lack of ability to meet the mandatory mortgage payments or of his or her critical requirements for cash. In situations like this, such homeowners will consent much of the time to selling the property for a substantial discount in order to achieve a fast sale.

In the past, banks dealt with such distressed asset mortgages almost entirely themselves. As a result of the American banks still repairing their heavily damaged balance sheets from the countless write offs and over leveraging that they engaged in over the past five to ten years, they can not keep up any longer with the enormous number of foreclosures on their books. This leaves them with little choice but to have to sell some of their mortgage property asserts at massive discounts to actual value in order to be able to create quick cash flow.

The end result is that distressed assets can present a potentially profitable investment opportunity for you. The still ongoing crisis in global liquidity and credit has banks selling mortgages to individual, as well as to large, investors at significant discounts. Such discounts to perceived value would never occur in the days of normalized conditions in the mortgage and credit market place.

This means that investors are currently able to purchase distressed home assets with discounts amounting to as much as 72.5%. With as little as

$100,000, smaller investors are able to get involved with this efficient and potentially lucrative investment strategy. Professional management teams are available to help small investors realize appropriate exit strategies whose goal is to generate an impressive 20% return on investment per year.

Purchasing distressed assets such as homes in mortgage payment trouble can offer ethical options and benefits as well. Investors are able to restructure the debt and payments of the home owner in such a way that distressed home owners are able to afford the new payments. This lets the troubled home owners stay in their houses so long as the investor owns the mortgage and the home owner is able to work with the newly arranged payment schedule.

Distressed assets of companies include many different types of assets. These might be commercial office buildings, commercial jets, and even factories and equipment sold at substantial discounts to real value. Many times, other corporations are able to acquire these distressed assets for their own uses at fantastic prices.

Distressed Securities

Distressed Securities refer to a corporation's financial instruments when the underlying companies are nearing or actually undergoing bankruptcy presently. Because such a firm is unable to cover all of its various financial responsibilities, its financial instruments will have undergone a dramatic decline in value. Yet thanks to the implied volatility that comes along with such inherent risk, the instruments actually provide investors with the very real possibilities of enormous returns. Such securities might be comprised of corporate bonds, trade claims, bank debt preferred stock, or common stock shares.

In the challenging investing climate of today, there are often many investors competing for opportunities which are bargain priced that might come with higher risk in the form of such Distressed Securities. There are scenarios where investors will carefully study up on the company plight and determine that it is not actually so serious as the market and public perceive it to be.

Because of this, they believe that their investments bought at a steep discount may increase dramatically in value as the situation of the company's finances becomes finally resolved. There are other cases where the investors agree with analysts that the firm may fall into bankruptcy. Yet they might be confident at the same time that the liquidation proceeds will be sufficient to cover the value of the securities which they obtain at a drastic discount to face value.

Individual investors should be extremely familiar with what will happen to such Distressed Securities should the company slide into either Chapter 7 or Chapter 11 bankruptcy. With the overwhelming majority of these bankruptcies, the common share equity will be completely wiped out. This means that investing in distressed stocks is highly risky. Yet many of the senior-most debt instruments like bonds, trade claims, and bank debts can provide some amount of payout after liquidation.

This is particularly the case when businesses elect to file a case of Chapter 7 bankruptcy. This halts operations and forces liquidation. The resulting funds will then be collected and dispersed out to the creditors according to their various degrees of seniority. With Chapter 11 bankruptcy, the corporation will restructure and resume its business operations. Assuming that such reorganization becomes a success, the distressed securities in the form of either corporate bonds or company stock could return incredible profit percentages as they stage a massive recovery alongside the company's improving fortunes and future prospects.

The trick is to understand at what stage such securities become Distressed Securities. Analysts will commonly label them as such when the firm that issues them cannot effectively meet a great number of its financial obligations. In the overwhelming majority of such scenarios, these securities will have been previously downgraded to junk credit rating status, as in CCC or lower by the major credit ratings arms of the debt rating agencies like Moody's Investor Services or Standard and Poor's.

Distressed securities are not necessarily always junk bonds though and should not be confused as such. Junk bonds only need to feature a credit rating of BBB or lower in order to be classified as junk. The underlying firm of the bonds is not in bankruptcy nor imminent to go there just because its bond issues carry the junk bond rating and label.

It is worth noting that the expected rate of return for distressed securities will be greater than 1,000 basis points (ten percent) over the rates of return for risk-free assets. This would include U.S. government bonds or Treasury bills' effective rates of return. It means that when the yield on five-year Treasury bonds amounts to one percent, then the Distressed Securities corporate bond should offer a rate of return of at least 11 percent.

Dividend Payout Ratio

The Dividend Payout Ratio refers to a ratio of all dividends which have been paid out to the total shareholders as compared to the complete net income of the company. In the end, the percentage of earnings paid to shareholders in the form of dividends is what this amounts to. Any amount of earnings which does not become payable to shareholders remains with the company in the form of retained earnings which the company keeps in order to reinvest for expansion or in other core operations or to pay down their company debt.

This Dividend Payout Ratio may be calculated out as the annual dividend per share divided by the company's earnings per share. Another way of figuring it is by taking the number one and subtracting the retention ratio.

This Dividend Payout Ratio delivers a figure for the total sum of money which a company gives back to its shareholders as opposed to how much they decide to hold for such things as increasing cash reserves, reinvesting in growth, and paying down debt. This is commonly referred to as retained earnings.

It is always important to consider a number of factors when deciding on how to read the Dividend Payout Ratio. This starts with the maturity level of a given company under consideration. Those firms which are newer and heavily skewed towards growth will want to expand, create and launch newer products, and also attempt to grow into completely new markets. They would naturally keep to reinvest the majority of or even sometimes all of their aggregate earnings. This would excuse them maintaining an extremely low or even zero percent payout ratio.

The same does not go for a company which is older and far better established. If they return only a small percentage of their earnings to the shareholders, then investors will complain. It might not only angry the individual corporate investors, but cause the so-called activists to intervene in the company board and management in retaliation.

Consider the interesting case of Apple. In the year 2012, the technology giant finally started paying a dividend for its first time in around twenty years at that point. It was because the new Chief Executive Officer believed that the enormous cash flow of the tech giant company meant that it was no longer justifiable to offer a zero percent payout ratio. The downside to this decision is it put Apple in the somewhat awkward position of joining the ranks of those corporations which believe they have passed their strong initial growth stage and so make a large dividend ratio payout to compensate. It signals that the company share prices will not likely continue to appreciate rapidly any longer.

The Dividend Payout Ratio has another helpful use. It can be deployed in order to determine how sustainable a dividend is from a given firm. Corporations do not like to cut back their dividends once they establish them. It can cause the stock price of the company to free fall and often reflects poorly on the skills and capabilities of management. When the firm has a higher than 100 percent Dividend Payout Ratio, it means that they are giving back a larger amount of money than they are earning. This would require that they reduce the dividend or eliminate it altogether in the near future.

Companies may decide to ride out a bad year in the market place without cutting their payouts though. This is why analysts like to contemplate the future earnings expectations of a firm to calculate up a forward looking payout ratio in order to put their last payout ratios into better perspective. Longer term payout ratios are similarly significant. Those ratios which are steadily increasing might be indicative of a maturing and growing business. Spiking ones might indicate that the dividend was quickly becoming unsustainable though.

Due Diligence

The phrase due diligence is utilized to discuss a wide variety of legal obligations, assignments, investigations, and reports. These all are practiced in business, manufacturing and law. The most commonly used version of the phrase has to do with businesses.

In business, the concept of due diligence pertains to the process gone through by venture capitalists in advance of pouring funding into a start up company. Also involved with this are investigations that continue later into the ways that the monies are being spent. Large companies similarly engage in such due diligence before making the decision to buy out a smaller company.

Venture capitalists practice a particular brand of due diligence that involves researching the present and past players and structures of the firm that is looking for venture funding. Venture capitalists are careful about putting money into firms that do not feature principals who showcase either a track record that is well proven or at least impressive credentials.

Such a due diligence investigation could be stricter or more relaxed based on the prevailing amount of caution held by the investment community at any given time. With most venture capitalist firms, there will be more than a dozen investigators employed who spend their time investigating particular information on the personal histories of the corporation's personnel. This task has become far easier than ever before thanks to the rise of the Internet and all of the subsequent access to information that is now available. Looking into an individual's experience and associations is now far quicker and more convenient.

Due diligence is also used for background checks. When venture capitalist decision makers make up their mind concerning the prospective firm, they will order these done. Most of the time, such venture capitalist partners will want to give funds to individuals that they either feel confident can be trusted, or to whom they have disbursed funds before with other ventures.

Despite the practice of due diligence, it does not guarantee that the investment will not fail. Companies that are comprised of successful proven people with tremendous educational backgrounds and practical experience still fail all of the time because of competition that no one foresaw coming, difficult conditions in the market, or even technical difficulties with products.

Due diligence involves a different understanding from one company to the next firm. Within the business of manufacturing, some environmental protections have to be taken. These are checked out in the due diligence report having to do with environmental site assessments. Such a report contains specifications in a checklist, as well as available sections for commentary.

Due diligence is also used by law firms concerning care that should be taken by companies or individuals in a particular scenario. An example of this might be a company making certain that their product was thoroughly checked out in advance of selling it and then finding out that it might be poisonous or harmful in strangling incidents. Should they not do this due diligence, then they may be charged with criminal negligence.

Earnings Per Share (EPS)

Earnings per share refer to the given total of earnings that a company has for every share of the firm's stock that is outstanding. There are several formulas for calculating earnings per share. These depend on which segment of earnings are being considered. The FASB, or Financial Accounting Standards Board, makes corporations report such earnings per share on their income statement for all of the major components of such statements including discontinued operations, continuing operations, extraordinary items, and net income.

To figure up the basic net earnings per share formula, you only have to divide the profit for the year by the average number of common shares of stock. With discontinued operations, it is only a matter of taking the discontinued operations income and dividing it by the average number of common stock shares outstanding. Continuing operations earnings per share equal the continuing operations income over the average number of common shares. Extraordinary items works with the income from extraordinary items and divides it by the weighted average number of common shares.

Besides the basic earnings per share numbers, there are three different types of earnings per share. Last year's earning per share are the Trailing EPS. These are the only completely known earnings for a company. The Current earnings per share are the ones for this year. These are partially projections in the end until the last quarterly numbers are released. Finally, Forward earnings per share are earnings numbers for the future. These are entirely based on predictions.

Earnings per share calculations do not take into account preferred dividends on categories besides net income and continued operations. Such continuing operations and even net income earnings per share calculations turn out to be more complex as preferred share dividends are taken off of the top of net income before the earnings per share is actually calculated. Since preferred stock shares have the right to income payments ahead of common stock payments, any money that is given out as preferred dividends is cash which can not be considered to be potentially available for giving out to every share of the commonly held stock.

Preferred dividends for the present year are generally the only ones that are taken off of such income. There is a prevalent exception to this. If preferred shares prove to be cumulative then this means that dividends for the entire year are taken off, regardless of if they have been declared yet or not. Dividends that the company is behind on paying are not contemplated when the earnings per share is calculated.

Earnings per share as a financial measuring stick for a company are extremely important. In theory, this forms the underlying basis for the value of the stock in question. Another critical measurement of stock price is price to earnings value, also known as the PE ratio. This PE ratio is determined by taking the earnings per share and dividing them into the price of the stock. Earnings per share are useful in measuring up one corporation against another one, if they are involved in the same business segment or industry. They do not tell you if the stock is a good buy or not. They also do not reveal what the overall market thinks about the company. This is where the PE ratio is more useful.

Equity Financing

Equity Financing refers to raising capital via selling shares within the enterprise itself. This comes down to selling an ownership stake in the corporation in order to come up with much needed funds for business enterprises. This type of financing could cover a wide array of different activities in both scope and scale. It might be only several thousand dollars which an entrepreneur raises from his family and friends. It could also be enormous IPOs initial public offerings that amount to literally billions of dollars and come from such household favorite names as Facebook and Google.

The phrase is most often applied to mega financing of major public companies which are listed on a stock exchange. This could also cover financing of private companies too. Equity financing is more or less the opposite to debt financing. In debt financing, funds will be borrowed form a business to be paid back at a later date and time.

There is more to Equity Financing than only selling common shares of stock. It might also involve other forms of equity (such as preferred stock) or even semi equity instruments like convertible stock shares or equity units which come with either warrants or common shares. Startup companies that evolve into highly successful firms often go through a few rounds of such Equity Financing as they grow and mature. These startups commonly attract varying types of investors at the different points in their growth. They will often rely on differing equity instruments for the various financing needs which arise throughout the newer company's history.

Consider an example to better understand the concept. Venture capitalists and angel investors are two different investors who are commonly the initial investors in startup companies. They generally prefer convertible preferred shares of stock instead of common shares of stock for their early rounds of funding. This is because those convertible shares offer a much higher possibility for upside potential as well as a little bit of downside protection.

After the firm has expanded enough to think about going public, they might begin to sell common shares of stock equity to retail and institutional investors. It might be that later they decide they require additional capital.

At this point, they might go out for secondary equity financing. This could include rights offerings or even offering various equity units which include warrants to sweeten the deal.

Financing via equity has rules and regulations which govern it. National securities regulators such as the SEC Securities Exchange Commission have the jurisdictional authority. This is intended to safeguard the investing public from any unscrupulous practices and operators who simply trick investors out of their funds then vanish. This is why such equity financing will usually come alongside a prospectus or at least an offering memorandum.

These provide a huge amount of useful information which assists the investors in taking highly informed decisions on the merits of the company and its financing offers. This data will usually cover the activities of the firm, provide information on the directors and other officers, explain the uses for the financing proceeds, offer financial statement disclosure, and revel the various risk factors.

The appetite which investors display for the various equity financing offerings heavily depends on the equity markets status as well as the financial market demand. When there are steady equity financing deals in the works, this represents an evidence of high investor confidence. Too many financing deals might mean that optimism is exuberant and a top in the market is coming.

When the Initial Public Offerings of dot coms and technology firms touched incredibly high record levels at the end of the 1990's, the writing was already on the wall. From 2000 through 2002, NASDAQ crashed and burned in a slow motion but extremely painful train wreck from which it needed more than a decade to recover. The speed and frequency of equity financing fell off substantially after this sustained correction in the markets because investors quickly became risk averse in the wake of the massive market selloff.

Equity Securities

Equity securities prove to be those asset classes which feature shares of stock in a given corporation. Investors hold these as reported by a company's official balance sheet. Corporations issue such securities in an effort to raise business capital via the financial markets. They use this money for significant company life events, such as for product development, merger and acquisition activity, or internal expansion. The funds are seldom for daily operating needs.

When investors buy equity securities, they gain a partial stake in the underlying firm. This is a primary alternative to turning to the bond markets to borrow money in taking on debt via the publicly traded bond markets. When a company first issues such equity securities, this is called an IPO initial public offering. Companies often raise enormous amounts of cash in this means, since investors are always hunting for new stock issues that will enable them to possess a part of a new and exciting opportunity.

The total number of shares that an IPO released varies wildly. It comes down to the amounts which the companies obtain permission to issue in their financial documents which they file with the regulatory overseer for their area. Corporations are allowed to sell a specific amount of stock shares in a given price range on the actual IPO day. After these shares have been dealt out to the public via the financial markets, the price of their equity will go up and down on the stock markets every trading day. This movement all depends on the perception of investors and the accompanying demand for the shares on any given day.

It is not common for such a firm to issue its entire inventory of available stock shares in a single offering. Rather than do this, they commonly reserve a certain quantity of shares to be issued at a later date in a second offering. This is called a follow on offering or secondary offering. The management of a company would elect to do this as they know they will likely need to raise fresh additional capital in the future in order to pay for hoped for expansionary plans.

When corporations continue to issue out their equity securities via the financial exchanges there is a downside for the existing shareholders and company investors. As additional shares are available to be bought, the pre-existing stake holders have their equity stake diluted as a percentage of the total. As an example, a major share holder could possess a huge quantity of shares that equate to fully 10 percent of all outstanding company shares which can be traded. Should the company choose to boost the total number of shares which are tradable, the equity of the shareholders will immediately drop in terms of the percentage ownership of all available shares.

The main alternative to issuing equity securities lies in issuing debt securities These publicly issued bonds offered via the bond markets by a company (or even government) raise money by taking on debt which must be repaid one day, known as the maturity date. Investors who buy debt instruments like these become de facto creditors of the bond issuing entities. The main disadvantage to such issuance in debt is that the company issuing has to provide continuous interest payments to the bond holders throughout the life of the bond contract. The company is able to maintain its ownership in itself in exchange for this trade off of interest payments.

Factoring

Factoring refers to a financial transaction which is considered to be debtor finance. In such an arrangement, companies actually sell off their invoices or accounts receivable to a third party factor for a discount. There is a major reason why a company would be interested in doing this. They may require cash for immediate needs which cannot wait for the accounts receivables to be effectively paid. When exporters engage in selling off their receivables in international trade finance, this is alternatively known as Forfaiting.

Factoring itself is typically also called invoice factoring, accounts receivable factoring, and accounts receivable financing. The foremost trade association for factoring proves to be the Commercial Finance Association. It handles both factoring transactions as well as asset based lending.

It is important to differentiate between factoring and invoice discounting. With factoring, receivables are actually sold off. Invoice discounting refers to a form of borrowing that utilizes for collateral on the loan the various accounts receivable assets. This is not the case in the United Kingdom however. Discounting is a type of factoring in the British market, which merely pertains to assigning receivables. This means that in Great Britain, this activity is also not deemed to be a form of borrowing. Confidentiality proves to be the principle difference between invoice discounting and factoring in the United Kingdom.

Four main events cover the factoring transaction. Each of these must be accountant-recorded by the individual financial professional who bears the responsibility for recording the transaction in its entirety. In the first step, the factor receives its fee. Next the interest expense must be paid out to the factor for advancing money on the transaction.

In the third step, the seller must allocate a certain percentage of the fees as bad debt expense. This relates to those receivables which the seller does not have confidence in being collectible. Finally, the seller will have to arrange a merchandise returns amount in the form of a "factor's holdback receivable." This category also covers any potential other gains or losses the seller will be forced to concede to the process of the invoice collecting.

There will be times when the charges the seller pays out to the factor will cover considerations such as extra credit risk, a discount fee, and additional services rendered by the factor. The final profit for the factor will amount to the ultimate difference between the amount it paid to obtain the invoices on accounts receivable and the actual money it finally recovers from the debtors. Any money which the factor loses because of non-payment is subtracted from this profit total.

With industries like clothing and textiles, companies which are completely financially sound will factor off their accounts. This results from the particular historical means of financing production in this industry. It permits the firm to cover its current cash needs and allows companies to operate with lesser cash balances. This leaves a larger amount of cash free for investing in future growth opportunities of the firm.

This debt factoring also serves a useful purpose as a means of improving cash flow control for those firms that find themselves in the unenviable position of possessing many accounts receivable that have various terms of credit which must be actively managed. Such a firm will often sell off its invoices at the appropriate discount because it decides that it will benefit financially in utilizing the resulting proceeds to improve growth. This serves them better than in acting as a de facto bank to their various clients.

This effectively means that factoring will happen at any point in any industry where the return rate for the proceeds put into future production is higher than the costs to factor out the receivable accounts. This is why the difference in money spent to factor must be carefully evaluated to ascertain if the value of producing additional goods will be higher than the money the company pays to work with the factor. A side but still important consideration revolves around how much cash the company possesses on hand for its operations and future growth potential.

Federal Funds

Federal Funds refers to the excess reserves which financial institutions such as commercial banks choose to deposit with their regional Federal Reserve Bank. These are also often called Fed Funds. Such funds may be lent out to other participants in the market who lack enough immediate cash on hand to cover their own mandatory minimum reserves and lending opportunities. Such loans are never secured and are offered at comparatively lower interest rates. This rate is known as the overnight rate or the Federal Funds rate. The name comes from the time period over which such loans are actually offered.

Such Fed Funds aid the commercial banks in their daily needs to attain their required reserves. These represent the sum of money which the banks must keep on hand with the regional Federal Reserve Bank. It is actually the total volume of a bank's customer deposits which determine the level of their particular reserve requirements. The Fed establishes either a range or alternatively a particular target rate for its fed funds rate. This is then adjusted from time to time according to monetary needs and economic conditions in the country.

Within the U.S., the market for fed funds operates on a parallel basis with the Eurodollar offshore deposit market. These Eurodollars trade on an overnight basis. Not surprisingly their interest rate proves to be nearly equal to that of the fed funds rate. Yet the transactions have to be actually booked from anywhere outside of the borders of the U.S. In fact many international banks will commonly employ their branches residing in Panama or the Caribbean (such as the Cayman Islands or Bermuda) to run such accounts. This is ironic, given that such transactions are typically executed from trading rooms located within the United States. Each of the two markets is wholesale and covers any transactions which range from at least two million dollars on up to in excess of a billion dollars.

The Federal Reserve carries on an important function using its Fed Funds. They deploy their famed open market operations in order to control the amount of money flowing through the national level economy and utilize adjustments to short term interest rates. This translates into the Fed selling and buying up a portion of the government bills and bonds it has previously issued out to commercial banks. Doing so actually decreases or increases the total money supply for the country. As a benevolent side effect, it then raises or lowers the shorter term time frame interest rates. It is actually the Federal Reserve Bank of New York (FRBNY) that physically carries out these open market operations.

As a point of fact, this federal funds rate is most similar to the shorter term time frame interest rates in the commercial markets. It means that their actions and the ensuing market reactions literally impact not only U.S. rates, but also LIBOR rates in London and Eurodollar rates. At the conclusion of every trading day, the Fed announces its daily effective fed funds rate. This proves to be the weighted average transaction rate for all tallied transactions throughout the business day.

There are a variety of participants in this enormous fed funds market. The key players prove to be the American- based commercial banks, American branches of the foreign
-based banks (like USB, Credit Suisse, HSBC, Barclays, RBS, RBC, Societe Generale, and BNP Paribas, to name just a few), government sponsored enterprises like Fannie Mae and Freddie Mac, savings and loan entities, agencies of the federal government, and securities companies.

Finance Controller

A Finance Controller turns out to be an employee who carries the responsibility for the higher level accounting, financial activities, and managerial accounting for a given firm. Such an employee will usually report to his or her supervisor the company CFO Chief Financial Officer. In smaller corporations and companies, the two positions may be one and the same. There are many important duties for these controllers. Among them are overseeing the duties of financial reporting, preparing the de facto operating budgets, and handling all critical affairs pertaining to payroll and many times staff development and continuing education.

It is a natural fact that controller duties and jobs will be different from one firm to the next because of the complexity, nature, and size of the particular firm and its industry as well. Some firms for example call their Financial Controllers comptrollers. This tends to be more of a senior position which is most typical in not for profit organizations and government departments. Naturally small firms will expect their controllers to wear more hats, while at bigger and multinational firms; they can delegate even some of the controller functions out to a broad spectrum of finance people, such as the Treasurer and Chief Financial Officer.

Financial reporting and auditing are critical functions and duties of many Financial Controllers. They are typically the point man responsible for keeping a close eye on the day to day financial condition of the firm. This position will work closely with the company or corporation's external auditors to be sure that the correct standardized reporting is being done. Controllers also set up, monitor, and even enforce the internal controls on financial reporting aspects. With the mega publically traded firms, the controllers often receive the thankless but essential task of handling the company's all-important quarterly public filings with the SEC.

A second important duty for the Finance Controller centers on the crucial role of budgeting for a firm. He or she will be expected to prepare the budget for the corporation and then to go through the important schedules for budgeting with the various departments and members of the organization in question. This will necessarily involve the collecting, analyzing, and consolidating of all relevant financial information on the company. The controller may not be the one who is ultimately tasked with maintaining the yearly budget, yet the position certainly monitors for discrepancy, investigates unexpected deficiencies, and summarizes trends of the finances within the firm. It will be the controller tasked with reporting any meaningful variances on the annual budget or expenditures to the upper level echelons of management on the board.

Besides these important roles, many financial controllers will also be expected to monitor any changes coming out or new legislation in the offing which may materially affect the company operations and their particular tax situation. Among the jobs in this category is to look for future risks while making sure that all necessary licenses, permits, and requirements for operating are attained. This is more than just filing crucial mandatory financial reports. The controller can also expect to handle tax preparation tasks like actually filing for federal and state taxes as well as various industry duties and taxes.

Finance Controllers also handle the development of staff from time to time. This might involve hiring, recruiting, and even training of some staff. It will require the person be able to appraise a result done in a job, delegating disciplinary actions when required and leading various employees or even temporarily small departments as necessity dictates. The controller will often be responsible for the company educational programs such as continuing professional educational requirements which are offered in the form of webinars, seminars, conferences, and other training events off site.

Financial Analyst

A Financial Analyst refers to a salaried individual who handles analysis, financial planning, and projection for both corporations and smaller companies. These accounting field experts create future forecasts for expenditures and revenues in order to come up with projected costs and capital budgeting for company projects. Those analysts who are senior level have the opportunity to work with executives in the corporate team and Chief Financial Officers to help determine across the company investments, policies, and future strategies.

These Financial Analysts draw on strong backgrounds in compliance and accounting in order to evaluate historical financial information, to forecast results for the future, and to push policy and process improvements. Their daily responsibilities include many different elements. They must analyze past and current financial performances and information. They have to evaluate depreciation and current capital expenditures. They must also consider various opportunities for investments of the company. These professionals do a great deal of projections and report preparing using their analyses. They work to find trends in the financial performance of the firm and offer suggestions for improving them. The analysts also evaluate and establish profit plans. Finally, they deliver financial projections and models for the finance team and executives to review.

There are a number of other positions which are related to this important job in a corporation or company. Some of these include financial analysis manager, senior financial analyst, investment analyst, and financial reporting manager. It means there are always opportunities for advancement in such a career path.

In today's increasingly technologically interconnected world, it should not come as a surprise that technology plays a major part in the careers of today's financial analysts. The ones who will be most successful in this field will gain as much exposure to these systems, tools, and platforms which service the field as they possibly can. Among the most typical technological requirements of these positions nowadays is having a complete grasp of the ERP enterprise resource planning systems. Second most in importance proves to be a command of both big data systems and data analytical systems. This is increasingly the case because firms more often rely on data-driven decisions now instead of the old school intuition-driven ones.

This job has a bright outlook for the future, according to the authority in the careers and employment industry--- the United States Bureau of Labor Statistics. In fact this organization states that the career outlook is tremendously positive for this position. The field will increase by approximately 16 percent during the years from 2012 to 20122.This makes it a more rapidly growing job opportunity than the average of every other career path in the U.S. The reasoning behind it is that corporations have put the recession and global financial crisis in the perspective of the past and so are putting on more financial analysts who they feel will help them to increase both their overall corporate growth and profits for the coming years.

The bureau similarly finds that these positions remain among the most heavily demanded jobs in either finance or accounting. This is the case not only for senior level positions, but also even entry level financial analysts. The respected industry publication U.S. News and World Report recently listed these jobs as among the top 100 Best Jobs, at number 63 in the United States. For the category of Best Business Jobs, they award it the number 13 best position in the nation.

This helps to explain why in the year 2014, financial analysts who possessed even from no to two years of experience earned average salaries amounting to $49,459 with an average range of from $39,252 to $60,352. The variance and range depends heavily on the industry, size of firm, location, and other factors of the employer. Senior financial analysts who possess over four years of experience can count on earning an impressive average $74,265 salary each year.

Financial Forecasting

Financial Forecasting refers to the corporate or government fiscal management tool for delivering information based on estimates from past, present, and anticipated future financial conditions of a firm or national government finances. It is extremely useful in projecting future revenue streams or expenditures. These can create a longer term or short term impact on corporate or government goals, policies, spending, and other activities. Such forecasting proves to be an indispensable component in the yearly budgeting activities.

Financial Forecasting is also the implementation of historical data in order to prognosticate future financial directions and trends. Companies employ such means of forecasting so they can decide how best to allocate out their budgets in order to plan for expected expenses over a future time period. This prediction model will commonly be derived from the forecast for demand of the corporate services and goods they purvey.

Investors can also employ such forecasting techniques to their advantages. They may run scenarios to decide if corporate events, including sales or revenue expectations, will boost or lower the stock price in a given firm. It gives the companies themselves a crucial means of benchmarking, which requires a longer term perspective on company operations.

Stock market and economic analysts also utilize Financial Forecasting in order to extrapolate the way that economic trends like unemployment and GDP will alter in the future quarters or even years. The problem with this is that it is not a precise science ultimately. As a forecast is farther removed from the present, the chances for it to be inaccurate only grow with time.

Statisticians also use Financial Forecasting for those scenarios that need future predictions. Data on customer satisfaction and how it will shift when a business' hours change can be gathered and measured using it. Similarly they can quantify and predict the impact of shifting working conditions on the company staff morale.

Stock analysts deploy a range of forecasting techniques in order to decide the ways that a given stock price will fluctuate over the future. They could begin by investigating a corporate revenue stream and contrasting this with national economic indicators for the country as a whole. They would have to measure any changes to statistical or financial data in order to ascertain the interconnecting relationship of numerous variables. Such relationships can be derived from particular events or the normal passing of time. Sales model forecasts could rely on a given event which is anticipated, such as buying the business of a competitor.

Financial Forecasting also takes on data sets or problems. Economists are able to engage in assumptions that pertain to a certain situation or simulation. They will select the most relevant data set to manipulate. After analyzing the information, they come up with their prognosis. Finally, there will be a reasonable verification time frame during which the analysts will compare their forecast to the real world results. They do this so that they can create still more accurate forecasting models for the future.

There are two types of specific Financial Forecasting techniques. The first particular kind is Qualitative forecasting models. Analysts utilize these to create prognoses that have a more limited scope. Such models will be greatly dependent on the opinions of experts. They benefit most heavily any short term forecasts. There are a number of examples of qualitative forecasting models available. Some of them are polls, market research, and survey which employ the Delphi method.

On the other hand, the alternative type of Financial Forecasting is quantitative forecasting. This means of forecasting will rule out expert opinions. It employs statistical data reliant on quantitative information. These quantitative forecasting models cover such series as discounting, methods, econometric modeling, and analysis of lagging and/or leading economic indicators.

Financial Statement

Financial statements are official records of a business' or personal financial activity. With businesses, financial statements present any and all pertinent financial activity as usable information. They do this in a clear, organized, and simple to comprehend way.

Financial statements are commonly comprised of four different types of financial accounts that come with an analysis and discussion provided by the company's management. The Balance sheet is the first of these. It is known by several other names, including statement of financial condition, or statement of financial position. The balance sheet details will outline a corporation's ownership equity, liabilities, and assets on a particular date. This will give a good picture of the general strength and position of the company.

Financial statements similarly include income statements. These can also be called Profit and Loss statements too. They outline numerous important pieces of company information, such as corporate expenses, income, and profits made in a certain time period. This statement explains all of the relevant financial details to the business' operation. Sales and all associated expenses are included under this category. This section of the financial statement proves to be the nuts and bolts of the whole document. It provides a snap shot of the company's ability to generate sales and turn profits.

A statement of cash flow is also a part of a complete financial statement. As its name implies, this section will share all of the details regarding the company's activities pertaining to cash flow. The most important ones that will be outlined include operating cash flow, financing, and investing endeavors.

The last element of a financial statement includes the statement of retained earnings. This section of the document makes good on its name to detail any changes to a corporation's actual retained earnings for the period that is being reported. These four sections of a financial statement are all combined together to make the consolidated financial statement, once they are combined with the analysis and discussion of management.

With large multinational types of corporations, such financial statements are typically large and complicated, making them challenging to read and understand. To assist with readability, they may also come with a group of notes for the financial statement that also covers management's analysis and discussion. Such notes will go through all items listed on the four parts of the financial statement in more thorough detail. For many companies, these notes for financial statements have come to be deemed a critical component of good and complete financial statements.

Financial statements are used by several different groups of people who are looking at a company. Investors use them in order to determine if the company and its stocks or bonds make a sound investment with a chance of providing good returns on investments and profits in exchange for limited risks. Banks utilize these financial statements to decide if a company is a good credit risk for their loan dollars. Institutions and other groups that may be considering a cash infusion or buyout of the company use such financial statements to decide if the company is a viable investment or acquisition target.

Financing Terms

There are two different financing terms available for businesses. These are short term financing and long term financing. In today's economic environment following the financial collapse and Great Recession, many businesses require both types. The two types of financing involve more differences than only the time frames.

Short term financing is commonly utilized for the daily business operations' funding and needs. This is also known as working capital. The financing terms for these short term facilities commonly require the short term loans to be paid back in a year or less.

Long term financing is more often utilized for the upkeep or purchase of fixed asset types. This might include a building or machinery that a firm owns. The financing terms for long term loans are for periods of time that are greater than a year.

Among the short term financing means are bank loans, bank overdrafts, trade credit, and leasing. For individuals, bank overdrafts prove to be the most common means of short term finance, since their finance terms permit an individual to draw out a greater amount of money that the person has in the bank, up to a predetermined amount.

Trade credit is useful for small businesses who may require the ability to buy goods and services or supplies before they receive payments and incoming receipts. With such trade credit facilities, the finance terms are commonly from thirty to ninety days to pay the full balance.

Long term financing might also involve bank loans, as well as corporate bonds or mortgages. With corporate bonds, a company is borrowing money from investors and members of the public. The financing terms of these types of instruments commonly require periodic interest payments that are known as coupon payments. The principal is then repaid on the agreed upon day. Many corporate bonds also feature a recall option that allows a company to pay off its long term debts early. This might be of interest to such a firm if they feel that they can borrow the funds for less money elsewhere or with lower interest rates.

Mortgages are extremely long term financing options made available to individuals or consumers for the purchase of a house or commercial property. These financing terms commonly run to thirty years or longer. Mortgages involve complex calculations for figuring out payments that often involve property taxes, mortgage insurance, and loan repayments.

Financing terms can also relate to the specifics of a particular loan, mortgage, or credit facility. They would spell out the interest rate, due dates of payments, and number of payments anticipated. In many cases, they would also specify the amount of interest that would be paid over the course of the loan or credit facility, as well as the penalties for not making the payments on time.

Fixed Assets

Fixed Assets refers to tangible property which are longer term holdings by their very nature. Companies and corporations both own and utilize them in their normal everyday business operations to produce their revenues and profits. They do not typically become converted back to cash or consumed any quicker than in under minimally a year time frame. Many corporations refer to their collective fixed assets as "the plant." Classic examples of these types of assets include real estate, factories, office space and buildings, furniture, computer equipment, and other operating equipment.

There are longer term assets that do not typically qualify as fixed assets though. Among these are patents and trademarks. They are generally considered to be simply intangible assets on company balance sheets.

Such assets also go by the names of property, plant, and equipment (PP&E). Corporations purchase fixed assets to create and supply services and goods. They might also rent them out to third parties to generate a revenue stream. They could simply deploy them within the company's own internal organization as well. These often include such tangible assets as office equipment, computers, and laptops, as well as manufacturing equipment and factories. Copyrights, goodwill, patents, and trademark could fall into either the fixed or intangible assets categories, depending on the accounting method favored by the firm.

There are many different types of equipment that fall under the classification of fixed assets. Among these are office buildings and plants, software and computer equipment, land, furniture, vehicles, and machinery. It often helps to consider a real tangible example when discussing difficult concepts like this one. Think about the company Amazing Fruits and Vegetables. They sell and even deliver fresh produce. This makes their delivery vehicles a fixed asset. The firm's distribution center would also be such a fixed type of asset. Even the parking lot where customers park while they shop the fruits and vegetables stand would be considered a fixed asset.

There are several reasons why it is helpful (and often times even essential) to have reliable information on the assets of a given company. The most important is that it leads to concise and precise financial reporting, as well as a better valuation of a going concern via financial analysis. Investors rely on such reports in order to ascertain the true financial health and real value of a given company. It enables them to make well- informed choices as to whether they should trust the firm enough to loan it money or instead invest in the equity of the corporation. One thing that makes it more confusing for investors is that firms have a choice of acceptable means of recording, depreciating, and disposing of their own assets. It requires qualified analysts who are willing to read the fine print and notes on the financial statements of the company in question in order to accurately determine on what basis the numbers were compiled.

It is an inevitable fact of life that fixed assets will gradually decline in value terminally as they grow older. They do offer long term income generation, which explains why they become expensed differently than do other company items. While tangible assets become subjected to occasional depreciation, intangible assets are subjected instead to amortization. A specific portion of the costs for the asset will be expensed out yearly. The value of the asset will correspondingly diminish alongside the amount of depreciation on the balance sheet of the corporation. The firm is then allowed to match up the cost of the asset in question with the longer term value of the item.

The method that a given firm utilizes to depreciate its assets will change the book value of the firm which is based on the amount they paid for the asset. This will make the equity book value different from the current market value of the asset in question. An exception to all of this depreciation and book value discussion concerns raw real estate. Land cannot be depreciated since it does not become depleted. The exception is when it is natural resource land, as with oil land, gold or silver mining land, or timber lands. These resources are finite and become expended over time and culling.

Fixed Income Markets

The Fixed Income Market refers to the bond market. This market is actually over twice the size of the better known (and more popular with investors) equity stock markets. The truth remains that it is mostly less well publicized by the media or followed and comprehended by the overall investing public. In fact equities differ from fixed income in many ways.

Trading is the first and most important difference. There are countless more securities available on the fixed income market. For example, GE stock is a single issue. GE bonds offer literally thousands of different GE securities from which to choose and in which to invest. As another real world example, in the Federal Government Treasuries markets, investors possess literally hundreds of different offerings.

The upside to having such a wide-ranging variety of debt issues from which to choose lies in the fact that investors are able to select a particular security which nearly identically meets all of their varying needs. There is also a flip side to this in that investors must develop an effective procedure for distilling all of their needs down to an exact formula so that they can next carefully screen through the fixed income industry to choose the security which most perfectly aligns with said requirements.

Price transparency is the second significant difference between equities and fixed income markets. The pricing on stocks are instantly relayed to both participants and countless media outlets. This means that investors have a high degree of confidence in their ability to obtain a fair market price for the purchase when they are ready to invest. With the bond markets, the trades become executed on the basis of dealer to investor or dealer to dealer.

With no central record for all the various transaction prices across the fixed income markets, the prices can and do differ substantially from one trade to the next. It also means that some particular bond issues might not actually trade over days, weeks, or months since the enormous volume of individual issues affects the volume per issue.

The problem to all of this is that investors can never have any concrete certainty on what an individual bond's fair market price really is. This brings up the second major difference between equity and fixed income markets. Institutional investors are the overwhelmingly dominant and critical players in the bonds market, though they are also important in equities markets as well. This is simply because retail investors are commonly far more active in the equities markets than they ever would be in the bond markets. Another factor that discourages the smaller retail investors from the fixed income markets is that the bond markets exact penalties on smaller sized trades.

In fact the institutions nearly completely dominate the bonds' markets. This makes the typical sized trade enormous, even in the millions of dollars in bonds. Any investors who tried to take on less than a million worth of them would pay a penalty in the pricing on the issue.

Yet there are a few advantages that smaller individual investors do possess in the bond markets. First among these is that the longer term investors do not have to worry over the noise of the daily price movements in the markets. This means that the individual investors can look for appealing longer-term opportunities and not have to worry about intervening price fluctuations along the way till maturity.

Individual investors can also contemplate a bigger variety of issues than most institutions. This is because the institutional investors are often strictly limited by their own investment rules and policies which state what kinds of issues they may or may not purchase and hold.

Finally, individuals have the ability to quickly move in and out of issues as their valuations deteriorate. Managers of bond mutual funds and other large institutional holdings do not have such options. They must instead simply buy the bonds when the money comes in or out of their underlying fund.

Follow-On Public Offer (FPO)

A Follow-On Public Offer is also known by its official acronym FPO. This occurs when a public company which is already listed on a stock market exchange issues additional shares to investors. Such FPOs are useful and practical for those firms which wish to raise extra equity capital from the capital markets via stock issues. These methods are popular with publically traded corporations.

Such firms like to avail themselves of these FPO issues by selling more shares to investors. They have to complete an offer document in order to accomplish this. FPOs are never to be confused with IPOs. IPOs refer to the initial public offering a company uses to issue equity shares to the public for the very first time. FPOs are instead supplementary issues which they make once the firm is already exchange-established and -trading.

There are two main types of Follow-on public offerings available to companies today. The first kind dilutes existing investors. The Board of Directors must agree to boost the level of shares floating. It raises money for paying down debt or internally growing the company business. It ultimately raises the numbers of outstanding shares as well.

The second kind of FPO proves to be non diluting. It is the preferred method when the major shareholders or corporate directors elect to sell their own personal shares of the company stock. Since no new shares become created, it does not dilute the holdings of existing investors in the company. This is generally known as a secondary market offering. Neither the firm nor the present shareholders gain an advantage from this type of method.

Because there are two different means of selling shares with such Follow-On Public Offers, this makes it extremely crucial to know who the stock sellers are on any given offering transaction. This way, investors are able to learn quickly and easily if the new offering will prove to be net dilutive or not.

Such Follow-On Public Offerings prove to be increasingly commonplace within the world of investing. Corporations appreciate that they can quickly and easily collect additional fresh capital to utilize for any common purpose they deem appropriate or expedient. Their share price might drop as a result of such an FPO announcement. This upsets shareholders who are the main losers in such a scenario. Many times these secondary share offerings will be made at prices that are lower than the present market prices. In any case, they will almost certainly dilute the power and voting rights of their presently existing shares of company stock.

It always helps to look at some tangible examples to better grasp a challenging concept such as this one. Back in the year 2013, corporations deployed enough Follow-On Public Offers to raise an impressive $201.7 billion in additional equity. This was the greatest single-year amount that they raised for four years. Facebook outperformed in this respect by selling off an additional $3.9 billion worth of shares. This made them among the biggest single beneficiaries of the FPOs for that year.

Investment banks love secondary offerings. They benefit directly from them since they receive a portion of the fee structure pricing. In that same year of 2013, leading American investment banking operation Goldman Sachs handled $24.7 billion in secondary offerings to be the number one FPO underwriter.

The year 2015 subsequently saw a great number of firms which had only gone public a year earlier decide to issue Follow-On Public Offerings. Shake Shack proved to be one of these. They announced their secondary offering and witnessed their shares decline as a result. The stock plunged an eye-watering 16 percent on the news that a major secondary offering was in the works for a price lower than the then-current share price. Naturally, investors in Shake Shack were unhappy, but they were completely powerless to prevent the deal from going through.

Fortis

Fortis refers to the now defunct Belgian-based multinational financial giant that had huge presences in insurance, investment and asset management, and traditional and private banking around Europe and beyond it internationally. Up to the year 2007, the jointly Brussels- and Utrecht-headquartered company continued to grow and prosper with massive operations placing it in the slot of twentieth biggest company in the globe (based on its revenue). Yet the Global Financial Crisis proved to be the match and eventual ruin of the firm which dated back to 1990.

The home base of operations and greatest strength of Fortis N.V./S.A. lay in what observers call the Benelux nations Belgium, the Netherlands, and Luxembourg. Their banking operations proved to be substantial in these countries especially. They included commercial banking, retail network branch banking, and merchant banking operations. In insurance, the behemoth boasted lines including life, property and casualty, and health insurance. Its many and varied products sold via a range of brokers, independent agents, its own bank branches, and financial planners. The bank had listings on Euronext Amsterdam, Euronext Brussels, and the Luxembourg stock exchanges.

It was in the heart of the 2008 based Global Financial Crisis that the firm began to encounter serious problems after two decades of tremendous growth and success. The initial signs of weakness in the firm appeared after Fortis joined a consortium of banks which were jointly acquiring ABN AMRO, the Dutch banking and investment giant. The Belgian/Dutch bank was partnered with Banco Santander of Spain and Britain's Royal Bank of Scotland Group in this takeover transaction. Yet the Belgian-based insurance and banking giant ran into critical problems in being able to finance its commitment for this joint acquisition target. The writing was on the wall for Fortis at this point, as the hedge fund wolves were looking eagerly around the world for signs of weakness to exploit in shorting and ruining financial companies to make vast profits at the expense of these faltering banks and insurance companies.

In no time at all, Fortis had to be jointly bailed out by the governments of Belgium, the Netherlands, and Luxembourg working together, as the bank was as large as the financial positions of the governments of Luxembourg and Belgium. At this point once the bank had been saved from collapse, it was split apart into four different pieces.

French banking giant BNP Paribas bought up the Belgian bank branches and its operations and renamed them BNP Fortis Belgium. BNP acquired the rights to the brand name for Belgium in the transaction. Meanwhile the Dutch government proceeded to nationalize all of the failed bank's Dutch banking and insurance subsidiary companies. In an ironic twist of fate, the Dutch national government re-launched them as their former buyout target of ABN AMRO. Eventually the Dutch split this up into Fortis Bank Nederland for the banking operations. Meanwhile the failed insurance and investment banking companies (including the Dutch insurance arm) they split off into ASR Nederland.

What little remained of the once-enormous company Fortis were its nascent insurance operations in Belgium and Luxembourg. The firm still proved to be the biggest insurance provider in Belgium. As the company had lost the rights to its brand name there to BNP Paribas, it was forced to change its name to Ageas by April of 2010. This greatly reduced insurance business in the smaller two of the three Benelux nations is all that remained of the once mighty Fortis Holdings. This turns out to be one of the most striking examples in Europe of the devastating consequences of the greatest financial collapse since the Great Depression in the 1930's. It helps to explain why the crisis became known as the Great Recession and Global Financial Crisis of 2008.

Franchise

A franchise can be defined in many ways. The definition from the International Franchise Association describes franchising as a means to expand a business so that goods and services can be distributed more effectively via a licensing relationship. The word itself legally means a specific kind of license. Ultimately, franchising refers to the personal relationship which a franchisor maintains with its franchisees.

In this arrangement, the franchisor licenses out its trade name as well as its operating methods, or systematic way of doing business, to a particular franchisee. In exchange for this arrangement, the franchisee pledges to run the business as per the terms of this license. The operating method here refers to the franchisor's system and way of doing business.

Franchisors guarantee their franchisees will have their support and help. They also maintain a certain level of control over specific parts of the franchisee business. This is critical for the franchise owner to safeguard its intellectual property rights as well as to be certain that the franchisee keeps to the guidelines of the brand itself. The quid pro quo of this is that the franchisee typically delivers a one time start up fee (known as the franchise fee) to the franchisor. The franchisees also pay a royalty fee to the franchisor, which is periodic and continuous. This enables the franchisee to utilize the franchisor's operating system and trade name.

The franchisor itself carries little responsibility for involvement in the daily management of the business of the franchisee. This is because franchisees exist as independent operators. Neither are they joint employers with their franchisors. This gives the franchisees a free hand in hiring employees, paying them according to their wishes, scheduling their shifts as they see fit, arranging their employment rules and practices, and even disciplining their own employees, all without requiring any approval from their franchisor. However, the uniforms which the employees wear will be stipulated by the brand and operating system of the franchisor.

Franchising is about a contractually defined relationship between the two parties. The franchisees and franchisor will share the brand in common. Despite this, both are distinctly separate businesses in both real terms and legally. The role of the franchisor is simply to build up its business and brand as part of supporting the various franchisees. The part which the franchisees play is to operate and manage their own business according to the specific terms of the franchise agreements.

It is interesting that definitions of franchises range from one state to the next according to the various laws which different states enforce. Some states include among the various elements of franchising the responsibilities of the franchisor to deliver a marketing plan to its franchisees. Others insist that the franchisor maintain an interested community of the business jointly with the franchisee.

Business Format Franchises are the most readily recognizable types of these arrangements for the everyday individual. These relationships typically cover the whole of the business and its format, not only the products, services, and trade name of the franchisor in question. In this common type, franchisors are expected to give their franchisees training, operating manuals, standards for the brand, a marketing plan and strategy to carry it out, quality control monitoring, and more.

Examples of the idea make these distinctions clear. Pizza Hut does not license out pizzas or breadsticks. Burger King does not license out hamburgers or chicken sandwiches. The two mega franchise operations instead license out components of their intellectual property. In this case it includes both their business systems and their trade marks, or their ways of producing these food items and company-described premises and atmosphere.

The history of these and other brands demonstrates that both services and products have changed significantly over the decades. Among the various advantages to these types of business format franchises and their arrangements is that they have the flexibility to do so effectively.

Today there exist numerous kinds of franchises throughout a constantly expanding array of industries and market segments in not only the United States and Canada but around the globe. Estimates state that more than 120 separate industries utilize the concept and practices of franchising now. The greatest share of franchising by far is still the food and restaurants businesses. Nowadays even medical services and home based health care rely on franchising though.

Franchise Model

Franchises are businesses where the owners sell the rights of their business to third parties. The owners of the franchise are known as franchisors. The third party operators who buy the rights are called franchisees. The franchise model is the precise way the business is run to insure uniformity among the different regional or national franchise outlets.

This model of business offers advantages to the sellers and the buyers of the franchise. Franchisors who sell their rights gain the ability to grow their business brand faster than they might with their own capital or by using the help of lenders or investors. They are able to harness other individuals' money to build up the business footprint faster than they can alone. They still maintain control over the brand.

Franchisors receive both an upfront franchise fee and continuous royalties. They avoid the deadlines of loan repayments with this model. With the royalties and fees that the franchisors gain, they are able to run the corporate headquarters operations, advertise and market the business brand, support and train their franchisees, build up their brand in the industry, and make improvements on the service or products that their business provides.

Franchisees also gain many benefits. Their franchise has a greater likelihood of succeeding than if they start up their own business. This is evident in many ways. They receive upfront training and continuous support. The time to open is less. Buyers also receive the recognition of a brand that is known, help in finding the best site for the new location, lesser costs because of group purchasing power, and better advertising exposure through regional and national campaigns.

Besides this, they receive leads that are generated by call centers and websites, the established franchise model, and moral support and counsel from fellow franchisee peers. A more recent benefit for franchisees pertains to help getting funding secured for startup and ongoing operation costs.

The model has been wildly successful particularly with nationally known franchises such as McDonald's, Subway, and Panerra Bread. Yet there are still downsides to the franchise model. These disadvantages apply to franchisees. Most importantly, they have little independence. This is evident from their services and goods they provide to franchise wide promotions that might not be effective in their own individual market.

Franchisees will have to utilize the company colors and approved paint colors on their walls. They can be made to redesign their units at significant expense. Most dangerous of all is the possibility that the franchise transforms after the franchisee signs a 10 to 15 year long contract. The ownership or management could completely change and force the brand to go in a different direction that the franchisee does not like or at all want.

The franchise model is all about following the system. This idea is central to the success of a franchisee's efforts. The reason that a franchisee purchases the franchisor's model and system is because they have confidence in it. Franchisees feel they can succeed and make money if they follow the system perfectly.

A good franchisor considers appropriate regional variations and suggestions for some changes. They also know that if they leave the system without gaining approval from the franchisor first, they may violate the franchise agreement. This could cause them to have their rights to use the franchisor's name and business model revoked.

Franchisees are also required to keep confidential any trade secrets or proprietary methods of business. They are also made to sign and abide by a non-compete clause agreement.

Gross Development Cost (GDC)

Gross Development Cost (GDC) refers to the aggregate costs of a given company project. It could also be called the sum of all means of finance which a company employs on a particular project. This is similarly the total costs which a firm incurs from the conception of to the final implementation of a certain project. Any costs that occur after the project's completion will be treated as operational expenses. Some analysts refer to the GDC as the expenses associated with developing either improved or new products.

Two main project cost estimate categories exist in the world of business. These are project planning estimates and project design estimates. The former will be deployed in justifying and receiving approval for a given project, analyzing alternative projects, programming the sequence of project events, and receiving the final project go ahead. The latter sum up the projected project costs pertaining to sourced materials and contracted work.

One thing about such cost estimates is that they never become complete until a given project is final. In fact, insightful companies will constantly review their estimates in an effort to ensure they remain current and accurate as possible. Project engineers carry the burden for making sure the projected cost stays updated all during the project development process. At the same time, the responsible project manager carries the responsibility for both reviewing and ultimately signing off on every estimate for the costs of the project.

Current project cost estimates prove to be the ones which are the most current estimates on file in the design and planning phases. Alternatively, project planning cost estimates will be the ones compiled before a project becomes fully approved. Project planning costs estimates can be categorized according to several different breakdowns. These include project feasibility, project initiation, draft estimate project report, and project report.

Projects rarely begin without a company coming up with a project initiation cost estimate. This is an expanded version of the estimates on project feasibility in greater detail. This estimate is the one that ultimately underlies the program project costs. This is why a highly reliable estimate is critical at this juncture. It proves to be the initial benchmark against any other and future estimates.

Next in the natural progression of a potential project comes the draft project report. This estimate utilizes the identical format to the project initiation cost estimates but naturally comes with far greater detail. In such an estimate, every competing project alternative option has to be compiled with current data derived from units actually involved with the project in question. This includes elements like structure design, materials, labor unit costs, hydraulics, right of way, etc.

The next project estimate in the progression of a project will be the Project Report Cost Estimate. Once again, this stays with the identical format as with the previous project planning cost estimates. The estimate for project costs should be more conclusive at this stage. Finally, once a project is fully approved will come the project design cost estimates.

The Project Manager will update such estimates during the project development. The Project Design Cost estimates can be labeled as either final or preliminary. Such design cost estimates concentrate on the project's construction costs. These estimates should be the most detailed, up to date, and accurate of the various planning cost estimates. They should cover everything from upfront project evaluation to construction design data and costs as available. Such data permits the project manager to develop the most detailed cost estimate possible in the ongoing progress of the project in question.

Gross Income

Gross income can be several different things in the United States. In tax law for business, gross income signifies all proceeds realized from every source minus the cost of goods that have been sold. It is also used for individuals and pertains to all income earned from any and every kind of source.

As such, it is not simply cash that has been realized, but it can also be income received in kind, as property, or as services. For a taxpayer, gross income is commonly believed to be all of the monies and values received. Although most income is tallied into this figure, a few kinds of income are excluded deliberately.

For companies, individuals, trusts, estates, and others, gross income is necessary for figuring up the mandatory income taxes within the United States. Taxes are figured up using a taxable income number that starts with gross income and then subtracts permissible tax deductions. Taxes are then calculated based on the resulting taxable income.

Many different types of income are considered to be a part of the gross income category. Wages are the earnings for work performed payable as tips, salaries, and related income. Income made as a result of such personal service is always tallied up in a person's gross income. Gross profits made from selling an inventory of products are also considered gross income. Gross profits result from sales prices of items minus the cost of the goods actually sold.

All interest received is also considered to be a part of gross income. Dividends, along with distributions of capital gains from companies or mutual funds are similarly a part of gross income. Gains on property that has been disposed of are also tallied into the gross income total after the extra proceeds beyond the adjusted cost in the property is determined. Also included are royalties and rents from intangible and tangible items.

A number of other non traditional types of income are also considered to be a part of this. Pensions, income from life insurance, and annuities income are counted. So are alimony, child support, and other maintenance payments. Shares of partnership income that are distributed fall under this category. Even the proceeds from national and state tax refunds are considered to be gross income.

The Internal Revenue Service claims that such gross income includes all forms of income from any source of which they are derived. As such, gross income can result from any gains having to do with labor, capital, the two together, or profits having to do with the sale of anything or a capital asset. A notable exception to gross income includes gifts and inheritances. While these could be taxed under the category of estate taxes or gift taxes, they are not deemed by the IRS to be a part of gross income.

Gross Margin

Gross Margin is also known as gross profit margin. This concept represents a business formula that companies compute. It is best expressed as the firm's total revenue less its cots of goods sold which is then divided by the total revenue. This provides the answer as a percentage. In other words, Gross Margins are the percentage of revenues the corporations keep after paying their direct expenses of creating both their services and goods. Higher percentages mean a company keeps a larger amount of every dollar worth of sales. This greater amount of retained income provides it with more money for servicing debt, making new investments, retained earnings, and paying out dividends to shareholders.

Gross margin equates to the amount from every sales dollar that the firm is able to keep for their gross profits. Consider a concrete and tangible real world example to better understand this idea. If HSBC Bank has a gross margin in a quarter of 30 percent, then this means it keeps 30 cents from every dollar in revenue it creates. The other 70 cents would go into the Cost of Goods Sold (COGS) category. Since all of the bank's COGS are already considered, the other 30 cents per dollar in revenue may be applied to general overhead, paying down any debt, expenses on interest, and shareholder dividend distributions.

Corporations utilize this gross margin in order to ascertain how their costs of production are measuring up against their revenues. When a corporation's gross margin is declining, it will try to find ways to reduce its costs of suppliers and labor costs. The supplier costs can be slashed by finding alternative suppliers who will supply the goods at lower prices. The other solution is to try to raise the prices on the company goods and services so as to increase the value of the corporate sales revenues.

Another effective use of gross margins lies in predicting the amount of money which they will retain towards general operating costs. Companies with 45 percent gross margins know they will have to work with 45 cents on each dollar of revenue they collect in order cover their remaining administrative and operating costs. The measure also allows for firms to measure up their efficiency as a company. Investors and analysts are able to compare and contrast two or more corporations of varying sizes against one another with the metric as well.

Gross margin should never be erroneously confused with net profit margin. Gross margin simply considers the connection between the cost of goods sold and the sales revenue. On the other hand, net profit margin covers every expense a corporation has. Calculating up the net profit margins requires firms to start with their revenues and subtract out their cost of goods sold and other expenses. This includes sales rep wages, distribution of product costs, taxes, and various operating costs.

Another way of looking at the differences between the two related but still different concepts is that the gross profit margin allows firms to determine the level of their manufacturing operations' profitability. Alternatively the net profit margin assists firms in considering their level of all around profitability.

Consider another example for calculating up gross profit margin. If a company brings in two million dollars in sales revenue, it might spend $800,000 on its labor expenses and another $200,000 on the manufacturing inputs. Once these costs of goods sold of one million dollars are subtracted out, a full million dollars remains in total gross profits. When individuals take the gross profits and divide it by the total revenue, the result is 0.5. Turned into a percentage, this equals a gross profit margin of 50 percent.

Hedge Fund

A hedge fund is an investment fund which are commonly only open to a specific group of investors. These investors pay a large performance fee each year, commonly a certain percent of their funds under management, to the manager of the hedge fund. Hedge funds are very minimally regulated and are therefore are able to participate in a wide array of investments and investment strategies.

Literally every single hedge fund pursues its own strategy of investing that will establish the kinds of investments that it seeks. Hedge funds commonly go for a wide range of investments in which they may buy or sell short shares and positions. Stocks, commodities, and bonds are some of these asset classes with which they work.

As you would anticipate from the name, hedge funds typically try to offset some of the risks in their portfolios by employing a number of risk hedging strategies. These mostly revolve around the use of derivatives, or financial instruments with values that depend on anticipated price movements in the future of an asset to which they are linked, as well as short selling investments.

Most countries only allow certain types of wealthy and professional investors to open a hedge fund account. Regulators may not heavily oversee the activities of hedge funds, but they do govern who is allowed to participate. As a result, traditional investment funds' rules and regulations mostly do not apply to hedge funds.

Actual net asset values of hedge funds often tally into the many billions of dollars. The funds' gross assets held commonly prove to be massively higher as a result of their using leverage on their money invested. In particular niche markets like distressed debt, high yield ratings, and derivatives trading, hedge funds are the dominant players.

Investors get involved in hedge funds in search of higher than normal market returns. When times are good, many hedge funds yield even twenty percent annual investment returns. The nature of their hedging strategies is supposed to protect them from terrible losses, such as were seen in the financial crisis from 2007-2010.

The hedge fund industry is opaque and difficult to measure accurately. This is partially as a result of the significant expansion of the industry, as well as an inconsistent definition of what makes a hedge fund. Prior to the peak of hedge funds in the summer of 2008, it is believed that hedge funds might have overseen as much as two and a half trillion dollars. The credit crunch hit many hedge funds particularly hard, and their assets under management have declined sharply as a result of both losses, as well as requests for withdrawals by investors. In 2010, it is believed that hedge funds once again represent in excess of two trillion dollars in assets under management.

The largest hedge funds in the world are JP Morgan Chase, with over $53 billion under management; Bridgewater Associates, having more than $43 billion in assets under management; Paulson and Company, with more than $32 billion in assets; Brevan Howard that has greater than $27 billion in assets; and Soros Fund Management, which boasts around $27 billion in assets under management.

High Yield Bonds

High Yield Bonds turn out to be bonds that possess a lower credit rating and higher yield than those corporate, municipal, and sovereign government bonds which are of investment grade. Thanks to the greater risk of them defaulting, such bonds yield a higher return than the bonds which are qualified investment grade issues. Those companies that issue high yielding debt are usually capital intensive companies and startup firms that already possess higher debt ratios. Investors often refer to such bonds as junk bonds.

The two principal corporate rating credit agencies determine the breakdown of what qualifies as a High Yield Bond and what does not. When Moody's rates a bond with lower than a "Baa" rating, or Standard and Poor's (S&P) rates then with an under "BBB" rating, then they become known as junk bonds. At the same time, all of those bonds which enjoy higher ratings than these (or the same rating at least) investors will consider to be investment grade. There are credit ratings that cover such categories as presently in default, or "D." Those kinds of bonds holding "C" ratings and below also have high probabilities for defaulting. In order to compensate the investors who take them on for the significant risks they run of not receiving either their original principal back or accrued interest payments by the maturity date, the yields must be offered at extremely high interest rates.

Despite the negative label of "junk bond," these High Yield Bonds remain popular and heavily bought by global investors. The majority of these investors choose to diversify for safety sake by utilizing either a junk bond ETF exchange traded fund or a High Yield Bonds mutual fund. The spread between the yields on the higher yielding and investment grade types of bonds constantly fluctuates on the markets. The at the time condition of the global and national economies impacts this. Industry-specific and individual corporate events also play a part in the differences between the various kinds of bonds' interest rates.

In general though, High Yield Bonds' investors can count on receiving a good 150 to 300 basis points more in yield as measured against the investment quality bonds in any particular time frame. This is why mutual funds and ETFs make imminent sense as an effective means of gaining exposure to the greater yields without taking on the unnecessary risk of a single issuer's bonds defaulting and costing the investors all or most of their original investing principal.

In the last few years, various central bankers throughout the globe have decided to inject enormous amounts of liquidity into their individual economies so that credit will remain cheaply and easily available. This includes the European Central Bank, the U.S. Federal Reserve, and the Bank of Japan. It has created the side effect of causing borrowing costs to drop and lenders to experience significantly lower returns.

By February of 2016, an incredible $9 trillion in sovereign government debt bonds provided yields of only from zero percent to one percent. Seven trillion of the sovereign bonds delivered negative real yields once adjusted for anticipated levels of inflation. It means that holding such bonds cost investors money, or provided them a real losing return.

In typical economic environments, this would drive intelligent investors to competing markets that provide better return rates. Higher yield bond markets have stayed volatile though. Distressed debts which pay minimally a yield higher than 1,000 basis points greater than a comparably maturing Treasury bond were notably affected. Energy company high yielding debt bond prices collapsed by approximately 20 percent in 2015 as a consequence of the problems in the energy sector which resulted from plummeting energy prices.

High Yield Preferred Stocks

Preferred stocks are a special type of stocks that many companies issue. These types of stocks provide investors with a different level of ownership in a given company. A preferred stock holder obtains a higher priority on the earnings and assets of a company than a common stock holder would enjoy. These preferred stocks also pay a higher dividend that has to be given out before any dividends can be paid to the common stock holders.

As such, they represent a hybrid type of security on the stock markets. They are like common stocks in that they are bought and sold as stocks and represent ownership in a company. These stocks can also trade up and down in price like a common stock. Unlike a common stock, they do not come with any rights to vote for a company board of directors or items on a company ballot at the annual meeting.

They are also like bonds in that they pay a higher dividend that must be paid out unless the company lacks the earnings to pay these holders. In this way preferred stocks have elements of bonds with their fixed rate of dividends. Every preferred stock comes with its own unique details that are set when the company issues the stock.

Preferred stocks are often higher yielding issues. They are most commonly issued by companies that are in industries such as financials, real estate investment trusts, utilities, industrials, and conglomerates. Despite this higher yield that makes them like bonds, they can be traded on the major stock exchanges. They are typically found on exchanges including the NASDAQ and the New York Stock Exchange.

As preferred stocks are a type of equity legally, they show up as equity on any company balance sheet. Both common and preferred stock holders are owners in the company. There are several advantages to preferred stocks that investors like about them.

In the past, individual retail investors were less aware of preferred stocks, but this is changing. Part of the reason they have gained in popularity surrounds market volatility. As common stocks have seen wild price swings in recent years, investors have been looking for more stable instruments in which they can invest.

Preferred stocks fit this need as they tend to be more stable in price than do common stocks. With more baby boomers looking for investments that provide higher yields, this has brought preferred stocks into the spotlight. The retirees gain the advantage of better yields and the opportunity for the price to increase in the issues as well.

Preferred stocks are not new. They have existed from the time when modern day investing began. Institutional investors have known about and invested in them for many decades. Many individual investors did not because they lacked the information they required to select and trade them.

In the past, individuals did not have any lists of preferred stocks from which to pick. The information available was difficult to come up with before the Internet made this kind of information much more readily available. Now there are tools smaller individual investors can find that provide calendar searches for ex-dividend dates.

There are also screening filters that allow individuals to narrow down their search for the best high yielding dividend preferred stocks. Preferred stocks represent another way to diversify an investor's portfolio and earn higher yields on dividends at the same time.

Holdings

Holdings refer to the asset contents in a given portfolio which an entity or individual possesses. Pension funds and mutual funds are good examples of organizations that have holdings. These positions can include all sorts of different investment assets and classes. Among these are stocks, mutual funds, bonds, futures, options, ETF exchange traded funds, and private equity assets.

It is both the kinds and amounts of such holdings in any portfolios that determine how well-diversified the portfolio actually proves to be. Well-diversified portfolios often include various sectors of stocks, bonds from a range of maturities and companies, and a variety of other investments that do not correlate with either stocks or bonds. Alternatively, only a few positions in several stocks that come from only one sector would be indicative of poorly diversified portfolios.

It is actually the mix and amount of various asset classes in any portfolio that will substantially determine what its total rate of return will be. The biggest positions will exert a larger impact on the return of a portfolio than marginal or tinier holdings in such a portfolio will. Many investors make it a practice to closely scrutinize the lists of positions which the world's most successful money managers maintain in an effort to follow their trades.

Such investors try to imitate the trading prowess of these superior results money managers in a variety of ways. It might be the manager has purchased stocks, in which case the imitating investors will try to stake out a similar company position. If these managers sell out of a stake, the investors will similarly sell off their assets in the company. The problem with such a follower strategy is that there is often substantial lag time between that point where the money managers make their moves and when this information becomes public domain knowledge.

There is another variation on the idea of mutual funds, hedge funds, and pension funds. This is the concept of holding companies. Such organizations are groups where the investors organize their positions and assets as an LLC Limited Liability Company. The reasons for this are varied. It might be they wish to decrease their own risk exposure, pool their investment dollars with fellow investors, and/or reduce their taxes as much as possible. Such companies rarely operate their own businesses directly. Instead, they are generally only a vehicle utilized to own various investments and companies.

Probably the best-known example of such an LLC company is the internationally followed Berkshire Hathaway, Inc. This Warren Buffet-dominated Omaha, Nebraska- based corporation originally began as a clothing textiles' manufacturing firm. Over the last numbers of decades, the corporation has solely existed as Warren Buffet's personal vehicle to buy out, maintain, and sell out his numerous and wide-ranging investments in various companies. Among the greatest and most significant positions which Berkshire owns are large stakes in the Coca-Cola Company, Dairy Queen Inc, and their wholly controlled subsidiary GEICO Government Employees Insurance Company.

The simplest way to envision these holdings is to mentally picture a large bucket, which represents the mutual fund. Every rock within the bucket stands for an individual bond or stock position. When analysts add up all of the rocks (as stocks or bonds), this equals the aggregate numbers of all holdings.

Figuring out the best mix of these holdings is the challenge that mutual funds, pension funds, and hedge funds all grapple with on a regular basis. It all comes down to the type of fund which they represent. Those bond funds or index funds would anticipate having many positions. This could mean from hundreds to thousands of different bonds and stocks. With the majority of other funds, too many or too few positions is risky and dangerous. Those funds that hold merely 30 positions would be subject to extreme volatility and single stock risks. If they had 500 to 600 different stocks or bonds then the fund would be as large as many indices like the S&P 500.

Income Statement

An Income Statement refers to a corporate financial statement that relays the performance of the company for a specific accounting time frame. Analysts measure such performance through reading the summary of the business revenues and expenditures in its non-operating and operating endeavors together. This statement reveals the net loss or net profit which the business experienced in the particular accounting time period. These documents are also referred to as statements of revenues or profit and loss statements.

As one of three important financial statements, these become contained within the yearly 10-K and corporate annual reports. The other two critical documents are the statement of cash flows and the balance sheet. Every publically traded firm is required by law to deliver such legal documents to the investing public via the SEC Securities and Exchange Commission. These three combined statements relay all of the critical information on the firm's financial affairs. Yet the income statement is special in that it alone reveals the company's net income and overall sales' overviews.

Income statements are different from the balance sheet in at least one critical way. Balance sheets provide a single moment in time snap shot of corporate performance. Income statements on the other hand deliver useful information on an entire time frame or period. They start with the company sales figures and conclude with the total net income and appropriate EPS earnings per share figures.

These income statements become sub-divided into two sections. The first is operating. The second proves to be non-operating. Operating sections of the statements on income reveal all of the pertinent data on expenses and revenues which result directly from the normal principal daily operations of the business. It helps to look at a real world example to better understand the concept. If a company makes computer equipment, then it will mostly earn its revenues through manufacturing and selling such computer equipment.

In the non-operating segment of the income statement, investors learn about the expenses and revenues associated with extraordinary operations of the firm. Continuing on with the prior example, the computer equipment firm may also sell some investments and real estate properties. Any and all gains it realizes on the sales would be included under the non-operating items portion of the statement.

Analysts find a number of important uses for these income statements. Among the key ones is figuring up critical financial ratios like ROA return on assets, ROE return on equity, gross and operating profits, EVIT earnings before interest and taxes, and EBITDA earnings before interest, taxes, and amortization. As such, these statements will commonly be portrayed in a standardized format that lays out every line item as a percentage of the sales. This method allows for analysts and investors alike to quickly and easily determine the expenses that comprise the greatest amount of the sales.

These statements may similarly compare and contrast both the QOQ quarter over quarter performance and the YOY year over year performance. This is why the income statement commonly delivers at least two and often three years of comparable historical data for analysts to consider. There are also two methods for presenting the income statements. They might be offered in a multi-step format. Accountants for the company could also portray them in a single step format. Each of the two methods is consistent with the important GAAP standards. They also both provide the identical net income final numbers. In fact their figures are formulated in more or less the same way. It is only their compilation and format which proves to be different from one another.

Initial Coin Offering (ICO)

An Initial Coin Offering refers to a non-regulated process in which the funds for new crypto-currency projects become raised. This is also popularly known by its acronym of ICO. These ICOs allow for entrepreneurs to sidestep the heavily regulated process of raising capital through more traditional means involving banks, venture capital, angel investors, or IPOs initial public offerings on stock exchanges.

With any ICO offer campaign, at least some of the crypto-currency will be sold off to those backers of the venture who become involved early. They receive this in compensation for providing traditional currency or alternative currency investment from the likes of Bitcoin. These ICOs are also known as IPCOs, or Initial Public Coin Offerings sometimes.

The process for engaging in an Initial Coin Offering is straightforward and relatively easy to do. The startup outfit begins by producing and releasing a whitepaper-based plan that reveals all of the key details on the venture. These include the needs this operation will meet when it is up and running, what percentage of the new virtual currency project pioneers will keep, what kinds of funding is allowed, the amount of cash required to make the venture a success, and what time duration the campaign will run.

In this campaign, the investors and supports of the new initiative will purchase part of the alternative coins of the new venture with real or virtual money. Such alt coins will be called tokens. They function in much the same way as do shares of stock which corporations sell their investors during an IPO initial public offering.

In cases where the funds raised are not sufficient to carry out the project requirements as set out by the firm in the white paper plan, invested sums will be given back to the investors as the ICO becomes a failure. Yet in those many cases where the funding objective are attained within the set out duration, then the money will be utilized to fund the new enterprise (or to finish it in other cases).

Naturally the upfront investors have their own motivation in purchasing such crypto-coins in the project. This is because they believe that the operation will be a success following launch. This would lead to a potentially massive gain in the value of their tokens.

One highly successful ICO proved to be the platform for the introduction of smart contracts to the world, known as Ethereum. Its coin tokens are called Ether. The Ethereum project came out in 2014. The ICO garnered $18 million worth of Bitcoins for the project's completion. This meant that the Ether tokens cost forty cents apiece. Following the live launch of Ethereum in 2015 and growing success in 2016, Ether roared higher to more than $14. In 2017, it has even topped $400 each at one point. Early investors who held to $400 realized gains of an eye-watering over 1,000 percent in less than five years.

It is true that many ICO events go off successfully. These Initial Coin Offerings are in fact highly disruptive and innovative means of fundraising. Yet they are not a serious rival to traditional stocks by a long shot. Many ICO campaigns have been deemed to be fraud. Without the imperative regulation provided by the SEC Securities Exchange Commission, their volume is likely to remain a tiny fraction of that done in IPOs on traditional exchanges for at least the foreseeable future.

ICOs have suffered from official national opposition which has hindered them as well. The People's Bank of China fully banned all ICOs in September of 2017. They declared them to be financially unstable and disruptive to an orderly economy. Banks were forbidden to provide any services having anything to do with ICOs. At the same time, these new tokens were no longer allowed to be utilized as a currency on Chinese markets. It caused the Bitcoin and Ether enthusiasts to realize that crypto-currency regulation is in the future cards. This temporarily crushed the prices of both main alternative currencies as investors realized what a serious setback it represents.

Initial Public Offering (IPO)

An IPO is the acronym for an Initial Public Offering. Such IPO's represent the first opportunity for most investors to start buying shares of stock in the firm in question. Initial Public Offerings commonly generate a great deal of excitement, not only for the company involved but also for the members of the investing community.

Private companies decide to issue stock and become publicly traded companies for a few different reasons. The main two motivating factors revolve around the need to raise more capital, as well as the desire to permit the original business owners and investors to take profits on their time and investment that they originally put into starting up the company.

It is true that private companies are limited in the amount of capital that they are able to raise, since their ownership turns out to be restricted to certain organizations and individuals. Public companies have the advantages of allowing any investor to take a stake through buying stock shares on exchanges that are publicly traded. It is far easier for them to raise money as public companies.

Initial Public Offerings that go well translate to large amounts of cash for a company. They use this for future expansion and development. Those who began the company or who were initial investors typically make enormous gains at that time in compensation for their time and effort.

Initial Public Offerings take huge amounts of preliminary work. Great amounts of paper work have to be filled in and filed with the regulatory oversight groups. A prospectus has to be created for investors to study and consider. Advertising campaigns for the first shares that will be sold must be developed. On top of these tasks, the company has to continue its normal operations. Because of this, financial firms such as Morgan Stanley or Goldman Sachs are commonly engaged to perform these tasks on the company's behalf. Such a firm is called the IPO underwriting company. With enormous sized IPO's, these tasks could even be divided up between a few different IPO underwriting companies.

Contrary to what many people think, the majority of IPO's typically do not do well initially. Besides this, a percentage of the companies will not make it, meaning that all of the investment in the IPO stock could be lost. Because of this, there is great risk and often lower rewards for sinking money into Initial Public Offerings than in traditional well established companies and stocks. Many investors buy into the enthusiasm and excitement that surrounds Initial Public Offerings. Another explanation for their euphoria may have to do with believing that there is something special in being among the first investors to acquire the next possible Apple, Coca Cola, or IBM. Whatever their reasoning proves to be, investors continue to love Initial Public Offerings and the somewhat long shot opportunities that they represent.

Insolvency

Insolvency refers to the point where an individual, business, or even governmental organization is not able to cover its various financial obligations any longer. This means that it is unable to settle debts with its creditors and lenders as they are due. Many times, before such an indebted individual, company, or government becomes embroiled in any type of insolvency or bankruptcy procedures, they will try to enter into informal negotiations with creditors. This could involve setting up other payment schedules and arrangements.

Insolvency can happen for a variety of reasons. Among these is a decrease in cash flow and profitability forecasts, poor management of cash resources, or a rapid expansion in costs and expenses. Where businesses are concerned, this type of insolvency is classified according to one of two separate categories. The first of these is Cash Flow insolvency. This happens as a corporation or company simply can not pay the business debts as they become due. The second form is Balance Sheet insolvency. This type results from a company reaching the point where it possesses a negative net asset position. It simply means that the corporation's aggregate debts are greater than its total assets.

It is entirely possible for firms to be solvent by balance sheet figures but at the same time be insolvent by cash flow. The opposite scenario could also occur. If a company is bankrupt according to its balance sheet while still solvent by cash flow, it simply means its incoming revenues permit it to cover its current financial obligations. There are numerous companies which possess longer term debt obligations that continuously operate in this balance sheet-bankrupt status.

Technically, insolvency and bankruptcy are not exactly the same thing. The former is a condition of being in financial trouble or at least difficulties. Bankruptcy is instead a court order. It describes the ways in which a debtor which is no longer solvent will continue to meet its obligations or instead have its assets sold off to settle with the creditors.

This means that it is entirely possible for a company, individual, or government entity to be no longer solvent but not yet be officially bankrupt.

This could result from a temporary or sometimes fixable problem. The reverse is never the case. An entity can not be bankrupt yet still be solvent. Such a lack of solvency often translates into an eventual bankrupt state when the debtors are not able to improve their financial conditions.

Corporations and firms that have become insolvent are able to improve their financial state. They might slash costs, borrow money, sell their assets, renegotiate the terms of their debts, or seek out a bigger corporation to acquire them. The buyer could settle their debts as part of the assumption of their services, products, technology, and proprietary trademarks.

Several unfortunate events can lead to a company becoming insolvent. If they do not have enough management in human resources or accounting departments, this could contribute to the problem. A lack of qualified accounting staff could cause a company's budget to be either ignored or misappropriated.

There might also be sharply increasing vendor prices which the company is powerless to stop. Higher prices for their goods and services mean that companies will have to raise their prices in an effort to pass these along to the consumer. The problem arises when customers then shop another company or product to get a better price. Lost clientele nearly always translates into a drop in cash flow. This means that they no longer have the cash coming in to cover the bills due to the company creditors.

There could also be lawsuits brought by employees or customers that break a company's finances. The firm could be forced to pay enormous bills for both defense and in settlement damages which make it impossible for them to continue ongoing operations. As operations cease and revenue naturally drops, the ability to pay bills disappears quickly.

A final reason centers on the lack of evolution in a company product line. It might be customers simply change their needs and therefore purchasing habits. This could lead them to rival firms which offer a broader product range or line. The company which could not or did not adapt its products will find its revenues and profits decreasing to the point where they are unable to cover their expenses with their remaining income.

Intangible Assets

Intangible assets refer to the possessions of a company that are not physical. They are difficult to quantify for several reasons. These types of assets can not be physically measured. They also represent an unknown or undetermined cash value to a company. Several criteria for intangible assets are that they are invisible and can not be touched. Despite this interesting characteristic they are intrinsically valuable. These assets prove to be critical to the overall success of any business.

Intangible assets are typically classed in two categories. These are legal assets and competitive assets. Legal assets are easier to understand than are competitive assets. Legal assets include the wide varieties of intellectual and creative property. In this category are such important holdings as patents, copyrights, brand names, trade secrets, and trademarks.

Each of these can be owned and has value, though it is not easy to assign a value to these elements. Patents are the rights to inventions. Copyrights give ownership of writings and similar creative property. Brand names are a company's physical name or product, such as Coca Cola, McDonald's, or Big Mac.

Trade secrets refer to a company's ways of making things that are not known to rivals and competitors. The formula for Coca Cola is a well-known example of a trade secret. Trademarks are the ownership of popular company or product slogans or phrases as used in advertising.

The second category of intangible assets is the competitive intangible assets. These are more abstract and difficult to grasp. Competitive assets refer to reputation and the knowledge of how to do things for the business. Such assets as these can be obtained with experience mostly. These types of assets include human capital, know how, leveraging, reputation, and collaboration. Naming such ideas is hard enough, but assigning them values is a matter of conjecture.

There are reasons why coming up with values on such intangible assets is so incredibly hard. Valuing properties means that an analyst must gaze into a company's future to determine the ways that these assets will impact its bottom line in the coming years. In the process they take the assets' cost and allocate it through the expected life of the asset. Some intangible assets are valued in legal terms. An intangible asset will never be given a longer life span than forty years. When the analysts and accountants do this allocation, it is referred to as amortizing the intangible assets.

Another division of intangible assets is the category of either definite or indefinite assets. With definite assets, individuals are referring to those that will endure for a specific amount of time. Contract agreements are good examples of these types.

Indefinite assets can last for an indefinite time span. A well-known example of this is a company's brand name. Such an asset will endure so long as the enterprise keeps making the products.

Intangible assets may be hard to value, but they are still valuable for a company. Clearly an intangible asset can not have the same easily assessable value that a physical plant or other equipment would. Such intangible assets are often of great value to the company though.

There are many cases of such a property being instrumental in the company's eventual success or failure. McDonald's is so wildly successful because of the tremendous value it gains from consumer recognition of its brand name. This recognition can not be physically touched or seen.

The results of its impact on the company profits are unquestionably valuable to McDonald's. The strength of their global brand pushes sales around the world on every year. These intangible assets like brands are so powerful precisely because they make an impact on customers' choices. This allows companies to charge higher prices for their products.

Interim Financing

Interim financing is a way of obtaining funding on a short term basis for a project. It can also be called gap financing or bridge financing. People or companies elects for this kind of financing for a specific purpose.

They may be seeking to get funding so that a project can be finished and start creating revenues. This would keep them from having to take resources away from other projects. This concept generally refers to loans. There are also cases of interim financing where companies utilize grants or other types of financial assistance.

A short term loan proves to be among the most frequently employed types of interim financing. These kinds of loans can be crafted so that the borrower will pay back the entire principle of the loan along with all of its interest in twelve months or less from the loan issue date.

This is the opposite of long term financing. In the longer term variety, the borrower receives several years to repay the loan. Loan deals on gap financing often come with interest rates that are a little higher than with longer term loans. For individuals or companies with excellent credit, financing companies can often offer extremely competitive interest rates on these short term loans.

A common use of interim financing is with construction projects that need to be finished. On an individual level, a consumer may wish to renovate either a room in the house or the entire home. The borrower may decide to obtain a short term loan at a better interest rate to cover the costs of labor and materials at the beginning of the project. This can save the borrower on the more substantial interest rates and fees for using credit cards or store credit with the various vendors. The end result is that the consumer spends significantly less money on the improvement project than he or she would by not utilizing the interim financing.

Real estate deals are another common use for this interim financing. A home owner may wish to move forward and buy a new house. The owner may need their present house to sell first. Short term loans like these can prove to be an optimal answer to the problem. Using the bridge loan the owner buys the house. The borrower can then repay the loan once their original house sells. This kind of strategy will help to push through the sale of the original house as well. The previous owners have already moved, which means the new owners can occupy the property without delay.

The goal of interim financing is to offer a short term bridge loan for the individual or business concerned. Despite this, sometimes a situation develops where the borrower will not be able to repay the loan as quickly as hoped. In this case, longer term or additional financing becomes necessary. Many lenders will work with the borrower in such a case to come up with a longer term financing program.

This will completely pay off the short term original loan. Additional money will usually be provided so that the borrower has the funds necessary to complete the project. This is especially the case with construction companies. It works out better for the borrower to engage in a rollover longer term loan than to take out another short term loan. The reason for this is that the longer term loans' finance rates are nearly always lower than the most competitive rates lenders will offer borrowers for short term bridge loans.

Internal Rate of Return (IRR)

The IRR is the acronym for internal rate of return. This IRR proves to be the capital budget rate of return that is utilized in order to determine and compare and contrast various investments' profitability. It is sometimes known as the discounted cash flow rate of return alternatively, or even the ROR, or rate of return. Where banks are concerned, the IRR is also known as the effective interest rate. The word internal is used to specify that such calculation does not involve facts that are part of the external environment, such as inflation or the interest rate.

More precisely, the internal rate of return for any investment proves to be the interest rate level where the negative cash flow, or net present value of costs, from the investment is equal to the positive cash flow, or net present value of benefits, for the investment. In other words, this IRR will yield a discount rate that causes the net current values of both positive and negative cash flows of a specific investment to cancel out at zero.

These Internal Rates of Return are generally utilized to consider projects and investments and their ultimate desirability. Naturally, a project will be more appealing to engage in or purchase if it comes with a greater internal rate of return. Given a number of projects from which to choose, and assuming that all project benefits prove to be the same generally, the project that contains the greatest Internal Rate of Return will be considered the most attractive. It should be selected with the highest priority of being pursued first.

The assumed theory for companies is that they will be interested in eventually pursuing any investment or project that comes with an IRR that is greater than the expense of the money put into the project as capital. The number of projects or investments that can be run at a time are limited in the real world though. A firm may have a restricted capability of overseeing a large number of projects at once, or they may lack the necessary funds to engage in all of them at a time.

The internal rate of return is actually a number expressed as a percent. It details the yield, efficacy, and efficiency of a given investment or project. This should not be confused with the net present value that instead tells the particular investment's actual value.

In general, a given investment or project is deemed to be worthwhile assuming that its internal rate of return proves to be higher than either the expense of the capital involved, or alternatively, than a pre set minimally accepted rate of return. For companies that possess share holders, the minimum IRR is always a factor of the investment capital's cost. This is easily decided by ascertaining the cost of capital, which is risk adjusted, for alternative types of investments. In this way, share holders will approve of a project or investment, so long as its Internal Rate of Return is greater than the cost of the capital to be used and this project or investment creates economic value that is viable for the company in question.

Investment Banking

Investment Banking refers to a particular subdivision of banking. This investment type of banking pertains to developing capital for governments, organizations, and corporations. Investment banks will come up with new equity and debt securities to float and sell them on behalf of any corporation. They also facilitate mergers and acquisitions and company reorganizations. They help to sell the securities and broker major trades for private investors and institutions. Besides this, they give guidance to those issuing stocks on the placement and floating of stock issues.

A great many of the bigger investment banks prove to be associated with (or wholly or partially owned by) bigger financial and banking institutions. A number of them have evolved into house hold known names. The biggest of these famous investment banks are Goldman Sachs, JPMorgan Chase, Morgan Stanley, Bank of America Merrill Lynch, HSBC, and Deutsche Bank.

In general, such investment banking fosters huge, complex, often international in nature financial transactions. This might come with advisory services on the best ways to structure deals when the customer is interested in engaging in a sale, merger, or acquisition. Other firms may want to know how much a certain company is worth. The investment banks may need to float and sell securities in order to raise money for the groups of clients. Someone will have to develop the documents which the SEC Securities and Exchange Commission requires in order for companies to be taken public.

The investment banking groups hire investment bankers who assist their clients (the governments, organizations, and corporations) in planning for, setting up, and managing enormous projects. This saves a great deal of money and time for the clients through identifying any risks common to the project before the project starts. The idea is that investment bankers are highly trained experts in the financial services fields. They are supposed to have a wealth of knowledge, background, and advice to offer their clients for the best way to plan developments so the company can pursue the best recommendations for the current state of economics pertaining to the company's particular project.

One can also think of the investment banks as not only an advisor but a middle man. They offer the useful go-between for companies and the investing public who want to purchase such new bond and stock issues. Investment banks package together financial securities and instruments so that the companies can optimize their revenues and safely come through the often complex regulatory environments.

For example, in many cases where companies launch their first IPO initial public offering, the underwriting investment banks will purchase most or all of the new shares straight off of their client the company. They then re-sell these IPO shares on the stock markets. The company gets a big single payday upfront this way and the investment bank acts as a contractor for the actual IPO underwriting. The investment banks typically profit well, as they usually re-price the shares with a nice markup on their original purchase price. This also entails a serious amount of risk though. If they overprice the stock shares, then they may not be able to sell all the shares and instead could end up selling them at a loss to the price they initially paid for them in the first place.

It is not at all uncommon for various investment banks to compete with each other for the best new IPO underwriting opportunities, and sometimes they end up working together on enormous ones. It could lead to a higher per share price being realized for the company which is going public. When the competition for the project becomes particularly intense, it can hit the investment bank's profit margins. In these cases what often happens is that several of the major investment banks will underwrite a portion of the securities, often in different jurisdictions such as EuroNext, NYSE, and London Stock Exchange. The advantages to the investment banks are that the risk becomes spread around and reduced this way.

Joint Venture

Joint ventures are businesses or projects that two or more companies create together. They typically have shared risks and returns, ownership, and control structure. Companies form joint ventures for a primary reason. Usually they are trying to combine their various resources in order to achieve some specific goal. It could be for an existing or a new project. Each of the JV owners is ultimately liable for the losses, profits, and costs that come with it. The joint venture itself is a separate company that has different objectives from the main interests of the owning companies.

Companies form joint ventures as a means to pool their expertise in the industry, their business reputation, their technology and abilities, and their separate human resources. This gives them the advantage of combining resources on a project as they are able to share the costs, liabilities, and risks associated with the job.

Joint ventures are most often temporary partnerships between two or more companies. They draw up contracts that spell out the joint project terms for which every participant will be responsible. At the end of the joint venture, every participating party gets its shared percentage of the losses or profits. They sign an agreement that the joint venture is over and dissolve the original JV agreement. These are among the advantages for forming such joint ventures.

There are many disadvantages to these joint ventures as well. Because of these, as many as half of the JVs ever formed end with conflict in under four years' time. Among the problems that plague joint ventures are greater liability, reduced outside opportunities, and unfair divisions of resources and work.

Greater liability is a serious and real issue for the owners of joint ventures. Most joint ventures become set up with structures of limited liability companies or partnerships. Each of these types of business structure comes with its own liability. Only if they form a business entity that is separate can they avoid this increased liability for the JV. All participating owners equally share responsibility for any claims that are filed against the JV. This is true regardless of how much they are involved in the activity that instigated the claims.

Contracts with joint ventures also typically reduce the amount of outside opportunities for all of the companies participating. This lasts so long as the joint venture project is ongoing. There are often non-compete agreements and exclusivity arrangements made in the process. These agreements will impact their business dealings with vendors and customers alike. The idea is to keep all parties focused on the joint venture's success and to reduce conflicts of interest between their various businesses. These limitations will end after the project concludes. In the meantime, they can negatively affect the main business and operations of the various partner companies.

Unfair divisions of resources and work are a final problem that haunts many joint ventures. The parties involved all share control and ownership. This does not mean that the employment of resources and amount of work done will be fairly divided. One company might only have to put people to work on the project while another has to provide facilities, technology, or access to distribution. This may mean a lot more work and resources are committed by the one partner.

Despite this unfair burden, the shares of the profits are the same for all contributors. It does not matter that one partner often contributes much more to the project. Such unfair distributions of work and resources often cause conflicts among the owners of the JV project. Conflicts like this can create a lower rate of success for the project in the end.

Junk Bonds

Junk bonds are almost the same as regular bonds with an important difference. They are lower rated for credit worthiness. This is why in order to understand junk bonds, individuals first must comprehend the basics of traditional bonds.

Like traditional bonds, junk bonds are promises from organizations or companies to pay back the holder the amount of money which they borrow. This amount is known as the principal. Terms of such bonds involve several elements. The maturity date is the time when the borrower will repay the bond holder. There will also be an interest rate that the bond holder receives, or a coupon. Junk bonds are unlike those traditional ones because the credit quality of the issuing organization is lower.

Every kind of bond is rated according to its credit quality. Bonds can all be categorized in one of two types. Investment grade bonds possess medium to low risk. Their credit ratings are commonly in the range of from AAA to BBB. The downside to these bonds is that they do not provide much in the way of interest returns. Their advantage is that they have significantly lower chances of the borrower being unable to make interest payments.

Junk bonds on the other hand offer higher interest yields to their bond holders. Issuers do this because they do not have any other way to finance their needs. With a lower credit rating, they can not borrow capital at a more favorable price. The ratings on such junk bonds are often BB or less from Standard & Poor's or Ba or less by Moody's rating agency. Bond ratings such as these can be considered like a report card for the credit rating of the company in question. Riskier firms receive lower ratings while safe blue-chip companies earn higher ratings.

Junk bonds typically pay an average yield that is from 4% to 6% higher than U.S. Treasury yields. These types of bonds are placed into one of two categories. These are fallen angels and rising stars. Fallen angels bonds used to be considered at an investment grade. They were cut to junk bond level as the company that issued them saw its credit quality decline.

Rising stars are the opposites of fallen angels. This means the rating of the bond has risen. As the underlying issuer's credit quality improves, so does the rating of the bond. Rising stars are often still considered to be junk bonds. They are on track to rise to investment quality.

Junk bonds are risky for more reasons than the chances of not receiving one or more interest payments. There is the possibility of not receiving the original principal back. This type of investing also needs a great amount of skills in analyzing data like special credit. Because of these risk factors and specialized skills that are needed, institutional investors massively dominate the market.

A better way for individuals to become involved with junk bonds is through high yield bond funds. Professionals research and manage the holdings of these funds. The risks associated with a single bond defaulting are greatly reduced. They do this by diversifying into a variety of companies and types of bonds. High yield bond funds often require investors to stay invested for minimally a year or two.

When the yield of junk bonds declines below the typical 4% to 6% spread above Treasuries, investors should be careful. The risk does not become less in these cases. It is that the returns no longer justify the dangers in the junk bonds. Investors also should carefully consider the junk bond default rates. These can be tracked for free on Moody's website.

Ledger

A Ledger is also often called a general ledger. It refers to a firm's set of (numbered) accounts that it maintains for its corporate accounting records. With such a record, the firm has a full history of all its financial transactions it has entered into throughout the entire existence of the firm. In this master set of company books, the firm keeps all of the necessary information it must have to compile its financial statements. The data will always cover such useful facts and figures as liabilities, assets, cash flow and positions, revenues, expenses, profits, and owners' equity.

Accountants work with these general ledgers as part of their book keeping system for drawing up the company financial statements. All transactions must be included in the master document. Accountants will first pursue creating a trial balance. This represents a report of all account balances and the corresponding accounts. It is this adjusted trial balance which will be employed to create all relevant corporate financial statements.

These general ledgers are employed continuously by those firms which utilize the method of book keeping known as the double entry system. In such a methodology of accounting, every financial transaction will impact minimally two different ledgers and accounts. It also signifies that every entry will have an equal and opposite credit and debit transaction. Such double entries will be arrayed in two separate columns. Generally the debit postings will be to the left while the credit entries will be posted to the right column. It is imperative that all credit and debit entries balance out all the time.

It helps to look at a concrete example to better understand this challenging concept. When a customer pays a $300 invoice, the cash account will rise. The accountant will book a $300 credit to cash. At the same time, he or she will then log a $300 debit on the other column for the accounts receivable. In this way, both the credits and debits will equal out.

There are four key financial statements which accountants can produce from these general ledgers. The balance sheet is one of them. Under balance sheets there are sub divisions including accounts receivable and cash accounts reports. The formula for any balance sheet proves to be assets minus liabilities equals equity. The one cash account in the example above gains by $300 while the accounts receivable category becomes reduced by the amount of $300. Thanks to this simultaneous increasing and decreasing of the balance sheet equation left side, the equation will stay in perfect balance.

A second critical financial report which is impacted by the general ledgers proves to be the income statement. It also has a formula, which amounts to revenue minus expenses equals net income (also called profit). It is crucial that this formula similarly remains balanced for the financial statements to be correct. A single given transaction might also affect both the income statement and the balance sheet. Consider another example. Firms might bill their clients $750. They would note a $750 debit on to the accounts receivable category. At the same time, they would put up a $750 credit on to the revenue (or cash) categories. Both the credits and debits grow by $750 this way. The two totals remain in balance.

This double entry accounting contrasts with single entry accounting methods. In either methodology of book keeping, the common element will be the accountant or book keeper working with a general ledger of some type.

Lender of Last Resort

Lender of Last Resort refers to an official central financial institution which provides emergency loans to commercial and savings banks as well as other financial institutions which are suffering from extreme financial hardship or are believed to be nearing collapse. Generally such a lender turns out to be a national central bank. Within the U.S., it is the Federal Reserve which functions as the last case lender to those institutions which find themselves without any other way to borrow funds quickly. Their inability to gain access to funds and credit could lead to a devastating consequence for the greater economy in general. This is why the central banks will provide credit extensions on an expedited basis to those financial institutions which are undergoing extreme financial stress and so in consequence cannot get funds from anywhere else.

The principal job of such a Lender of Last Resort is to maintain the financial system stability and the banking system integrity through safeguarding the deposited funds of individuals and businesses. This is critical to foster confidence in the financial system and to prevent wholesale panic from taking hold of depositors who might otherwise cause runs on the banks by attempting to draw out all of their funds at once. Such an action would create an illiquidity event for the bank and force them to close their doors.

It has been over a century and a half since central banks made it their missions to head off great depressions through being the effective Lenders of Last Resort when financial crises erupted. The action does deliver the liquidity funds with a penalty interest rate. As open market operations take over the funding facility, the interest rate drops for safe assets as collateral. The process also includes direct support to the market.

Commercial banks do not enjoy borrowing from the Lender of Last Resort at any time. It would be a sure fire warning that the bank was undergoing financial stress or even experiencing a crisis of liquidity and a crisis of confidence would next follow. This is the reason that critics of this type of arrangement feel that it tempts banks into taking on a higher level of risk than they should in a form of moral hazard. This could happen because they believe that consequences for engaging in risky financial behavior will not be so severe.

The alternatives to a trustworthy central banking institution not functioning as a Lender of Last Resort can be serious. Bank runs are what result in times of financial crisis when the customers of banks begin to show concern over the solvency of their home financial institution. These customers can be seized with sudden panic and descend en masse on the bank demanding to withdraw all of their funds when confidence in the individual bank or the banking system as a whole erupts.

Banks only maintain s tiny percentage of their deposited funds on hand in their vaults. This is how a bank run can result in the liquidity of a bank rapidly disappearing. Literally these panicked customer actions can set into motion a self-fulfilling prophecy which leads to the bank failing as a result of insolvency.

This actually occurred in 1929 and throughout the 1930s. Bank runs led to catastrophic and widespread bank failure throughout the United States after the 1929 stock market crashes. This snowballed into the Great Depression which gripped the country and developed world economies for the next roughly fifteen years. The American federal government responded too late with tough new legislation which mandated severe reserve requirements on the banks. It required by law that they keep a specific minimum percentage of their deposits as available cash reserves.

Levied Taxes

Levied taxes are taxes that are forcefully collected from an individual, business, or other entity. Among the many taxes most frequently collected these days are income taxes. These taxes could be said to be levied, since the law requires that an individual's income tax is levied for the government by the company where they work.

Three main types of tax systems are in effect in the world today where income is concerned. These include progressive, proportional, and regressive tax systems. Progressive taxes levied are those that employ progressively greater rates of tax as earnings are higher. As an example, the first $10,000 that an individual makes might be taxed at only five percent, while the next $10,000 is possibly taxed at a rate of ten percent, and income above this could be taxed at a twenty percent rate.

Proportional taxes use a pre set flat rate of tax. This applies to all earnings, no matter how high or low they are. With a ten percent flat rate, everyone will pay their ten percent of income as taxes levied, regardless of what amount of money they actually make.

Regressive taxes are said to hurt the poor by shifting the tax burden to lower income earners. This type of tax levy only taxes income to a certain dollar level, such as the first $80,000. Any money made above this amount would simply not be taxed. In reality, most tax systems employ the various kinds of tax levying methods to address various forms of income.

Levied taxes also apply to corporations and businesses. The income of a company is taxed in what is known as a corporate tax. This is sometimes alternatively referred to as a profit tax or corporate income tax. With corporate taxes levied, the net income is generally the figure that is taxed. Net income refers to the difference of gross income and expenses and other allowable write offs.

With individuals, the total income for a family or individual is commonly taxed. Some deductions are usually allowed before the taxes to be levied are determined. Income may be reduced by a certain amount as a result of how many children a family has to support, as an example.

There are many other forms of taxes levied in modern capitalist countries such as Great Britain and the United States. More than two hundred different types of taxes can be identified in the U.S. alone. These include such various taxes levied as income tax, sales tax, property tax, estate tax, capital gains tax, dividends tax, gasoline taxes, leisure taxes, luxury items taxes, and so called sin taxes on items such as cigarettes and alcohol. The United States has been called the most heavily taxed society in all of world history.

Liabilities

Where a business is concerned, liabilities prove to be amounts of money that are owed by the company at any given point. These liabilities are displayed on the firm's balance sheet. They are commonly listed as items payable, or simply as payables.

There are two types of liabilities. These are longer term liabilities and shorter term liabilities. Long term liabilities turn out to be business obligations that last for greater than the period of a single year. Mortgages payable and loans payable are included in this category.

Short term liabilities represent business obligations that will be paid in less than a year. There are many different kinds of short term liabilities. They include all of the items detailed below.

Payroll taxes payable are one of these. They represent sums automatically collected from the employees and put to the side by the employer. They have to be given to the IRS and any state taxing agencies at the pre determined time.

Sales taxes payable are another short term liability. The business collects them from its customers when sales are made. They hold them until it is time to give them to the proper revenue collecting department within the state.

Mortgages and loans payable are another short term liability. These represent payments made every month on mortgages and loans. They are not large single payments or the total amount of a loan that is eventually owed, but instead represent recurring monthly obligations.

Liabilities for individuals are another type of liabilities altogether. They also represent money that has to be paid out. For people, they are debts owed, as well as monthly cash flow that goes out of the individual's accounts.

Liabilities and assets are the opposites of each other, yet people often get them confused. While assets are things that contribute positive cash flow to a person's finances, liabilities are those that create negative cash flow, or money that leaves an individual's accounts every month. For example, a house that an individual owes money on and makes monthly payments on is a liability, not an asset. The house takes money from the person in the form of monthly mortgage payments each month. For a house to be an asset, it would have to be completely paid off. Even still, if monthly taxes and insurance payments are being made, then technically it would still be a liability. Houses can only be assets really and truly when they are rented out and the rental income that a person receives is greater than all of the expenses associated with the house every month, including any mortgage payments, taxes, insurance, upkeep, and property management fees. When the net result of a property is money coming in, then it is an asset and not a liability.

Liquidation

The meaning of liquidation depends on the use of the word. In financial terms, there are three different definitions of it. In economics or finance it refers to a failed company. A company that is insolvent is unable to pay its bills when they are owed. Liquidation is the process of winding up the company. The operations of the company cease at this point. The assets would then be divided up among its creditors and stock holders. This is done based on whose claims have priority.

Insolvent companies that choose to go into liquidation generally do so under U.S. bankruptcy code Chapter 7. This legal statute gives the rules on liquidation of companies. Companies that are still solvent but are in trouble may also file a Chapter 7 bankruptcy. This is less common. There are also bankruptcies for companies that do not force liquidation. One such provision that covers this scenario is Chapter 11. In a Chapter 11 filing the trustee saves the company and restructures its debts.

When the process of liquidation occurs, the company halts all operations. All of its assets are tallied up and then distributed to the various claimants. After this is finished, the trustee finally dissolves the business. The debts actually have not been discharged in this process. They still exist to the point where the statute of limitations on the debts expires. There is no debtor in existence to pay off these debts. Creditors simply write them off in practice.

The assets in this liquidation process are handled in a certain methodical way. The Department of Justice appoints a trustee. This individual supervises the process. Assets are distributed to those who have claims based on their priority. Secured creditors are first in line. This is because their loans are backed up by collateral.

The lenders are allowed to seize this collateral and then to sell it. Many times they receive far less than the actual asset value because there are limited time frames. Sometimes the assets are not enough to cover their debt. These creditors are compensated from any other liquid assets in this case.

Unsecured creditors come next in the process. In this category are holders of bonds, the IRS, and employees. Bond holders are a form of unsecured creditors. The company may owe the IRS taxes. Employees may be waiting on payroll or other money they are due. The last category to receive compensation is shareholders. If any assets are left they receive them. Preferred stock investors receive priority before the common stock holders. Usually there is nothing left for either class by the time the creditors are paid.

Another definition of liquidation surrounds huge sales. Sometimes a company needs to close out a great deal of inventory. They would do this by liquidating their inventory at deep discounts. Any company can do this. They do not have to file for bankruptcy in order to sell off inventory.

A third definition of liquidation involves closing out an investment. This generally occurs when an investors sells their holdings in exchange for cash. An individual might also liquidate out of a one position and into an opposite one. If he or she held long shares in a stock, they could instead take on the identical number of short shares.

Brokers can force liquidate trader positions in certain cases. Traders who have acted or traded recklessly with risk can have this happen. If traders' account values drop below the minimum margin requirements they can suffer from forced liquidation as well.

Liquidation Value

Liquidation Value represents the full value of a corporation's complete range of physical assets if and when it declares bankruptcy or actually goes out of business. This value is compiled when every asset on the company books and balance sheet becomes tallied up. This value then includes real estate, equipment, factories, fixtures, and inventory. Those assets that are intangible would never be a part of the firm's final liquidating value.

This is one of four key types of value assigned to a corporation or company's various assets. These include book value, market value, salvage value, and liquidation value. With every category of value, this delivers an alternative view point for both analysts and accountants alike to classify the total value of all assets. For individuals and investors who engage in workouts and bankruptcies, this Liquidating Value is absolutely essential to know.

Book value and market value generally vie for the crown of largest assets' category valuation. In cases where any group of assets' market value has deteriorated because of decreasing market demand instead of the business using it up, this proves to be true. With book value, the asset value equates to the one declared upon the corporate balance sheet. Since the company balance sheet declares these assets for their historical price and cost, this means that the book value could equate to more or less than the relevant market prices which apply on a given day. When the all around economy is growing and prices in general are rising, then this book value is traditionally less than the relevant market value.

With liquidation value, the sum represents the anticipated price for the asset after it has been sold, generally for a loss as compared the original price. Salvage value refers to the one assigned to the assets once they reach the conclusion of their natural and useful life. This then would represent the scrap value of assets. Liquidation value typically proves to be less than the book and market values yet still higher than basic salvage value. Liquidating assets are still valuable, they just sell for less than they otherwise should and would because of the proverbial fire sale in a shortened time frame. It causes them to be sold for losses versus their listed book value.

There are reasons why such liquidation values never include any intangible asset prices. Such intangible assets comprise the goodwill, intellectual property, and brand recognition of the company or corporation. When firms are sold off instead of being liquidated, the firm's value will include both intangible assets' value and liquidation value. This is why traditional value investors will consider and contemplate the variances between the ongoing concern value and the market cap value. They are able to decide this way whether or not the stock of the corporation represents a good value.

It is always useful to consider an example in order to clarify the concept of liquidation value. A given corporation the Snappy Pop Company has $550,000 in liabilities. They also possess book valued assets of $1 million on their company balance sheet. The auction value of these assets might be $750,000, which represents three-quarters of their fair value. At the same time, the salvage value is $75,000. To determine the liquidation value, analysts simply subtract out any liabilities (in this case $550,000) off of the auction value (in this case $750,000). This gives a value of $750,000 minus $550,000 for a grand total of $200,000 liquidating value.

Loan Discount Rate

The Loan Discount Rate refers to an interest rate which commercial banks and various other financial institutions pay on loans they take from the discount window of their regional branch of the Federal Reserve Bank. It can also pertain to the discounted cash flow or DCF analysis interest rate. This rate would set the current value of all future cash flows.

Where the DCF analysis is concerned, the discount rate considers more than simply the time value of money. It also factors in the insecure future cash flows. The higher a future uncertainty risk may be for the uncertain cash flows, the higher the discount rate will prove to be. There is also a third meaning to the discount rate term. This is the rate which insurance companies and pension plans utilize to discount their liabilities. In general, the first definition above is the primary one for this phrase, and the one we will mostly consider in greater detail throughout this article.

The Federal Reserve is the government institution tasked with setting and administering the primary interest rates which the Federal Reserve banks set. It is not the market that sets these rates. The Fed offers these loans via its discount window as a lender of last resort to its member financial institutions when they are in trouble. This window became extremely popular back in the end of 2007 and 2008 when the national economic and financial situation in the U.S. declined dramatically almost overnight.

The Federal Reserve then engaged in necessary emergency steps in order to deliver significant liquidity to the struggling financial system. That year, the borrowing from the discount window made a new all-time record high of $111 during this crisis peak of the Global Financial Crisis and Great Recession of October in 2008. The Board of Governors of the Federal Reserve System then slashed the loan discount rate to a low of .5 percent not seen since the end of the Second World War on the date of December 16th of 2008.

It is always instructive to consider a real world concrete example of a challenging concept such as this one. If an individual anticipates that he will receive a thousand dollars in a certain year, he may need to ascertain how much the present value of said thousand dollars is right now. To determine this, he would have to choose a given interest rate at which to discount the present value. If the individual employed a ten percent rate, then the money a year from now would be worth $909.09 today. This is $1,000 divided by 110%. If the anticipated receipt date of the thousand dollars was for two years in the future, then the present value of the money would today be $826.45.

Companies often need to figure out an appropriate discount rate to deploy on a given project. A great number of firms utilize the WACC Weighted Average Cost of Capital when the risk profile of the project proves to be similar to the company profile as a whole. In scenarios where the risk profile of the project is significantly different from the company's operations in general, they will instead utilize the CAPH Capital Asset Pricing Model. This delivers a project-specific discount rate which might more appropriately reflect the risk of the given project.

The loan discount rate should never be confused with discount points. These are a kind of prepaid fees in lieu of interest which mortgage borrowers are able to buy at their closing. They reduce the amount of the interest dollars which the borrowers will have to pay out in later re-payments. Such points typically cost a percent of the entire loan amount. Every point reduces the interest on the loan by from an eighth to a quarter of a percentage point.

Loan Syndication

Loan Syndication refers to the procedure of getting a few different lenders involved in delivering a few different components of a loan. This activity typically happens in those situations where borrowers need to borrow a huge amount of capital. In these cases, the money required might be more than any one lender will feel comfortable providing or could be higher than certain lenders' levels of allowed risk exposure. This is why many lenders choose to work hand in glove on such projects in order to deliver the financing a borrower requires.

Corporate borrowing typically involves this type of loan syndication such firms look for loans to cover a wide range of needs. It is most often needed as companies are attempting to perform an acquisition, a merger, or a share buyback, or for other kinds of capital intensive projects. With a capital project of this nature, significant loans will be involved. This is why these loan syndications are utilized for these types of projects or merger and acquisition activity.

This kind of Loan Syndication permits any single lender to be involved with more than only a single huge loan. It also allows it to keep a more manageable and sensible level of credit exposure since it is not the one creditor involved with the deal in question. In these types of multi bank underwritten deals, the various lenders' terms will commonly be identical to the borrower, although there are incidents where this is not the case and they instead vary. The various lenders will often require different amounts of collateral. These requirements can vary significantly. It is common however for there to almost always be a single loan agreement which governs the whole of the syndicate group.

With the majority of Loan Syndication, one financial institution plays the role of lead bank. They will then arrange all terms and particulars of the deal itself. This lead financial institution is commonly referred to as the deal's syndicate agent. Such an agent is commonly responsible to handle all particulars of the deal. This means they will arrange the upfront transaction, compliance reports, fees, loan monitoring, reporting, and repayment arrangements in the life of the loan. They do this on behalf of every lender who is a party to the deal.

There can be specialists brought in to help with some aspects of the deal in question. These are typically third parties which are not a part of the loan syndicate. They often handle such important administrative functions as monitoring and report making. With loan syndications, there are many times higher fees to cover the huge reporting requirements as well as to finalize, package up, and handle the loan servicing and processing. This means that fees can run up to 10 percent of the principal of the loan amount.

For the year 2015, the company with the greatest amount of loan funded syndications on its books was Charter Communications. They boasted of $13.8 billion in syndicate amounts thanks to the merger transaction with Time Warner Cable. The lead financial institution on the syndication was Credit Suisse. For the loan market of the United States, the banks which represent the foremost lead institutions with loan syndications prove to be Bank of America Merrill Lynch, Wells Fargo, JPMorgan, and Citi.

There is an umbrella organization which covers the corporate loan market. This is the LSTA Loan Syndications and Trading Association. There goals are to offer resources for those firms interested in participating in loan syndications as well as those companies that require the services of loans in this capacity. It brings together all of the various important players in the market, delivers market research on relevant topics, and even lobbies industry regulators to impact procedures for compliance in Washington, London, and other important loan syndication cities around the world.

Loan to Cost Ratio

Loan to Cost Ratio, or LTC, proves to be a measurement utilized by finance companies in extending loans for commercial real estate projects. It is employed ultimately to make comparisons of the offered financing for a given building project versus the expenses of completing said project. With the LTC ratio, lenders of commercial real estate loans are able to decide on the risks involved in backing a particular construction project via loans. The LTC ratio is similar to the LTV loan to value ratio. They both compare the amount of the construction loan to the value in fair market terms of the project in question.

Lenders work with the Loan to Cost Ratio in order to decide what loan percentage or dollar amount the financier is agreeable to finance. They do this with a basis on the firm costs stated in the construction project budget. After construction completes, these projects then possess a new and often times significantly higher value. Future values can often be double what the construction costs prove to be. This means that on a loan for $200,000 in construction, the future value of the project is likely to be $400,000 once it is fully concluded.

Consider how LTC will look in this example. With $200,000 in construction costs, and an 80% LTC ratio, the lender would be willing to loan out $160,000 on the total project. Using a similar 80% LTV ratio metric instead would significantly change the amount of money the lender is wiling to extend to $400,000 x 80% for $320,000.

Lenders never completely finance 100% of construction costs. This is because they feel that the builders also need to have significant exposure to the project in order to guarantee they will give their all to see them succeed. This is what is meant by the colloquial expression "skin in the game." It prevents a builder from simply getting up and walking away from a project gone bad. It is why the majority of lenders will require a builder to kick in minimally 10% to 20% of the construction costs to secure a financing deal.

Loan to value ratios are not the same as the Loan to Cost Ratio, though they have much in common up to a point. LTV evaluates the loan issued versus the project value once it will be fully completed. Since most banks assume that construction projects will double in value once they are finished, this is why an identical LTV percentage to the LTC ratio will yield twice the loan amount.

Lenders hold firmly to the LTC ratio. It helps them to clearly express the levels of risk in a given financing project for commercial construction. In the end, using a greater Loan to Cost Ratio will entail a significantly riskier project from the lender's perspective. This is why the overwhelming majority of reputable mainstream lenders will not surpass a pre-determined percentage when they consider any given project. They usually limit this amount strictly to a maximum of 80% of the project's LTV or LTC. When lenders are willing to become involved at a higher percentage and ratio, they will most always insist on a substantially greater project and loan interest rate to compensate them for the additional level of risk to which they are consenting.

Lenders will also have to consider other information and circumstances beyond simply Loan to Cost Ratio and Loan to value ratios when extending such financing. They take into consideration the value of the property and its location for where the project will be constructed. They also contemplate how much creditworthiness and experience the commercial builders in the application possess. Finally, they consult both the borrowers' loan payment histories on other loans and their credit record as demonstrated in their company credit report.

Market Capitalization

Market capitalization refers to a company's total value. Analysts determine it by multiplying the number of shares in existence times the price of the stock. This concept can also be utilized to measure the full value of a stock exchange. The New York Stock Exchange market capitalization would equal the value of all publicly traded companies on the exchange added together.

Market cap is another name for market capitalization. Examples of how this is figured make it easier to understand. Companies that have 2 million shares which have been issued that sell for $20 apiece have a market cap of $40 million. If an investor had enough money and could get the stockholders to agree to sell their shares, he or she could purchase the company for $40 million total. In practice many shareholders would want more than the current share price to sell their stock.

There are three different main sizes of market capitalization among traded companies. These are large cap, mid cap, and small cap corporations. Large cap companies are generally considered the least risky ones in which to invest. They typically possess substantial financial resources to survive economic downturns. They are also generally leaders in their industries. This gives them a smaller amount of growth opportunity.

Because of this the returns for these large cap companies are often not as spectacular as with successful companies in the other two categories. They also have a significantly greater chance of paying dividends out to their share holders. Large cap corporations have $5 billion and higher capitalization.

Mid cap companies are generally less risky than the smaller companies. They still do not have the same possibilities for aggressive growth. Mid cap companies commonly possess market capitalization of from $1 billion to $5 billion. Studies have shown that mid caps have outperformed large cap and small cap corporation stocks in the past 20 years.

Small cap corporations are those which possess under $1 billion in market capitalization. These tinier companies have often completed an Initial Public

Offering in the recent past. Such companies are considered the riskiest of the three types. This is because in economic downturns, they have the greatest chance of failing or defaulting. They also enjoy plenty of opportunity and space to expand. This means that they potentially could be extremely profitable if they succeed.

Proponents of using market cap as the primary means of valuing companies have a well thought out argument. Stock prices tend to reflect the beliefs of investors and analysts in the anticipated earnings of a company. Higher earnings should cause traders and investors to bid up the price of the stock. Multiplying this price by the number of shares gives a comparable means of valuing one company against another.

A downside to valuing businesses this way is that it can give companies without profits high valuations. In the dot com bust at the turn of the century, technology companies that had never turned a profit were valued in the tens of billions of dollars. This in theory made them more valuable than reliable companies that had actual assets and earnings. Companies in slower growing industries are also typically valued less than they should be since their stock prices are often undervalued. Critics of this way of valuing companies suggest that more accurate measures would include the value of a company's assets, its annual revenues, or its earnings per share.

Companies whose market capitalization falls substantially below their asset value become takeover targets. This is because corporate raiders are able to buy a company for less money than they will realize by selling off its various parts, businesses, and assets separately.

Market Value

With regards to real estate, market value is the price which a real property seller can anticipate obtaining from the property purchaser in normal open and fair market negotiations. In general, appraisers value a home or other piece of real estate property utilizing a number of critical factors. When markets are volatile, such prices will vary significantly. Real estate agents may place one value on a home or other piece of real estate, yet in the end, the true property value is only what an able and willing buyer will actually pay to acquire it.

It is crucial to be aware of the market value of a piece of property individuals or businesses are selling as this ultimately sets the asking price of the real estate in question. Those sellers who are not intimately aware of this will either overprice their houses or under price them. Either of these actions will often lead to poor financial results. Not being aware of a property's true value can cause homeowners to become victims to practices of predatory lending. In this unscrupulous lending behavior, the bank or other lending financial institution will prevail upon a borrower to take out a greater amount of money than their property is really worth.

It is real estate agents or better still professional appraisers who determine most accurately the market value of a house or piece of real estate through measuring it up to other properties in the area or neighborhood which share similarities with the one in question. Real estate agents and appraisers call such recently sold area properties "comparables." They will always seek to find houses which are as alike in style, size, and location to the one they are appraising as possible.

Such properties must have sold within the prior six months to a year. According to this strategy, the professionals will similarly discern what the typical price per square foot of the houses in the area actually is. This practice by itself will not set the market price of a house, but it will give the professionals a good starting point from which to set a reasonable and viable asking price for the property.

There are also various other factors which influence a property's market value. These include the condition of the property in question as well as any improvements which the seller makes. Where a home is concerned, bathroom and kitchen renovations and updates are the main ones which will boost the selling price. Other more cosmetic appearance improvements like new carpet, fresh paint, updated light fixtures, and special window treatments will help a house to show better and perhaps sell faster, yet they will not increase the all around value of the home.

Yet it is absolutely true that the overall condition of any piece of real estate will impact its total value. Houses that boast more current and better maintained appliances and systems, roofs, windows, and even entry doors will realize a significantly better final selling price than those which offer flawed structures or outdated appliances, systems, entry doors, and mechanics.

In corporations and investments, market value is the price for which a given asset will sell in the open market. This measure of value can often be applied to the market capitalization of any company which is publically traded. Determining the market cap value is a matter of multiplying out the current price per share by the quantity of total outstanding shares.

This measure of market value is simplest to calculate for those instruments which are traded on exchanges, like futures and stocks. This is because their market prices are readily available and commonly disseminated. With over the counter securities such as fixed income securities, it can be far harder to ascertain. Yet the most difficult to determine market values are those commonly associated with less liquid assets such as businesses and real estate. This is why business valuation experts and real estate appraisers determine the market values for such assets as these.

Merger

A Merger refers to a financial transaction which combines two preexisting companies into a single larger resulting firm. A few different kinds of mergers exist today. There are a variety of reasons for why companies engage in such mergers. These mergers and acquisitions often go through with an eye to extending a firm's customer base and product reach, increasing its market share, or moving into new markets and industry segments. In the end, the ultimate motivation is to make shareholders happy by adding shareholder value.

These combinations occur as two firms join forces into a new larger single company. They are nearly identical to takeovers and acquisitions. The main difference lies in the stock shareholders of each firm holding on to an interest in the share of the new corporation. With acquisitions though, a single company buys out all of or a controlling interest in the stock of the target company. This leads to an unbalanced ownership within the newly formed corporation. Practically the whole process of such mergers is generally kept under wraps so that the members of the investing public are completely unaware of it until after they are announced.

Most personnel at both companies are kept in the dark as well. In fact, the lion share of such merger efforts fail. With the majority of them completely secret, it is hard to say with any accuracy the number of possible mergers that become discussed and considered any year in question. The number ought to be extremely high as the quantities of successful ones prove how desirable such mergers are for a great number of corporations.

There are so many different explanations for why two firms wish to combine. Some of these are ideal for shareholders while others are actually not. A profitable company could be combined with a loss-making firm. This would allow the profitable company to employ the losses of the losing target as a tax write off against its own considerable profits. It would simultaneously grow the entire new corporation.

A good reason for these types of combinations is to boost the market share of a given firm. This is especially helpful with bigger corporations which cannot easily grow their market share organically any longer because of their sheer scope and size. When major competitors combine, the new company might be able to overwhelmingly dominate the industry, providing it with a wide range of choices in setting prices and buyer incentives. In these cases, the Sherman Clayton Anti-Trust laws often come into play to stop the merger and prevent the formation of a new monopoly.

There is another popular motivation to combining two existing companies. When they make products which are distinctively different yet still complementary, it presents an opportunity for cost savings. It could be that the acquiring firm wants to obtain the assets of a target firm which is a part of its product supply chain. As an example, there could be significant manufacturers who wish to obtain control over the warehousing chain. This would enable the buyer to save considerable costs on warehousing and to earn profits from the business it buys out at the same time.

A real world tangible example of this type of merger occurred when PayPal merged with eBay a few years ago. eBay became capable of sidestepping the considerable fees it had to pay PayPal previously. The complementary product line was actually a good match also.

It is usually investment bankers who handle the particulars details of and arrangements in a merger. They help with the transfer of ownership of the company itself via stock sales and strategic issuance. This does give incentive to investment banks to encourage mergers between existing clients. It could happen even when a merger would not be in the best interests of the two companies' underlying shareholders.

Mezzanine Financing

Mezzanine Financing refers to an unusual form of hybrid financing. This is a combination of equity and debt financing which provides lenders with the opportunity to convert their ownership and equity interest in the firm. They would want to do this to protect themselves from default possibilities. They would be third in line after both venture capitalists and other types of seniors lenders were paid back.

Mezzanine Financing should always be completed after performing appropriate due diligence by the lender. The borrower does not put up much or any collateral which is why it becomes treated as if it were equity on the balance sheet of the company.

In order to bring in interested parties on to Mezzanine Financing, the firm will have to showcase a solid track record within their industry. They will have to boast an established product and developed reputation, as well as a practical business expansion plan, and a corporate history of profitability. The business plan will need to show opportunities via an IPO initial public offering, acquisitions, or expansions.

Mezzanine Financing commonly attracts an interest rate of from 12 percent to 20 percent. This is because it represents a high return but also high risk form of debt. It usually takes the place of some of the capital which the equity investors would otherwise need to put up for a company to continue to operate effectively or to expand aggressively.

It always helps to consider a real world example in order to better understand a challenging concept like this one. If a private equity firm wants to buy a $200 million business, the senior lenders might consent to delivering $150 million in financing. While the private equity firm pours in $25 million of its own money, they might look for another $25 million in Mezzanine Financing as part of the effective buyout of the company which is the target. Through utilizing the concept of Mezzanine Financing, the buying firm is able to leverage its capital and increase its total return on the deal.

Such Mezzanine Financing can lead to lenders obtaining some equity share and stake in a company or at least warrants for buying in equity at a later point and time. This can dramatically boost the investor ROR rate of return. The Mezzanine Financiers also obtain interest payments which the borrower must make either annually, quarterly, or monthly according to their contract which they originally executed. As an example, if Britannia Capital Corporation is able to earn as much as 20 percent per year on all of its Mezzanine Finance investments, then this ROR proves to be far higher than today's pitiful interest rates which U.S. Treasury instruments pay yearly. These commonly provide around two percent only. The reason of course it that the Treasuries are perceived to be risk free, which of course is not at all true.

One reason that borrowers like Mezzanine Financing debt is because they may deduct the interest from their taxes. Consider the following example. If the standard tax rate for companies is 35 percent, then the pretax interest rate at 20 percent becomes reduced to 13 percent after taxes are factored.

The other reason is that this type of financing proves to be far more management friendly than competing debt structures since borrowers are allowed to figure up their interest into the loan balance. When borrowers are unable to pay their scheduled interest payment, they can defer part or even all of the interest. This type of choice is usually not available for other kinds of debts. Besides this, companies which are rapidly expanding in value are able to restructure the original mezzanine type of financing into another form of senior loan at a significantly lower interest rate. This will save them hugely on their costs for interest over the longer-term.

There is a downside to mezzanine financing though. The owners of the firm in question will sacrifice some control as well as upside potential since they are losing equity in the transaction. The owners will also be forced into paying a higher rate of interest, which becomes progressively more expensive as the financing remains in force for a longer period of time.

National Association of Securities Dealers (NASDAQ)

The NASDAQ is the acronym for the National Association of Securities Dealers Automated Quotation Systems, though the organization has dropped the Automated Quotation Systems part of the name as obsolete. This NASDAQ is the country's second largest stock exchange. It represents the principal rival to the NYSE, or New York Stock Exchange, which is the largest stock exchange in the country and only one larger than it.

The NASDAQ is also the largest equity securities trading market in the U.S. that is based on an electronic screen. When market capitalization, or the value of its stock per share multiplied by the number of outstanding shares, is considered, it is the fourth largest trading exchange in the world. The NASDAQ actually records a higher trading volume than does any competing electronic stock exchange on earth with its actively traded 2919 ticker symbols.

NASDAQ became established in 1971 by the NASD, or National Association of Securities Dealers. The system originally represented the successor to the OTC, or Over the Counter traded market. It later developed into an actual stock exchange of sorts. By 2000 and 2001, the NASD sold off the NASDAQ into the NASDAQ OMX Group, who presently own and operate it. Its stock is listed under the symbol of NDAQ since July 2 of 2002. The FINRA, or Financial Industry Regulatory Authority, oversees and regulates the NASDAQ stock market exchange.

The NASDAQ made major contributions to the world of electronic stock exchange trading as the first one of its kind on earth. When it began, it started out as a computer bulletin board system that did not literally put buyers and sellers in touch. Among its great achievements, the NASDAQ proved to be responsible for decreasing the spread, or the bid and the asking prices' difference for stocks. Many dealers disliked the NASDAQ in the early days, as they made enormous profits on these higher spreads.

In subsequent years, the NASDAQ evolved into a typical stock exchange through adding volume reporting and trade reporting to its new automated trading systems. This exchange became the first such stock market in America to advertise to the public. They would highlight companies that traded on the NASDAQ, many of which were technology companies. Their commercials closed out with the motto the stock exchange for the nineties and beyond, that they eventually changed to NASDAQ, the stock market for the next one hundred years.

The NASDAQ is set to become a trans Atlantic stock exchange titan with its purchase of the Norway based OMX stock exchange. This will only enhance its European holdings that presently include eight other stock exchanges throughout Europe. Besides its NASDAQ stock exchange in New York City, the group possesses a one third stake in the Dubai Stock Exchange in the United Arab Emirates. With its double listing arrangement in place with the OMX exchange, the NASDAQ OMX is set to become the major competitor for NYSE Euronext in bringing in new listings.

Net Operating Profit After Tax (NOPAT)

Net operating profit after tax is also called by its acronym of NOPAT. This refers to the potential earnings (in cash) of a corporation working under the pretense that it has no debt. This NOPAT metric is often utilized in so-called EVA economic valued added calculations. The formula for determining NOPAT is as follows: the operating income times the result of one minus the tax rate. For companies which are debt leveraged, this NOPAT proves to be a more precise and exact way of examining their operating efficiencies. As such it does not factor in the tax advantages which a number of corporations enjoy from their debt load.

Analysts and accountants consider a number of varying performance metrics when they are evaluating a corporation in which to invest. The two most frequent performance measures turn out to be sales (or revenue) and net income growth. With the revenue/sales figures, this delivers a top line performance metric. It does not say anything about the company's operating efficiency value though. Similarly the net income does include the operating expenses of a firm, yet it also factors in the net tax benefits and savings from the company's particular debt leverage.

This is where the Net operating profit after tax comes in as a useful hybrid form of alternative calculation. It permits the analysts to compare and contrast a company's performance against past metrics and other companies by removing the effects of debt leverage from the equation. This allows analysts to truly fairly measure one company against another, regardless of the two firms' net debt positions.

It always helps to consider a real world, concrete example with these complex terms. If a company's EBIT Earnings Before Interest and Taxes was $12,000 and their tax rate was 25 percent, then the calculation for NOPAT would translate to $12,000 times the result of one minus .25,(or .75). This equals $9,000 as a NOPAT. It is an after tax cash flow estimate that does not include the tax benefits of debt. For those companies without debt, Net operating profit after tax equals the same amount as does the net income after tax.

It is worth noting that analysts prefer to compare and contrast firms within the same industry when utilizing the NOPAT metric. This is because every industry has its own normal range of operating costs. Some industries' typical expenses turn out to be dramatically lower or higher than others' do.

For example, cable utilities would have extremely high operating costs associated with initially putting in, continuously upgrading, and maintaining their technology and physical hard-wired distribution networks. Soft drink businesses like Dr. Pepper/Snapple Group (DPS) have relatively low costs since they generally license out their products to other companies which produce and distribute them on their behalf.

Net operating profit after tax has other uses besides the helpful view of a company without its debt leverage being considered. Those analysts who follow and predict mergers and acquisitions utilize this NOPAT value all the time. It helps them to figure up the FCFF free cash flow to firm. This is equal to the NOPAT less any changes to working capital. It also equates to the net operating profit of the firm after taxes less the firm's capital.

These two metrics NOPAT and FCFF are commonly utilized by those types of analysts who hunt down targets for acquisition. The reason for this is that the financing of the acquiring firm will then substitute in for the present financing arrangement (their corporate debt).

Net Present Value (NPV)

Net Present Value refers to a principal profitability measure that companies utilize in their corporate budget planning process. It helps them to analyze the possible ROI return on investment for a particular proposed or working project. Thanks to the involvement of time value and its depreciating effect on dollars, the NPV is forced to consider a discount rate and its compounding effect throughout the term of the entire project.

The actual Net Present Value in an investment or business project considers the point where revenue (or cash inflow) is equal to or greater than the total investment capital that funds the project or asset in the first place. This is particularly useful for businesses when they are comparing and contrasting a number of different projects or potential projects. It allows them to draw a valuable comparison of their comparative profitability levels to make sure that they only spend their limited resources, time, and management skills on the most valuable ventures. The higher the NPV proves to be, the more profitable it is as an investment, property, or project in the end.

Another way of thinking about the Net Present Value is as a measurement of how well an investment is meeting a targeted yield considering the upfront investment that the firm made. Using this NPV, companies can also determine precisely what adjustment they need in the initial investment in order to reach the hoped for yield. This assumes that all else remains constant.

Net Present Value can also be utilized to effectively visualize and quantify investments in real estate and other asset purchases in a simple formulaic expression. This is that the NPV is equal to the Current value minus the cost. In this iteration of the NPV, the current value of all anticipated future cash flow is discounted to today utilizing the relevant discount rate minus the cost of acquiring said cash flow. This makes NPV essentially the value of the project less the cost. When analysts or corporate accountants examine the NPV in this light, it becomes easy to understand how the value explains if the item being purchased (or project being funded) is more or less valuable than the cost of it in the first place.

Only three total categories of NPV ultimate values are possible for any property purchase or project funding. NPV could be a positive Net Present Value. This means that the buyers will pay less than the true value of the asset. The NPV might also be a Zero NPV. This simply means that the buyer or project funder is paying precisely the value of the asset or project worth. With a negative NPV in the final categorization, the buyer will be paying too much for the asset technically. This will be more than the asset is actually worth. There are cases where companies or buyers might be willing to pursue a project or acquire an asset with a negative NPV when other factors come into play.

For example, they might be interested in purchasing a property for a new corporate headquarters whose NPV is negative. The reasoning behind such a decision could be the unquantifiable and intangible value of the location of the property either for visibility purposes or because it is next to the present company headquarter premises.

It is always helpful to look at a concrete example to de-mystify difficult concepts like Net Present Value. Consider a corporation that wishes to fully analyze the anticipated profits in a project. This given project might need an upfront $10,000 investment to get it off the ground. In three years time, the project is forecast to create revenues amounting to $2,000, $8,000, and $12,000. This means that the project is expected to provide $22,000 on the initial $10,000 outlay.

It would appear that the return will amount to 120 percent for a gain greater than the initial investment. There is a reason why this is not the case though. The discount rate for the time value of money has to be factored in, and this means a percentage of several points per year at least. The figure of 4.5 percent is often utilized on a three year project like this. This takes into consideration the fact that dollars earned three years from now will not be so valuable as today's earned dollars. This is why the corporate accountants will use business calculators in order to plug in the discount time value rates to figure the true NPV. Discounting by the 4.5 percent means that the project actually will return somewhere near $21,000 in terms of today's dollar value.

Net Profit

Net Profit refers to the remaining sales dollars which are left over after a firm pays for all of its operating costs, interest on debt, preferred stock dividends, and taxes. Common stock dividends are not included in the amounts deducted from the firm's aggregate sales revenue. Sometimes analysts call this type of profit the net income, the bottom line, and/or the net earnings.

A simplistic (but useful) way of thinking about this form of profit is that it is all of the money which remains after all of the expenses of the going concern are paid in full. Calculating the net income is done when aggregate expenses are subtracted from total revenue. Because these net earnings traditionally occur on the final line in an income statement, companies often refer to it as their "bottom line."

It remains true that this Net Profit is still among the most closely watched business indicators in the world of finance. Because of this, it has a substantial part in the computations of financial statement analysis and ratio analysis. Stake holders in the corporations also scrutinize this bottom line carefully since it ultimately proves to be the way they become compensated as shareholders in the firm. When corporations are unable to realize enough profits to pay their shareholders, stock prices plunge. On the other hand, when corporations are growing and in solid financial health, the more available profits become reflected in greater stock prices.

A common mistake that many individuals make is in their understanding of what net profits actually represent. Net profit is never the metric for the total cash earnings a firm realized in a certain period. The reason for this confusing fact is that income statements also showcase a range of expenses that are not cash-based. Some of these are amortization and depreciation. In order to understand the true amount of cash which corporations actually generate, investors and analysts must carefully review the cash flow statement.

In fact any changes to net profit will be constantly and thoroughly reviewed, examined, and discussed. When firms' net profits are negative or even lower than anticipated, there are a host of issues that could be causing it. It might be that the customers' experience is negative. Sales could be decreasing for one or more reasons. Expenses at the company could be out of control or simply poorly managed and monitored. New management teams may not be performing at the anticipated or promised levels.

In the end, the Net Profit will range wildly from one firm to the next and according to which industry they represent. One industry's profits will likely be substantially different from another industry's. It is not a useful comparison to make between one corporation and another since these profits are quantified in dollars (Euros, pounds, Swiss francs, or yen). It is also a fact that no two corporations will be exactly the same size by either revenues or assets.

This is why many analysts prefer to make comparisons between corporations and industries by utilizing what they call profit margin. This is the net profit of a company as a percentage amount of its total sales. Sometimes analysts and investors will also look at the P/E Price to Earnings Ratio alternatively. This widely cherished ratio reveals to considering investors what the price is (in the form of stock price) for every dollar of net profit the corporation actually generates.

Analysts still like the metric of net profit despite these limitations. A survey conducted querying around 200 marketing managers who were senior level revealed that an incredible 91 percent agreed that they believe this measurement to be very useful.

Operating Cash Flow (OCF)

Operating Cash Flow is also known by its abbreviated acronym OCF. It refers to a metric for the quantity of cash which a corporation or company's typical daily business operations produce. As such, it provides a good insight into a firm's ability to generate enough cash flow in order to either grow or at the very least maintain its existing operations. It might also prove that a going concern requires outside financing in order to fund its expansion plans.

Publically traded firms must calculate their Operating Cash Flows through employing an indirect method of calculation. This GAAP Generally Accepted Accounting Principles mandate means that they have to adjust their net income into a cash basis. They do this by making alterations to their accounts that are not cash. This includes accounts receivable, depreciation categories, and inventory changes.

In fact the Operating Cash Flow is a true representation of the cash portion of the firm's net income. This will also take into account other non-cash items thanks to the requirements which the GAAP sets out for net incomes to be done as accrual-based reporting. This means that amortization, compensation which is based upon stock shares, and incurred but as of yet not paid for expenses would be included in the calculations.

Besides this the actual net income has to be adjusted to reflect changes to working capital kinds of accounts in the balance sheet of the corporation. Especially important is the fact that any accounts receivable increases actually equate to booked revenues for which no collections have been completed. Because of this, these increases have to be taken off of the net income figure. This is partially offset at least by any reported accounts payable increases that are due but as of yet not paid, since this remains in the net income number.

Analysts have opined that such Operating Cash Flow represents the most accurate and basic form of outflows and inflows of cash as a company engages in its normal operations of the daily business. Where the health of a firm is concerned, this represents among the most crucial of metrics. Yet it most appropriately and usefully works for those corporations that are not overly complex.

The Operating Cash Flows focus on the both outflows and inflows which a corporation's principal business activities involve. This includes buying and selling inventory, paying employee salaries, and delivering services. It is important to remember that all financing and investing activities will not be included in the Operating Cash Flow. These become reportable separately. A part of these excluded activities would be purchasing equipment and factories, borrowing money, and engaging in share holder dividend payouts. Finding this cash flow number is easy by looking at the corporation's cash flows statement. This statement will break out the numbers into several categories including cash flows from operations, from financing, and from investing.

Operating Cash Flow is a very important number on a company balance sheet. Many financial analysts and investors would rather consider such cash flow measures since they reduce the impacts of confusing and opaque accounting tricks. It also delivers a better, sharper big picture for the business operations' health and reality.

Consider the following examples. When a firm concludes a big sale, this delivers a major increase to its revenues. This is irrelevant though if the firm can not collect on the money owed. It does not represent a real gain for the corporation. At the same time, firms could be producing elevated operating cash flow numbers. Despite this, they might have an abysmally low net income number if they employ an accelerated depreciation calculation or possess many fixed assets.

PEG Ratio

The PEG Ratio refers to the stock PE price to earnings ratio divided up by the earnings growth rate over a certain fixed time frame. This ratio itself is popularly utilized to ascertain the real value of a stock taking into account the firm's earnings growth. Many analysts consider it to be a better big picture view of the company and its progress than simply using the standard PE ratio.

The misleading fact is that a lower PE ratio tends to make any stock seem like a screaming buy. When one considers the growth rate of the company along with this in the form of the PEG Ratio, it may reveal that a stock is even more undervalued considering the performance of its corporate earnings. It is also true that the amount of a PEG ratio valuation and how it indicates an underpriced or overpriced stock ranges by the type of the firm and the industry in which it is. A good set of guidelines is that any PEG ratio under the number one is beneficial.

Besides this, analysts know that any PEG ratio's accuracy will ultimately depend on the quality of the information which is initially inputted. For example, if one deploys historical growth rates, this could deliver an unreliable PEG ratio, especially if the growth rates in the future are anticipated to be lower than the company growth rates have proven to be historically. This is why accountants and company analysts will often differentiate between the various primary methods of calculating the PEG Ratio according to whether they are relying on historical growth or anticipated future growth. To this effect, they will use the terms Trailing PEG or forward PEG to distinguish between the main two methods.

Figuring up the actual PEG Ratio is not difficult. Analysts and investors are able to do this by first computing the PE ratio of the firm under consideration. This PE ratio can be calculated out by taking the stock price of the firm and dividing it by the EPS earnings per share. After the PE has been compiled, it is easy to configure the PEG formula. One simply takes the PE Ratio and divides it out by the rate of earnings growth, whether he is using the trailing PEG or forward looking PEG.

This is a difficult enough concept that it makes good sense to consider a real world example to better understand the ideas involved. If Vodafone has a share price of $46 per share while its earnings per share for the year are $2.09, then last year's earnings per share might have been $1.74. At the same time, Telefonica Espana has a share price of $80 with earnings per share for this year of $2.67 and an EPS from last year of $1.78. Utilizing this data, the information on each of the two companies can be calculated. The Vodafone PE ratio is 22 while the Telefonica PE ratio is 30. Yet despite this fact, the growth rate of Vodafone is 20 percent to Telefonica's 50 percent. It means that Vodafone's resulting PEG would then be 1.1 while Telefonica would have a significantly superior .6 PEG.

Now the fact is that numerous investors would look at Vodafone superficially and say that it seems to be more appealing because it has the lower PE of the two cell phone operating firms in question. After further investigation though, Telefonica has the higher growth rate for its PE than does Vodafone.

This means that Telefonica stock prices trades at an effective discount to its company growth rate. In the end, those investors buying Telefonica corporate stock are coming out of pocket less money per unit of earnings growth in the company. All else being equal, it makes the Telefonica stock a better valued buy than the Vodafone one in this particular example.

Permanent Financing

Permanent Financing refers to a longer term loan or debt instrument. It can also be thought of as longer term equity financing or debt. Most of the time, such long term financing becomes utilized to buy or develop the kinds of long lasting fixed assets like machinery or factories. The payoffs and contributions from such longer term assets happen over grater lengths of time. This is why long term financing makes sense in order to lessen the risks that the principle will not be paid down or off, as could be the situation with debt financing.

With longer term debt financing, money will be borrowed from a third party source so that a business can finance a particular project and the associated assets or purchases. On the other hand, longer term equity financing centers on putting up company assets in exchange for obtaining funding for particular projects and their relevant asset purchases. There are many cases where a partial ownership stake in a corporation will be offered so that the firm is able to come up with the necessary capital for the projects. Both opposing options come with their own pros and cons. This is why the owners of the company or the corporate directors will be the ones who have to decide for themselves which choice works best for their particular enterprise and scenario.

Such Permanent Financing should never be confused with shorter term financing. There are several critical characteristics that differentiate the two types. Short term financing requires that the debt be paid back in under 12 months. The opposite idea of this is the long term debt option. Such debt will offer more than 12 months and often times many years or even decades to repay it. There are many types of longer term debt. Among the most popular of these are bonds, mortgages, and loans.

Another difference between short term and long term debt lies in the repayment schedule. Short term debt is often repaid in a single lump sum repayment. With the Permanent Financing or longer term debt, these payments can be either made annually, monthly, or in a few periodic lump sum repayments.

The reasons for such debt issues is another major difference between the two types. Short term debt has a purpose of financing daily operations. An example of this might be for those firms that operate in a seasonal industry and capacity. Christmas shops are one such example. They could need short term resources in order to cover their materials, payroll, and leasing costs up to the point that their Christmas products start selling in earnest. The revenue is then utilized to pay down short term debt.

On the other hand, longer term debt is specifically utilized for buying assets that require often a few or even many years in order to pay for their cost and upkeep. A Christmas shop might want to avail itself of this type of debt facility in order to pay for constructing a bigger Christmas ornament and goods production factory. They would be able to repay the longer term loan little by little over the ensuing years. It would allow them to take advantage of the rising revenue stream and resulting profits created by the higher production output of the long term new factory facility.

It is not only businesses that can take advantage of Permanent Financing. The sovereign governments of the world similarly use longer term financing routinely to pay for their annual budget deficits. In the case of the United States, these instruments take the form of longer dated and maturing Treasuries. Good examples of these longer term debt government obligations are both 10 year and 30 year Treasury Bonds.

Prime Rate

The Prime Rate is the most typically utilized shorter term interest rate for the United State banking system. All kinds of lending institutions in the United States employ this U.S. benchmark interest rate as a basis or index rate to price their medium term to short term loans and products. This includes credit unions, thrifts, savings and loans, and commercial banks.

This makes the Prime Rate consistent around the country as banks strive to be competitive and profitable in their lending rates which they provide to both consumers and businesses. A universal rate like this simplifies the task for businesses and consumers as they shop around comparable loan products that competing banks offer. Every state in the country does not maintain its own benchmark rate. This makes a California Prime or New York Prime identical to the U.S. Prime.

Commercial and other banks charge this benchmark rate to their best customers. These are those clients who have the best credit ratings and loan history with the bank. Most of the time banks' best clients are made up of large companies.

The prime interest rate is also known as the prime lending rate. Banks typically base it on the Federal Reserve's federal funds rate. This is actually the rate that banks loan money to each other for overnight purposes. Retail customers also need to be aware of the prime lending rate. It directly impacts the lending rates that they can access for personal and small business loans as well as for home mortgages.

The federal government and Federal Reserve Bank do not set the prime lending rates. The individual banks set it. They then utilize this base rate or reference rate to set the prices for a great number of loans such as credit card loans and small business loans.

The Federal Reserve Board releases a statistics called "Selected Interest Rates." This is their survey of the prime interest rate as the majority of the twenty-five biggest banks set it. It is this publication which reveals the Prime Rate periodically. This is why the Federal Reserve does not directly set this important benchmark rate. The banks more or less base it on the target level of the federal funds rate that the Federal Open Market Committee sets and changes at their monthly meetings.

Different banks adjust their prime lending rate at the same time. The point where they change it is generally when the Federal Open Market Committee adjusts their own important Fed Funds Rate. Many publications refer to this periodically changing reference rate as the Wall Street Prime Rate.

A great number of consumer loans as well as commercial loans and credit card rates find their basis in the prime lending rate. Among these are car loans, home equity loans, personal and home lines of credit, and various kinds of personal loans.

The rates above the prime lending rate that banks charge their less then prime (or subprime) customers depend on the credit worthiness of the borrower in question. The banks attempt to correctly ascertain the risk of default for the borrower. For the best credit customers who have lower chances of defaulting, banks can afford to assess them a lower interest rate than others. Customers with higher chances of defaulting on their loans pay larger interest rates because of the risk associated with their loans not being repaid.

As of June 15, 2016, the Federal Open Market Committee voted to maintain its target fed funds rate in a range of from .25% to .5%. As a result of this, the U.S. prime lending rate stayed at 3.5%. Once per month the Federal Reserve committee meets to determine if they will change the fed funds rate.

Principal

Principal has several different meanings. It most commonly pertains to the initial amount of money that a person either invests or borrows with a loan. A secondary meaning has to do with a bond and its face value. Sometimes the word pertains to the owners of a company or the main participants in any type of transaction.

Where borrowing is concerned, this term relates to the upfront amount of any loan. It also is utilized to describe original amounts which the individuals still owe on the loan in question. Looking at a clear example always helps to clarify the concept. When people obtain a $100,000 mortgage, this Principal is the same $100,000. As the individuals pay down $60,000 of this amount, the remainder of $40,000 that is left to pay off is similarly referred to as Principal.

It is the original Principal that decides how much interest borrowers will pay. If borrowers take out a loan with an initial amount equaling $20,000 that comes with a yearly interest rate at seven percent, then they would be required to pay $1,400 in annual interest for each year that the loan remains open. As borrowers pay the monthly payments to the loan servicer, the interest charges for the month will first be paid off. What remains goes toward the initial amount which the individuals borrowed. Paying down this original amount borrowed remains the only means of lowering the interest amount that accrues on a monthly basis.

Another form of mortgage that operates differently has the name of zero principal mortgages. Bankers think of these as interest-only loans. They represent a unique form of financing where the routine monthly payments of the borrower only apply to the loan's interest. This means that the initial loan amount never gets paid down unless the borrower makes extra payments. It also translates to no equity building up in the property which backs the mortgage loan.

Because of this, financial advisors will typically not recommend these types of mortgages to home buyers as they are rarely in the true interest of the purchaser. Despite this fairly obvious assessment, there are a few unusual cases when they could work out for certain people. When a home buyer is starting out on a career path that pays very little initially but will later on earn substantially more in the not too distant future, it could be worthwhile to lock in the home price now while it is lower. Once the income increases apace, the borrowers always have the ability to refinance into a more traditional mortgage which would cover payments on the initial amounts borrowed as well.

Another scenario where these loans make sense relates to unusual and fantastic opportunities for a particular real estate investment deal. When huge returns on investment dollars can be anticipated, it is practical to go with these mortgage's far lower payments that are interest-only. Meanwhile the borrower can plow the additional monthly payment money savings into the exceptional investment opportunity.

Principal also finds use describing the first initial outlay on an investment. This does not take into consideration any interest that builds up or earnings on the investment. Savers might deposit $20,000 at a bank in a savings account with interest. After a number of years, the balance will grow to $21,500. The principal remains the original $20,000 the savers gave the bank. The additional $1,500 will be called interest or earnings on top of this initial outlay.

It is interesting to note that inflation will not change the nominal value of a loan or financial instrument's principal. Yet the effects of inflation do very much reduce the real value of the initial amount.

Private Equity

Private Equity refers to an investment capital source that comes from those institutional investors and accredited individual investors who boast high net worth. The goals of these investors are to gain a significant equity ownership in corporations. The partners at these firms raise funds and then manage them to gain higher than average returns for their client shareholders. They commonly pursue this goal via an investment time frame of from four to seven years. Private equity is therefore not for those who require that their investment positions be readily liquid.

Such mega funds are often utilized to buy private companies or to privatize publically listed corporations in order to de-list them from the stock market exchanges in a go private arrangement. Each firm sets its own minimum investment threshold for the fund investors. This ranges depending on the needs of the funds being raised. There are many funds with a minimum $250,000 in smallest investment permitted, while still others look for at least millions of dollars per contributing investor.

The private equity industry has a long and storied history of gaining the best possible talent from the corporate world throughout America. This includes top-delivering CEOs and directors even from Fortune 500 firms as well as the best management consulting and top strategy firms. This is why private equity hiring managers often scout out major corporations, law firms, and accounting companies when they go recruiting for new talent. They require legal experience and accounting skills to provide the many support services that such large enterprises require in order to put together major corporate mergers and acquisitions and to properly advise the management companies on the effective management of their newly acquired portfolios holdings.

There are quite high fees involved with such firms. Typically they receive first a management fee and then a performance fee. This generally amounts to annual management fees at around two percent of all assets under management. The performance fees add up to 20 percent of all gross profits when they sell a company. There can be a great deal of variety in the ways that such firms receive their compensation and incentives to outperform.

It is not hard to understand why private equity has been so successful at recruiting and keeping the very best talent based upon the money they have to offer by way of compensation for performance. Consider that these firms which have a billion dollars' assets under management would likely have around only two dozen professional investment personnel. They receive $20 million in annual fees just for the assets under management. Add on to this the 20 percent performance fees based on all gross profits, and it is not hard to understand how they generate additional tens of millions of dollars in performance fees for the company.

Middle market level managers and associates generally expect to earn six-figure salaries and bonuses. The vice presidents pull down half a million dollars easily. Principals rake in a cool over million dollars per year in both realized and unrealized compensation.

Given the incredible rewards at stake, it should not come as any surprise that there are a range of types of private equity firms operating today. Many choose the route of passive investing to be strictly financiers. They depend on their appointed management to increase the size and profitability of the firm in which they invest so that the owners will realize generous, outsized returns. Other kinds of these firms choose to be more active investors. They deliver operational support to the management to ensure that they can build up a stronger and more profitable firm which they can then resell or spin off.

These private equity firms pride themselves on their expansive list of contacts and relationships with corporate boards. They leverage these CFO and CEO relationships to help them grow the company revenue as well as to recognize synergies and operational combination opportunities. One of the kingpins of private equity remains Goldman Sachs, the legendary investment bank. They facilitate the biggest deals and concentrate their time on forging acquisitions and mergers that have billions of dollars in notional values. For other smaller investment banking companies, the majority of deals run in the range of from $50 million to $500 million, while lower middle-market transactions vary from $10 million to $50 million in total.

Private Equity Firm

A private equity firm is a company that provides capital which is not from public stock exchanges. It is instead made up of private investors and funds. They invest their money directly into private companies or public companies via buyouts. When they take over a public company in this way, the entity becomes delisted from its stock exchange.

The capital or money for a private equity firm comes from a combination of retail and institutional investors. This money can be used for a variety of purposes. Some of these include acquiring other companies, funding startups and new technologies, improving an existing company's balance sheet, or improving working capital.

Private investors who contribute money to these private equity firms must be accredited. This means they can prove by their income and assets that they can afford to tie up significant amounts of money for longer time periods. Many of these investments require substantially longer holding periods for distressed companies to be turned around. Similarly it can take years for start up ventures to reach the status of a liquidity event like an IPO initial public offering or sale to another firm.

The private equity market has grown to be powerful quite rapidly since the decade of the 1970s. Nowadays, more than one private equity firm will often work together to pool funds so that they can buy out enormous publicly traded companies. When these come together to do this it is often referred to as an LBO leveraged buyout.

An LBO provides huge amounts of funds to finance a massive purchase. Once they have completed this transaction, the private equity firms will work to improve the company's balance sheet, financial health, and profits with an eye on ultimately reselling the bought out firm to another company or spinning the company back off using an IPO.

A private equity firm commonly receives two types of income from its investors. These are performance and management fees. Many of these companies assess an annual two percent management fee for all assets they handle. On sales of bought out companies, they commonly get 20 percent of all profits made.

Investment professionals are always interested in obtaining jobs with these private equity firms. The salaries can be enormous. With only a billion in AUM assets under management, such companies will usually employee two dozen or fewer investment professionals. These companies earn millions of dollars in fees between their management and performance fees.

Medium level volumes of from $50 to $500 million in deals will earn employees salaries in excess of $100,000. Vice presidents at such companies bring in around half a million dollars' pay. Principals can easily surpass $1 million in salary. Bonuses can be on top of this when the companies realize good years.

Transparency calls began to ring out in the private equity world starting in 2015. This was because the earnings, bonuses, and incomes of practically all employees at almost all of these companies were enormous. This led a few different states in 2016 to start working on regulations and laws for a greater clarity on the inside dealings of these private equity firms. The American Congress in Washington has been resisting these efforts and trying to limit the amount of information which the SEC Securities and Exchange Commission is able to access.

Private Equity Fund

A Private Equity Fund refers to a fund that is not carried by a public stock exchange and which does not have to be regulated by the SEC Securities Exchange Commission. Private equity itself is made up of the range of investors and funds who choose to invest directly in privately held companies. They might also pursue mergers and acquisitions to cause public companies to be delisted by taking private the companies which were public.

The capital for such private equity comes from retail and institutional investors. Such funding is useful for many types of purposes. It might bolster working capital, make possible research into a new technology, provide for acquisitions of public or other privately held companies, or simply improve a given company's balance sheet.

Such private equity funds derived most of their resources from accredited investors and institutional investors. These deep pocketed entities are able to allocate enormous amounts of money into an investment (that might possibly fail) for longer term time frames. Generally these longer investment holding time frames become necessary for such private equity investments. This is because working with distressed companies or waiting on liquidity events like IPO initial public offerings or selling the private company to a public one needs time.

This private equity fund market has grown rapidly from the 1970s to date. Nowadays, funding pools can be started by private equity firms so that they can take enormous public companies private. A substantial quantity of these private equity operations engage in what analysts call LBO leveraged buyouts. With an LBO, large purchases can be affected in the markets thanks to the pooling of enormous resources. Once the transaction is completed, the private equity firms will do their very best to better the profits, prospects, and all around financial condition of the newly privatized company. Their greatest hope and plan is to resell the company back via an initial public offering or alternatively through selling the company to another larger firm.

It is worth noting that the fee arrangements of these private equity funds are different from one fund to the next. They generally start with a management fee and add a performance-based fee to the costs as well. Some firms will assess an approximately two percent management fee each year based on the value of the assets under management. They usually also get 20 percent of all profits realized when selling any companies.

When investors hand over their money to one of these private equity funds, they are throwing their lot in with an adviser that is actually a private equity firm. These funds are something like a hedge fund or mutual fund in many respects. All three of them are comprised of pooled resources that an advisor combines to utilize for investment purchases for the common good of the fund. There are differences between these types of pooled funds though.

Private equity firms will usually concentrate their efforts on longer term time framed investment possibilities. They will often look for those assets that require significant amounts of time in order to sell investments. This given investment horizon will require many times at least 10 years and sometimes significantly longer than this.

A common strategy of investing with these private equity funds proves to be engaging in minority stake investments in startups or companies which are rapidly expanding in a promising industry. Others focus solely on the previously mentioned leveraged buyouts. In either case, transparency of these funds is an issue that has been growing since 2015. The high incomes for these funds have raised questions about what they are doing with the enormous sums of money they receive.

From 2016, some states began to pursue regulations and bills that provided more clarity on what the inner workings of such private equity firms is really like. The congress has so far resisted these investigations and tried to limit the ability of the SEC Securities and Exchange Commission to access the funds' privately held proprietary information.

Prospectus

In the world of finance and investments, a prospectus proves to be a legal document. This document is utilized by businesses and institutions who must describe in great detail the type of stock or bond securities that they are issuing for potential buyers. Such a prospectus generally offers great information to investors concerning stocks, mutual funds, bonds, and even other types of investments.

The information contained in a prospectus will be reports like the financial statements of the company, a detailed description of their business, biographies of directors and other officers along with their pay packages, lists of properties and assets, and information concerning any lawsuits with which they are involved.

When stocks are first being issued as in an IPO, or initial public offering, such a prospectus is given out to the interested parties of investor prospects by brokerages and underwriters. This prospectus should always be read by an interested investing party in advance of putting capital into their security. This is especially important so that you will know the risks that are inherent in the company's business and their stock or bond issue in advance of becoming involved with their securities.

In the U.S., securities may not be offered to the public until after a prospectus has been first placed on file with the SEC, or Securities and Exchange Commission. This is a component of a registration statement. Once the SEC states that the registration is in effect, the stock or bond issuing company is then allowed to utilize the prospectus to help finalize the shares of stock or the bonds in question. The SEC examines a prospectus to ensure that is maintains the appearance of abiding by the disclosure rules.

Some corporations are allowed to work with a simplified prospectus to issue stock and bond securities. These companies must be up to date with their Form 10-K filings with the SEC for a given amount of time, keep their level of market capitalization over a minimum amount, and engage in some procedures. Some scenarios do not mandate that an offering has to be SEC registered. In these cases, a prospectus is called either an offering circular or offering memorandum.

A good example of this is the offerings of municipal securities. These turn out to be exempted from the majority of federal security laws. Such municipal types of issuers usually make up a disclosure document type that is referred to as the official statement instead. This would not offer the depth and scope of a standard prospectus, but will still contain a great deal of helpful and useful information on the particular offering.

Companies generally do not have the time to put together a prospectus entirely on their own. Since this is the case, they commonly engage the help of an issue manager who is also the underwriter of the new issue. These issue managers are also known as book running managers.

Quantitative Risk Management (QRM)

Quantitative Risk Management represents the discipline which deals with the ability of an organization to quantify and manage its risk. This scientific approach to business is becoming increasingly critical in today's world as organizations need to satisfy stakeholders who demand it.

Government regulators similarly insist on clarity within organizations now, especially regarding the amount of capital financial institutions are holding. The firm executives are hunting for the best allocation of capital. Corporations and their boards are seeking justification to control expenditures. Project managers need to be assured they will make their timelines and meet budgets. All of these individuals and entities are looking for effective QRM nowadays.

These QRM capabilities give decision makers the facilities to both analyze their applicable risk data as well as to forecast the likely positive and negative effects in the future. It provides the organization with enormous advantages. Analyses that are more dependable and finely detailed will deliver information which management requires to make superior decisions that are ultimately better informed. As the Quantitative Risk Management process yields higher quality information and becomes more easily accessible to the relevant organizational members, the decision makers are able to more effectively utilize the techniques of QRM to decrease the amount of guesswork involved in the daily decisions of their business operations.

This allows them to obtain valuable insights into possible risks, so they can estimate their overall exposure to them and discern any weaknesses in their oversight controls. It also permits them to determine how practical new services and products will be and to consider the opportunities for up selling and also cross selling of company goods, information, and services. Finally, organization leaders will be able to evaluate any degrees of variance in their company cash flow so that they can streamline and better their ultimate operations.

Quantitative Risk Management is important as every one of those activities just mentioned contains at least some degree of risk. By quantifying and considering them all using a combination of techniques such as trending, modeling, stress tests, and metric evaluations, company decision makers can create faster and more effective responses. This allows them to benefit from any uncovered opportunities and simultaneously to deal with any possible negative effects before they actually materialize and cause significant damage.

There are numerous examples of the uses of and needs for Quantitative Risk Management in business organizations. Cash flow at risk, or CFaR, represents one of the most significant drivers of business. Company leaders require effective prognoses of their future cash flow in order to firm up important decisions for the business. These include confirming or pushing off investments, reducing expenses, reinvesting capital in the business model, or choosing to reengineer their critical operations. Correctly extrapolating cash flow involves proper understanding of such underlying factors as currency changes, sales, pricing of products and services, vendor viability, and operational costs.

Value at Risk, or VaR, is another critical measurement in an organization that benefits from Quantitative Risk Management. Bigger, international, and more complicated financial institutions such as JP Morgan Chase, Citigroup, HSBC, Standard Chartered Bank, BNP Paribas, and Banco Santander have to constantly evaluate where their risk exposures are in order to appropriately allocate the correct capital amounts to be capable of absorbing losses which they do not anticipate.

Project risk management is another area where this Quantitative Risk Management can save the day. So many projects exceed their allocated budgets, deadlines, and milestone markers simply because there is not a sufficient evaluation of the variables, uncertainty, and risk involved with the project itself. This is where the process of QRM can save enormous amounts of time, frustration, and ultimately resources by delivering on deadlines and budgets.

Reconciliation

Reconciliation refers to an accounting process. Its chief defining characteristic is that is employs two different records in order to make sure that the figures it portrays are both identical and accurate. This critical process ensures that money going out of an account measures accurately against the amount actually spent. In other words, it assures accountants that the two values will be in balance once the recording period concludes.

While no universally accepted standard exists for Reconciliation accounting, the GAAP generally accepted accounting principles prefer account conversion and double entry accounting for the primary best methods of reconciling. Individuals or companies may elect to reconcile their important records on an annual, monthly, or daily basis with either methodology.

It always helps to demystify a complex topic with real world examples. Julian like many consumers opts to reconcile his check book and credit card accounts at the conclusion of each month. He does this by comparing debit card receipts, cancelled checks, and credit card receipts along with the statements from the bank and credit card companies. It allows for Julian to determine if money is being withdrawn fraudulently or illegally. Besides this, it provides him with confidence that no bank errors have been made on any of his accounts at the various financial institutions. Julian finally benefits from a big picture view of his spending habits and patterns each month this way.

As accounts become reconciled, the ending balance should match up exactly with the transactions as noted on the statements for the month and also with the records of Julian or other account holders. Where checking accounts are involved, individuals must also be concerned with outstanding checks or pending deposits and the impact these will create on the real world balance as well as the statement balance.

Companies are also critically concerned with the processes of Reconciliation of their accounts. Corporations have to reconcile all accounts in order to make sure there are no errors on the balance sheets or that no fraud has occurred within the company at large. Larger firms and smaller ones alike will generally deploy one of several good accounting programs to take care of these internal processes. This is because there will be no computational errors when utilizing these programs. They prevent mistakes that can create major consequences for companies which are publically traded.

As an example of the usefulness of such Reconciliation, auditors will commonly do a final review of corporations' financial statements as the Sarbanes-Oxley Act and other federal regulations require. They might come across a significant error in this review. The firm would then be forced to publicly disclose this failure of internal controls. Otherwise it might have to declare it a material weakness or material misstatement. This is all critical since corporations cannot be expected to engage in intelligent decision making processes if they cannot rely on their own internal financial information.

With double entry accounting, the accountants will post each and every financial transaction according to a two-column entry on the balance sheet of the firm. When companies draw on a $50,000 longer-term loan, their accountants will credit the longer term debt category and also notate the payable columns with the $50,000 amount. They will simultaneously debit the cash column by the identical amount. The important rule is that as the amounts are all tallied together, they must reconcile to an even zero final amount.

If businesses acquire an invoice for repainting of their office building, they will then credit the invoice amount under the column for accounts payable while debiting the column for painting and other office expenses by the identical amount. As the firm pays its bill, the accountants will then debit the accounts payable while simultaneously crediting the column for office painting.

Resource Holdings

Resource Holdings, also known as Resource Land Holdings and RLH, is a private equity firm which focuses on purchasing huge pieces of real estate which are rich in natural resources. The company's ultimate goal with these acquisitions is to sell off those parts of the properties that do not generate cash flow so that they can reduce the cost basis of the property to as nearly zero as they can. At the same time, the work to maintain and improve the cash flow of the remaining piece of property to share this out to their investors. They also enter a number of partnership arrangements with original owners so that these parties remain actively involved in the management and success of the operations. The company is headquartered in Colorado Springs, Colorado in the United States.

Resource Holdings arose in 1998 because its founders wished to provide opportunities for and to invest themselves in timber, agricultural, and mining properties and operations throughout the United States. They work with a variety of local operators, brokers, and entrepreneurs in order to invest in this range of land parcels across a wide range of asset classes which are rich in resources. As of time of publication of this article, RLH had created and managed two individually funded entities along with four different private equity funds.

The first Resource Land Fund I they capitalized with $20 million worth of committed equity. It entered its first investment back in December, 2001. Their second Resource Land Fund II they established using $51 million in equity. It purchased its initial investment in July, 2003. Their Resource Land Fund III received a larger $175 million. It obtained its first investment March of 2006. Each of these investment funds received full investment and then was closed in turn. The Resource Land Fund IV closed with $316 million in committed funds back in August of 2010.

The firm seeks out investments in land across a range of asset classes. Their primary focus has always been on regional timber, agriculture, quarry, mining, and other resource rich properties which have typically been ignored or overlooked by the massive institutional investment world. Such regional entrepreneurs that require significant capital intense investment have found that the needed funds are often not available to them as economic cycles create financial and funding challenges for these medium sized operations. In these particular scenarios, Resource Holdings appears on the scene as a life saving potential source of capital. They often invest right along with local entrepreneurs and partners.

As part of their specific portfolio of investments and property holdings, Resource Holdings owns or invests in properties across 20 different states in the U.S. spanning from Florida, to Texas, to California. At time of publication, they had 46 different properties within their various funds and portfolios. Among these were a limestone quarry in Texas, a citrus operation in Florida, timber operations in California, sand quarrying in Alabama, a large coal surface mine in the Midwest, and apple orchards in Washington state.

As an example, Resource Holdings saw that there were positively growing trends within the building stone market. They used this basis to seek out and invest with two long standing operator-owner partners of two different limestone quarries found in the center of Texas. The owners continue operating the limestone quarrying firm with RLH as the capital partner.

In another instance, the investment firm saw an opportunity to become involved in a successful Florida citrus business a few years ago. They arranged a unique sale-leaseback with the owners which guaranteed the investment company both a minimum yearly return and a profit split with the operating partner-owners. Thanks to their sympathizing and working with the various concerns of the owners, they were able to obtain a high quality property that the markets never had an opportunity to seize. The final arrangement which the company struck with the owner operators allowed both of them to sit on one side of the table to share economic objectives and interests.

Retained Earnings

Retained earnings are a component of the earnings categories of corporations. They describe the portion of a company's net earnings that they do not give out to shareholders as dividends. Instead these earnings are kept by the firm so that they can pay down debt or reinvest in their core operations and business model. Balance sheets note earnings which are retained as part of the shareholder's equity column.

There is a formula for figuring out retained earnings. It adds the initial earnings with net income or subtracts net losses from it. Dividends must then be subtracted out from these earnings as they are paid out to stockholders.

Corporations have their reasons to keep a portion of their earnings. In the majority of scenarios, they wish to invest them into segments of the market where the firm is able to build opportunities or growth. This could be by spending money for additional research and development or in purchasing new plants, equipment, or machinery. Companies can also use these earnings to purchase other firms. Such acquisitions allow them to expand their market share or product offerings in this method of non organic growth.

It is possible for such earnings to become negative. This happens when the firm's net loss is larger than the initial retained earnings. Such a case creates a deficit. The general ledger for these earnings becomes adjusted each time an entry is placed for the expense or revenue accounts.

At the conclusion of the company's accounting period, such earnings that are retained become reported. This could be in the quarterly report or the annual report. They will either continue to be accumulated and be positive, or they can shift into negative territory and be recorded as a deficit. These changes in earnings from one accounting period to the next are not directly noted. It is easy to infer them by looking at the totals of ending and beginning retained earnings for the accounting period. Increases or decreases to the accumulated totals happen because of dividend payouts and net losses or net incomes for the period.

Every period, a firm's revenues and expenses must be closed out. This is done into an income summary that shows the total net income or loss. Finally these are closed out into the retained earnings column. Net income directly boosts or decreases these earnings this way.

Dividends are the other major item that decreases the retained earnings number. Such dividends can be paid out as stock or cash. Either type reduces the earnings which are retained. This is because cash dividends come out of the net income ultimately. The greater amount of dividends that a company distributes, the lower amount of earnings it will retain. Dividend accounts are also temporary in nature and are closed out to the earnings which are retained at the end of the accounting period.

Though newly issued shares given out as dividends do not reduce the net income, they must be reconciled on the balance sheet. This is done in the accounts for additional paid in capital on the balance sheet. The earnings which are retained category decreases by the identical amount as this paid in capital column.

Return on Assets (ROA)

Return on Assets is also known by its acronym ROA. It is also sometimes called return on investment. This proves to be an indicator of a company's profitability compared to its aggregate asset base. With ROA, investors and analysts can learn about the big picture of the efficiency of an organization's management compared to the deployment of their company assets which produces earnings.

This is figured up relatively easily. To calculate the ROA, simply take the corporation's annual earnings (or income) and divide these by the firm's total assets. The final answer is the percentage amount of ROA. Other investors will do a slight variation on the formula by adding back in the corporate interest costs to the net income. This allows them to employ operating returns before the net cost of debt.

Thanks to Return on Assets, analysts and investors can learn the amount of earnings that the invested capital or assets produced. Such a figure ranges dramatically from one publically traded company to the next. Every industry's ROA varies substantially. For this reason, analysts prefer to compare and contrast the ROA primarily against the company's own prior figures or alternatively versus another company which is both similar and in the same industry.

Company assets are made up of equity and debt together. The two kinds of financing will jointly fund most corporations' various operations and projects. Because of this Return on Assets number, investors are able to discern the efficiency with which the firm converts its investable money into actual net income. Higher ROA numbers are always considered to be superior. They mean that the corporations can bring in larger revenues and earnings on a smaller amount of investment.

Consider a real world example for clarification. If Imperial Legends Strategy Games produces a net income of $2 million on aggregate underlying assets of $6 million, then it has a Return on Assets of 33.3 percent. Another company Joy Beverages may enjoy the same earnings but against a full asset base of $12 million. Joy Beverages would have an ROA of only 16.7 percent in this scenario. This means that ILSG does twice the job of converting its all around investments into profits as does Joy Beverages. This matters because it speaks volumes of the quality of management. There are not too many managers who are able to turn over significant profits utilizing small investments.

The Return on Assets provides observers with a snapshot and analysis of a business that is distinctive from the usual return on equity formula. Consider that certain industries need to pay more careful attention to the ROA figure than other ones do. In banking, some firms managed to avoid the various banking crises of the last few decades. The ones that sidestepped the problems better than others had something in common. It was that they were more conservative based on the ROA they deployed. The more successful banks did not allow their return on assets numbers to become too unnaturally high. They did this by contemplating the underlying fine details in the loan book. Too many loans that yielded too high a return indicated that management was taking excessive risks. Yet in the business of software development firms, these enterprises are not leveraged, so this ROA comparison is less important.

An important difference separates asset turnover from Return on Assets. Asset turnover specifies that companies have sales which amount to a certain amount per asset dollar on the corporate balance sheet. Conversely, the ROA explains to investors the amount of post tax profit that a firm creates for every $1 of assets it has. This is to say that the ROA compares all of the company earnings relating to the entire resource base the company claims, including both long-term debt and the capital from shareholders. This makes the relevant ROA a strict test of shareholder returns. When companies possess no debt, then their two figures of ROA and ROE Return On Equity will be identical.

Return on Equity (ROE)

Return on equity proves to be a useful measurement for investors considering a given company. This is because it takes into account three important elements of a company's management. This includes profitability, financial leverage, and asset management. Looking at the effectiveness of the management team in handling the three factors gives you as an investor a good picture of the kind of return on equity that you can expect from an investment in such a company.

Return on equity is very easy to calculate. You can figure it up by collecting two pieces of information. You will need the company earnings for a year and the value of the average share holder equity for the same year. Getting the earnings' figure is as simple as looking up the firm's Consolidated Statement of Earnings that they filed with the Securities and Exchange Commission. Alternatively, you might look up the earnings of each of the last four quarters and add them up.

Determining share holder equity is easiest by looking at the company's balance sheet. Share holder equity, which proves to be the difference of total liabilities and total assets, will be listed for you there. Share holder equity is a useful accounting construct that reveals the business assets that they have created. This share holder equity is most commonly listed under book value, or the quantity of the share holders' equities for each share. This is also an accounting book value of a corporation that is more than simply its market value.

To come up with the return on equity, you simply divide the full year's earnings by the average equity for that year. This gives you the return on equity. Companies that produce significant amounts of share holder equity turn out to be solid investments, since initial investors are paid off using the money that the business operations generate. Companies that create substantial returns as compared to the share holder equity reward their stake holders generously by building up significant amounts of assets for each dollar that is invested into the firm. Such enterprises commonly prove to be able to fund their own operations internally, which means that they do not have to issue more diluting shares of stock or take on extra debt to continue operating.

The return on equity can also be utilized to determine if a corporation is a cash generating machine or a cash consuming entity. The return on equity will simply show you this when you compare their actual earnings to the share holder equity. You can learn at almost a glance how much money the company's present assets are producing. As an example, with a twenty percent return on equity, every original dollar put into the company is creating twenty cents of real assets. This is also useful in comparing subsequent cash investments in the company, since the return on equity percentage will demonstrate to you if these extra invested dollars match up to the earlier investments for effectiveness and efficiency.

Return on Investment (ROI)

ROI is the acronym for return on investment. This return on investment is among the most often utilized methods of determining the financial results that will arise from business decisions, investments, and actions. ROI analysis is used to compare and contrast both the timing and amount of investment gains directly with the timing and amount of investment costs. Higher returns on investment signify that the results from investments are positive when you compare them against the costs of such investments.

Over the past couple of decades, this return on investment number has evolved into one of the main measurements in the decision making process of what types of assets and equipment to buy. This includes everything from factory equipment, to service vehicles, to computers. ROI is similarly utilized to determine which budget items, programs, and projects should be both approved and allocated funds. These cover every type of activity from recruiting, to training, to marketing. Finally, return on investment is often employed in choosing which financial investments are performing up to expectations, as with venture capital investments and stock investment portfolios.

Return on investment analysis is actually used for ranking investment returns against their costs. This is done by setting up a percentage or ratio number. With the vast majority of return on investment calculation methods, ROI's that are higher than zero signify that the returns on the investment are higher than the associated expenses with it. As a greater number of investments and business decisions compete for funding anymore, hard choices are increasingly made using the comparison of higher returns on investment. Many companies believe that this yields the better business decision in the end.

There is a downside to relying too heavily on the return on investment as the only consideration for making such business and investment decisions. Return on investment does not tell you anything regarding the anticipated costs and returns and if they will actually work out as forecast. Used alone, return on investment also does not explain the potential elements of risk for a given investment. All that it does is demonstrate how the investment or project returns will compare against the costs, assuming that the investment or project delivers the results that are anticipated or expected. This limitation is not unique to return on investment, but similarly plagues other financial measurements. Because this is the case, intelligent investment and business analysis also relies on the likely results of other return on investment eventualities. Other measurements should also be used along side the return on investment to help measure the risks that accompany the project or investment.

Wise decision makers will demand more from return on investment figures than simply a number. They will require effective suggestions from the person making the return on investment analysis. Among these inputs that they will desire are the means of increasing an ROI's gains, or alternatively the means for improving the ROI through decreasing costs.

Revenue

Revenue refers to the amount of money which firms generate in receivables within a certain time frame. It includes deductions for merchandise which is returned as well as any applicable discounts. This is also known as the gross income or sometimes the "top line" amount. Net income can be figured out by subtracting the costs from the revenue.

Analysts and accountants determine the amount of revenue simply by taking the price for which services and goods sell and multiplying this by the quantity of units or the actual amount which the firm sells. Sometimes revenue is referred to as "REVs."

There are a number of other definitions and synonyms for revenues. Some call it sales in layman's terms. Whatever name businesses and individuals refer to it by, revenue proves to be the total amount of cash which a company garners through its aggregate business activities. The price to sales ratio is one measurement in business that relies on revenues for the denominator. This contrasts with the competing measurement of price to earnings ratio, which utilizes the profits instead for its denominator.

Revenue can be figured up by several different means. It is really up to the method of accounting which companies and corporations choose to employ. With accrual accounting, sales which the firm makes using credit also count among the revenues so long as the customers have taken delivery of the services or goods. This is why investors and analysts must review the company's cash flow statement in order to evaluate how effectively a firm actually collects on the money which its customers owe it.

The other primary form of determining a company's revenues is through cash accounting. This form of accounting utilizes only sales for the revenues' quotient once the money a customer owes has been collected by the firm in question. When a customer gives the money to a corporation or company, the firm recognizes it as a receipt instead of the general category of revenues. Companies can actually have receipts that do not include revenues. This is possible if a customer were to pay for a service in advance of receiving it or for purchased goods which they have not yet received.

Revenue can also be called "top line" since income statements display them first on the report. Analysts then take revenues and deduct the expenses so that they can come up with the "bottom line," which is also called simply profit or alternatively net income.

Many times investors evaluate both a firm's net income and revenues independently of one another so that they can ascertain how strong a business' health really turns out to be. The reason for this is that net income can increase while revenues remain flat. Cost cutting can actually cause this phenomenon. This scenario is not a positive sign for the longer term growth potential for a firm.

Analysts and investors often further subdivide the revenues from a given company or corporation according to the groups which generate the money. Company accountants can also divide up the receipts of the firm into several categories of operating revenues, the core business of the firm's sales, and non-operating revenues that come from secondary sources. Such non-operating variants are typically not recurring or can not be forecast successfully. This is why these are sometimes known as one-time gains or events. Examples of this could be money gained through lawsuits, investment windfalls, or receipts from selling an asset.

Where a government is concerned, revenue refers to the receipts they obtain as a result of fees, taxation, fines, securities sales, transfers, intergovernmental grants, resource rights and mineral rights, or any sales of government assets or state-owned and -run companies which they might make.

In the world of not for profit organizations, such revenues are commonly referred to by the phrase of "gross receipts." Among the components that make up these receipts are donations from companies, foundations, and individuals; investment returns; grants out of governmental agencies and entities; membership dues and fees; and fundraising endeavors.

Revolving Credit

Revolving Credit refers to lines of credit that customers draw on and then make payments on to their creditors. In order to have such a facility, the debtor must pay a commitment fee. This enables them to utilize the funds on an as-needed basis. Such a facility is typically deployed for operating expenses. It would therefore vary every month according to the present day cash flow requirements of the customer. Both individuals and corporations alike are able to take out these revolving lines of credit.

An agreement would be established upfront between the bank and the customer. Such a contract would guarantee the maximum potential amount that the bank will loan out to the client. Besides the initial commitment fee, there will naturally be interest costs for the corporate borrowers. These are called carry forward charges when the accounts are set up for consumers.

Banks and other financial institutions will contemplate a number of factors concerning the borrower and its ability to repay such a line before these revolving credit lines become issued. Where individuals are concerned, this means that his or her current income, credit score, and stability of employment will all be evaluated. Where organizations and corporations are concerned, the bank will typically review the income statement, balance sheet, and cash flow statement before making its final decision on approval and maximum line amount.

For those business entities and individuals who suffer from commonplace fluctuations in non-anticipated expenses and cash balance fluctuations, this revolving credit can be crucial and even lifesaving. They provide flexibility, versatility, and convenience, though this comes at a cost. The price for this is a more expensive interest rate which banks and lending institutions levy for revolving credit than they do on more traditional installment types of loans. Many times, this revolving credit facility will come alongside interest rates which are variable and can be quickly adjusted as appropriate.

The credit limit proves to be the highest dollar amount which the financial institutions will allow the borrower to draw. While there are many different examples of revolving credit facilities in the market place today, the most frequently cited ones are the personal lines of credit and the home equity lines of credit. These are also called HELOCs.

It is important to understand the differences between revolving credit and installment loans. Installment loans typically involve a pre-determined and –set number of payments which will be made on a monthly or quarterly basis over a fixed amount of time. By contrast, revolving funds only involve interest payments along with fees which are applicable per the contract established between the actual bank and the client.

When an individual or corporation receives this revolving credit line, it means that a customer has been pre-approved for receiving a loan. It is more convenient to use than taking out loans again and again, as one does not need to have his credit reevaluated or a new loan application taken every time they draw upon the revolving facility funds. This is why revolving facilities were created for smaller loans that are shorter term in nature. With more massive sized loans, the banks will want a better laid out structure that comes complete with installment payments.

There are differences between business credit cards and revolving lines of credit. No physical credit card is necessary with revolving credit lines. Also revolving lines do not require a preset purchase or amount. This credit can be transferred into the company or personal account for whatever reason they wish. This makes the revolving facilities more like cash advances with funds immediately available upfront and without questions asked regarding the purchase. The interest rates on revolving facilities are also commonly substantially less than are those associated with even business forms of credit cards.

Run Rate

The Run Rate refers to a company or corporation's financial performance. It utilizes the present financial information in order to forecast the firm's future time frame performance. This then allows analysts and accountants to extrapolate going forward based upon the present day financial performance. Naturally this rate takes as a granted the belief that the current financial conditions for the economy in general and the firm in particular will continue. It is also possible for the run rate to mean the company's average stakeholder ownership dilution on a yearly basis as a result of grants of stock options which the company has parceled out during the past three years and as featured within their annual report.

The idea of extrapolating such a future performance is based on the assumption that the current performance will indeed continue over the longer term. It always helps to consider a clear cut example to shed more light on difficult concepts like this one. If Nestle has sales of $10 billion in its last quarter, the Chief Executive Officer could reasonably extrapolate based on this data that the corporation is functioning on a $40 billion run rate. As such, the financial information is deployed in order to develop a year-long projection for the firm's likely performance. Analysts would then call this process annualizing.

Run rates are often useful for coming up with good performance estimates for those corporations which have only a short corporate history behind them, as in under a year. Alternatively, they are particularly helpful for assessing the longer term extrapolations of new departments, divisions, or even profit centers in a well-established firm. This is often the case for any company that is enjoying its first quarter in profits in a long time or ever. This run rate can similarly prove to be useful if fundamentals in the operation of a given business were shifted in some meaningful way that will have a major impact on the future performance and results of the business in question.

The problem comes in with the run rate often proving to be an ultimately deceptive measurement. This is particularly the case in seasonal industries. A useful example pertains to retailers considering the profits in the wake of the important winter holiday season. This proves to be the crucial time period where a great number of retailers make their greatest volumes of sales. When such information is utilized to develop a run rate, then the resulting estimates of the future forecast will likely be flawed and over inflated.

Another weakness to the run rate is that it is usually dependent on only the most recent information. This means that it might not fairly compensate for changes in circumstances which can lead to a false bigger picture. With technology producers like Microsoft, Google, Samsung, and Apple, they often bring in far greater sales surrounding the launch of one of their new products. If they employ only the data from the time frame following a substantial product release, this will likely result in falsely skewed data.

Another limitation to run rates is that they do not take into consideration any big one-time only sales. It might be that a factory receives a big contract and is fortunate enough to be paid upfront for the order. Whatever their delivery timetable for the services or goods, this will lead to higher sales figures for a single reporting period because of this unusual one-off purchase.

It is easy to calculate up a run rate if the company has quarterly data. All that must be done is to multiple the numbers by four. When monthly data is being analyzed, the number has to be multiplied out by 12.

S Corporation

S Corporation refers to the Subchapter S Corporation type of company filing which measures up to certain requirements set by the IRS Internal Revenue Service. This status provides a corporation which possesses a hundred or fewer shareholders all of the advantages of incorporation while also keeping the benefits of only being tax treated like a partnership.

One of the many benefits to this type of incorporation is that it is able to pass all of the company income straight through to the shareholders, thus avoiding the problems of double taxation which are a real issue with shareholders of public companies. There are some particular requirements that must be met to enjoy these advantages. The firm must be domiciled as a domestic corporation. It cannot possess over a hundred shareholders, and it may only count a single class of stock.

Such S Corporations can pass all of their credits, deductions, losses, and any income straight through to the various shareholders. They may then report this loss or income directly via their own personal tax returns. It allows them to pay out their taxes at generally considerably lower individual income tax rates. There are some built in gains on which the S Corporation will pay the taxes at the corporate level, but these are few and far between.

These S Corporations have to be domestically headquartered firms whose shareholders are estates, certain kinds of trusts, and individuals. A corporation, partnership, or non-resident alien can never qualify for this category of shareholder. There are also some financial institutions, domestic international sales firms, and insurance outfits that are not allowed to incorporate as an S Corporation.

There are some significant advantages to establishing an S Corporation. It builds up real creditability with employees, possible customers, investors, and suppliers as it proves the owner is seriously committed to the firm. Employees may also be shareholders in the company, which allows them to enjoy company salaries while also receiving any corporate dividends and distributions which are tax-free as compared to the investment in the company. This is certainly beneficial for morale.

Paying out distributions in the form of dividends or salaries allows the owners to lower the self-employment tax liability at the same time as it creates wage and expense deductions for the firm. Since this S Corporation will not pay any federal taxes at company level, such losses can be utilized to offset other forms of income for the tax returns of the shareholders. It is always helpful to save money on the onerous American corporate income taxes, particularly for new firms. It is another benefit to these companies that the various interests within the corporation can be easily transferred without creating tax liability events and consequences. Complicated accounting rules do not create restrictions nor does the company have to adjust the basis of property either.

Yet there are also a few downsides to establishing a company as an S Corporation. The IRS closely examines any and all distribution payments made to shareholders in the forms of either dividends or salaries to make sure that they are really employees working in the firm. If wages become characterized as dividends, then the company will lose its compensation paid deduction. Should dividends be characterized as wages, then the company will pay a greater amount of employment taxes. It is also easy for mistakes to be made in the areas of notification, consent, election, filing requirements, or stock ownership requirements that lead to the S Corporation being untimely terminated. There is considerable money and time investment in such a corporate structuring as well.

The owner will have to begin by filling in and filing articles of incorporation to the Secretary of State, get a registered agent on board for the company, and pay any relevant fees and costs involved. Owners often have to pay yearly reporting fees and franchise taxes along with ongoing types of fees. These may be inexpensive, but they can still be deducted under the cost of doing business category. Even if the investors possess non-voting shares of stock in this form of corporate structuring, they will still get distribution and dividend rights.

Sale And Leaseback

A Sale And Leaseback is also known as a simply leaseback. This arrangement involves an asset seller who first sells the asset or property in question then immediately leases it back exactly as it is from the buyer. These types of deals are fleshed out and contracted immediately following the asset in question's sale. The precise amount in payments and the specific time period to be covered are both set at this point. It amounts to the asset seller personally becoming the lessee while the buyer becomes the actual lessor under such an arrangement.

Many owners of small to medium sized enterprises (SMEs) find that they require a great deal of fresh capital in order to expand their operations. There are a number of different ways in which they can come up with such capital. Two of the more popular and better known ones are surrendering equity in order to obtain funds or taking on debt either as bonds or secured loans.

With equity, it does not have to be repaid to the provider. The cost for this is that a portion or even all of the ownership of the enterprise is surrendered. The tradeoffs for debt are that it has to be repaid one day (or in regular periodic payments). It also appears as debt on the balance sheet of the company, which may impact future opportunities for financing, debt purchases, or obtaining fresh capital via an equity offering.

Hybrid arrangements which are not either equity or debt are these Sale And Leasebacks. Instead they function more as a hybrid form of debt arrangement and product. The firm entering into the deal will not grow its debt load, yet it still manages to achieve the goal of accessing capital by selling assets. Some have referred to this as a company variation on the consumer-entered pawn shop arrangement.

Extrapolating on this example, the company in question goes down to the pawn shop and provides them with a valuable piece of property or asset. In tradeoff for this asset, the company receives an agreed upon amount of cash. The only point where this comparison breaks down concerns repurchasing the asset in question. In a sale and leaseback, no one expects that the company will attempt to repurchase the property or asset, only that they will make periodic payments in order to utilize the asset.

Consider the following example. The fictitious company Johnny Appleseed Orchards requires more funding to pay its increasing numbers of contractors and employees. It is unable to obtain funding from banks thanks to a downturn in the lending market brought on by the Great Recession and Financial Crash of 2007. The company decides it will sell half of its orchard acreage to an investment company which wishes to become involved in realizing an income stream from the sale of produce. The acreage is instantly leased back to the owner-operators of Johnny Appleseed. This benefits them if the cost to lease back the acreage is less than the interest rate and total interest payments on higher interest loans they would otherwise be forced to seek.

The most typical type of a sale and leaseback occurs with builders and those firms that have many expensive and fixed assets. This is useful when they require cash which is tied up in their costly assets to utilize for other capital needs or investments, yet they still require use of the equipment or assets so that they can continue to run their business.

Such sale and leasebacks and their arrangements also give the seller of the asset some beneficial tax deductions. The lessor gains the advantages of a stable payment and guaranteed lease arrangement which continues for a predetermined and contractually pre-set amount of time.

Such sale and leaseback deals do come with a whole different set of regulations for accounting purposes than do debt arrangements. Despite this, they are not called financing in most of the cases. This keeps them as off-balance sheet arrangements. Some analysts will therefore add on capitalized leases such as these to the category of longer term debt. They do this especially as they are attempting to gain the bigger picture view of the firm in question's aggregate debt obligations.

Securities and Exchange Commission (SEC)

The SEC is the acronym for the Securities and Exchange Commission. This Federal government agency actually governs the buying and selling of stock securities and other types of related investments. The SEC also works to safe guard investors against impropriety and fraud. They encourage the development of the market with the end goal of keeping America in the first place as the world's leading economic giant.

The Securities and Exchange Commission came into existence in 1934. The stock market crash in 1929 prompted a tremendous regulatory response where the national government observed that it had to oversee and monitor investments within the U.S. The SEC is headquartered today in Washington D.C. Its staff is comprised of five commissioners who are appointed, as well as the personnel working in eleven different regional offices throughout the country. They work together to create, amend, and enforce the laws that regulate investments in the country.

The SEC has various critical missions. Among the most significant one is their role in ensuring that the markets are transparent. To do this, they significantly regulate securities trading within the U.S. Companies are required to turn in a variety of legal financial documents during the year so that investors may obtain a true picture of the total financial health of the firm in question.

The documents are kept on file in a database that is available to the public. Anyone who is interested is allowed to inspect them by logging on to the SEC's website and working through their system of electronic documentation. The SEC has great powers that it exercises in enforcing the rules. It is able to mandate company audits if it has suspicions of illegal behavior. Those it finds in violation of its rules may be brought by the SEC to court.

In keeping with the SEC's mandate to help safe guard investors, they monitor the trading of stocks and the individuals responsible for selling them. This means that exchanges, their dealers, and all stock brokers are required to work through the Securities and Exchange Commission. They can be subjected to inspection from time to time to be certain that they are properly taking care of their customers. Consumers have the right to report practices that are unfair to the SEC directly. If you are an investor, you ought to avail yourself of the SEC's wide range of documents on the various publicly traded corporations that they keep in their database on their website.

The SEC additionally governs companies that are interested in undergoing Initial Public Offerings in order to become public companies. Such interested firms have to file a significant quantity of documents with them first. To help them accomplish this, the SEC engages a big staff. Their document database includes regulations and directions for filing such documents. Consultation help is available if companies run into difficulties.

The SEC also promotes education. If you are an investor who wants to learn more about safe investing, then simply go to their website. They have workshops and publications on the site to help all investors. This is in addition to all of the companies' documents kept on file there.

Seed Money

Seed Money refers to that capital which someone delivers to a business, initiative, or project at the beginning in order to get it started. This money is intended to be the seed that helps the upcoming project or company to grow and flourish. Offering such early stage funds can prove to be extremely risky. The project could completely fail, which would wipe out the initial seed money. Yet those investors who are in on the opportunity early on can make huge amounts in returns if the company or its project becomes a success.

A variety of sources exist for possible seed capital. There are also a range of financing choices for those new firms which require such Seed Money. This is why the seed raising prospects are often referred to as the "friends and family round" of funding. This means that much of this early startup capital literally does come from personal and close connections. Those family members and friends who personally know and would vouch for the entrepreneur could be better disposed to offering funds on a given project. If and when such a project fails, this can cause strained family relationships on the part of those who relinquished their funds only to lose them later in the project however.

Other traditional sources of Seed Money include some banks, venture capitalists, and sometimes various government agencies which may choose to invest in the entrepreneur once they get to know him or her. The money might be offered as loans or grants. Occasionally this money is offered in exchange for equity stakes in the company, as with equity financing. This provides the financiers with stakes in the new venture in return for their early stage investment. Later as the company develops exit events, the initial round investors may sell their stakes back to the firm or to another financier or investor.

It is in the earliest stages of research and development that seed money proves to be so very critical. There will always be entrepreneurs who deploy their own money for this stage in an effort to develop a viable project and saleable product before their seed money runs thin. With many others, they require outside-sourced funding in order to get them through that initial crucial timeframe for product development and launch.

This becomes all the more critical when a young company develops a project which proves to be time sensitive. It might be a computer software package that offers immediately useful applications and which may quickly run into competitors in the market place. Such seed money may actually increase the speed of the development process so that people still want and are interested in the new product when it effectively reaches market.

Obtaining seed money typically changes the project dynamics though. Entrepreneurs are no longer sole owners of the venture at this point. They will have to provide details and updates on the R&D progress in order to not only receive money, but appease their seed investors. It is no longer technically an exclusive or private project anymore at this point.

It gets difficult for some controlling entrepreneurs to let their projects go as they involve more and more investors. This can hurt the product development when the owners cannot make way for the new partial owners over the longer term. This is why it is so very important for the new investors to take on an active part in overseeing the project to ensure that the precious seed capital is being well- and carefully spent to further the project towards a timely product launch.

Share Consolidation

Share Consolidation refers to a reverse split. In this corporate operation, a number of shares of stock become merged together into only one single share. These share consolidations can take place either in the forms of reverse stock splits or as stock share funded buyouts.

With reverse stock splits, the corporation simply decreases the quantity of shares of its own stock available in order to increase the price per share. When a stock buyout takes place, the acquiring corporation creates more shares of its corporate stock with which to buy out the chosen target company. The target firm's shareholders then receive this newly created stock from the acquiring company in lieu of receiving cash payments for the target company shares they own.

There are a number of advantages to Share Consolidation buyouts done through stock funded purchases. The acquiring firm is able to buy the target corporation without having to deploy its own cash reserves or without getting a loan. This does not mean the transaction is free or completely without cost.

In creating the new shares, this diminishes the stock price of the buyer's shares. This can happen as investors decide that the target firm is worth less than the total number of shares which the acquirer is willing to pay. The present shareholders then own a lesser percentage of the firm and its future earnings. This is the case whether or not the value of their shares decreases or instead remains constant. It explains why many companies will instead utilize combination efforts of both cash and stock buyouts in order to successfully pay for an acquisition.

When a target firm becomes a part of the acquiring company, then its own corporate shares do not trade individually on the stock exchange any longer. One hundred percent of the target corporation's shares will be traded in exchange for the shares of the buying corporation as the transaction concludes. At this point, shares of the target firm will be delisted from all market indices they may trade in, as well as from the exchanges on which they were listed themselves. This also changes the aggregate value for the index the target company used to comprise. Managers of indices often choose to substitute in another corporation in place of the target corporation to maintain the same number of companies within the index in question.

The number of outstanding shares following the buyout will vary based on the relative values of the stock issues of both the selling and buying firms. When the shares of the seller prove to be higher priced than those of the acquirer, a greater number of shares will exist following the merger. As corporations merge their own shares in a reverse stock split, fewer remaining shares will exist following the operation or alternatively the combination.

When corporations choose to consolidate their shares utilizing reverse stock splits, this typically gives a warning that the corporation has run into trouble. The firm will quite possibly no longer be able to build up its share value via increasing its sales. This would be why they are trying to boost the share price to make it seem more valuable and expensive for the investors.

Once stock prices decline below the minimum allowed price set by the hosting stock exchange, they will be involuntarily delisted off of the exchange. This is why firms which are nearing bankruptcy may attempt to consolidate the price of their share to keep them over the threshold of this minimum price. For example, the NYSE New York Stock Exchange removes any corporation when the average price for its corporate stock drops under a dollar for any rolling 30 day long period.

Shareholder Value

Shareholder Value refers to the value of a company which stakeholders in the firm enjoy as a direct result of management growing revenues, earnings, and free flow cash in time. The actual value of any company comes down to the effects and results of the strategic choices that senior management makes and carries out for a firm. This includes both strong returns on their invested capital positions as well as making solid investments.

As value is built up over the longer term time frame, the price of the shares goes up and the company is able to pay out bigger cash dividends to its various stake holders. Unfortunately, the opposite is also true; share prices can fall while dividends can sometimes be cut out of dire necessity. Rising dividends is usually the sign of a healthy and growing company, while falling dividends are a sign of a weakening and sick firm.

The balance sheet of a given company will reflect a higher and growing shareholder value. This is tallied in the equity section on the corporate balance sheet. The formula for this balance sheet is stockholder's equity equates to the company assets minus the corporate liabilities. Stakeholder equity also includes retained earnings. These are the company's sum of all net income minus the cash dividends from the inception of the firm.

When the management of a company in question affects strong strategic choices which boost company earnings every year, the firm will gain the ability to either keep higher retained earnings to build up the business organically or to dole out a bigger cash dividend to its shareholders.

The EPS earnings per share of a firm can be appropriately defined as the earnings available to the shareholders divided up by the number of shares of common stock which are outstanding. This ratio proves to be the primary indicator of the shareholding value of a corporation. As the firm grows its earnings then such a ratio will also increase. It will cause the corporation to be looked on more favorably and valuably by investors.

Corporations have to raise significant amounts of capital in order to purchase assets. They utilize said assets to generate revenues.

Corporations which are effectively managed optimize their asset use in order to run the business with lesser investments in the assets. Take a concrete example to help understand this challenging concept. A plumbing firm may utilize both a truck and equipment in order to finish a residential plumbing job. The full cost of such assets amounts to $100,000. The higher the sales which the plumbing firm is capable of generating with the truck and plumbing equipment, the greater the shareholder value the company will create for its stakeholders. Companies which are valuable are able to generate higher and higher earnings using the identical amount of dollars in assets.

It is also true that creating enough cash inflows is necessary to run the business with solvency. This represents a critical shareholder value indicator. It also allows the firm to operate its company and grow the sales without having to resort to issuing additional shares of stock or borrowing additional sums of money from bondholders or alternatively from banks. Such firms are able to rapidly boost their cash flow through effectively collecting on their accounts receivables and quickly converting their existing inventory into sales.

This is why the rate of cash collection is so very important to any firm. It can be quantified via turnover ratios. Corporations will try to boost their sales without having to order and hold greater amounts of inventory or without needing to boost the typical dollar amount in actual receivables. A larger rate of accounts receivable turnover and inventory turnover will result in building up the share holders' value with time.

Shares Outstanding

The Shares Outstanding refers to the quantity of shares in a given company's stock which are presently owned by all of the shareholders in total. This also includes the larger share blocks owned by the institutional investors. It also encompasses the company officers' and insider shares which are restricted ones. Every corporate balance sheet will display this number under the category title of "Capital Stock."

This key company metric is utilized in determining such important attributes of a publically traded company as their market capitalization, their CFPS cash flow per share, and their EPS earnings per share. The number of shares for a particular firm is never static, but in fact can range significantly over the years. The concept is also referred to as outstanding shares.

The only type of company shares that are not a part of this Shares Outstanding figure are the treasury stock which the company holds itself. Corporate share numbers can and do change for a variety of reasons. When firms choose to float additional shares, this raises the total numbers. They often do this in an effort to raise fresh capital via equity financing or as employees choose to exercise their employee stock option benefits. It is also possible for total number of outstanding shares to decrease over time. This especially occurs when corporations buy back their own shares from the open market using a share repurchase program. These rebought shares then become additional treasury stock for the firm.

Corporations are required by the SEC Securities and Exchange Commission to make publically available the numbers off both outstanding and issued shares. This information will not only be included in the annual reports and company balance sheets, but also in the corporate websites under the sub pages of investor relations. They can also be determined from the stock exchange websites as well. This information is similarly contained within the quarterly filings with the SEC.

When companies engage in a 2 for 1 stock share split, this will double the total number of Shares Outstanding. Similarly, this total number will be reduced by half if they should engage in a reverse stock split of a 1 for 2 shares consolidation. The main reason a corporation would be interested in this mathematical trick with the share prices is because they want to reduce the company share price to an easier buying price range for smaller-pocketed individual investors. It will similarly boost the liquidity when they do so.

A company might also decide to consolidate their shares if their company share price has taken a severe hit. This will double the share price and restore it to what is often times an exchange-mandated minimum price range so that it meets the ongoing listing requirements. It might harm the stock's overall liquidity in the process, but it will likely discourage short sellers' targeting the issue since it makes it considerably harder for them to borrow shares for the physical short sales.

It always helps to consider a real-world example to demystify confusing concepts like this. In June of 2015, NFLX Netflix, Inc. revealed that they would engage in a seven for one stock split. The idea was to reduce the stock price drastically so as to make it more affordable. This would also increase the numbers of investors in the stock issue, they hoped. They did manage to increase the numbers of shares by a full seven-fold and cut the underlying price per share to one-seventh of its prior levels in the process.

With Blue Chip Stocks, increasing the number of Shares Outstanding generally boosts the value of the stock and the overall market capitalization of the issue as well. Because these larger and more successful companies tend to deliver success in the form of greater earnings and higher dividend payouts over the years, their prices which reduce in the wake of the stock split tend to float gradually back to where they were before the split.

Standard and Poor's (S&P)

Standard and Poor's is a global ratings agency that is also responsible for the S&P and Dow Jones indices in the stock market. Besides providing ratings on companies and products, they also rate governments' sovereign credit ratings. This company is based in the United States but has 26 offices throughout the globe. The corporation has shortened its name from Standard and Poor's Ratings Services to S&P Global Rating as of April 28, 2016.

The history of Standard and Poor's goes back over 150 years. Today they provide market intelligence that is high quality and well respected. They offer this in the form of their well known credit ratings, global research, and thought leadership. The company operates primarily as S&P Global Market Intelligence and S&P Dow Jones Indices.

Their division S&P Global Market Intelligence proves to be among the world leaders in delivering research and information on a variety of asset classes. They provide this with thought provoking analysis via a number of advanced platforms. Every year the company gathers more than 135 billions individual points of data in the pursuit of this goal. They cover 99% of all the market capitalization in the world. Standard and Poor's wants to be more than just the provider of financial data and intelligence. They are looking to be a creative force for transparency, growth, and the provision of value in the world's capital markets.

Each day this division of the company gathers, scrubs, analyzes, and interprets enormous amounts of data and content. They take this raw information and transform it to intelligence investors can act on covering industries and companies in the worldwide financial markets. Standard and Poor's Global Market Intelligence offers not only data but also valuable insight that helps readers to make more educated and intelligent investment and business decisions that impact the future.

This division boasts several core beliefs. These are relevance, accuracy, timeliness, and completeness. The group proves to be a foremost purveyor of analytics, news, research, and information to a variety of groups around the globe. Beneficiaries of this information include corporations, government agencies, universities, and professionals.

The solutions and data which lead the industry come from their subsidiaries SNL Financial and S&P Capital IQ. These combine to put together data from individual sectors and the comprehensive market with news and analytics. The tools that result allow the group's clients to perform a wide variety of functions. They can track their performance, identify ideas for investments, generate alpha, grasp dynamics of the competition in an industry, determine credit risks, and produce valuations.

This division boasts over 10,000 employees operating in 20 countries around the globe.

The other principal division of Standard and Poor's is the S&P Dow Jones Indices. This group turns out to be the biggest international source for concepts, research, and data on indices. It counts among its legendary financial indicators the Dow Jones Industrial Average and the S&P 500 indices. It has been working with these indicators for more than 120 years to create forward thinking market solutions which help to meet needs of both retail and institutional investors.

They began with launching the Dow Jones Industrial Average in 1896 and later produced the S&P 500 in 1957. This has made them an engine in many of the most critical financial creations of the 20th century. They now offer in excess of 1 million different indices that run the spectrum of many different asset classes throughout the world. The company claims that more assets have been invested in different products that are based on their indices than with any other company on earth.

Structured Finance

Structured Finance refers to the possibility of and procedures for issuing loans because of a reliable history of strong corporate cash flow. Instead of using assets for a loan's collateral, the funds are given out based upon the past history that shows a consistent cash flow in the business of the borrower. This cash flow will provide for the orderly and on- time pay back of the loan principle and interest. This type of financing is usually opted for when the more traditional methods either fail or are simply not practically available to a business.

It is also fair to say that structured finance proves to be an intricately involved and even complex financial instrument. This vehicle permits big companies and financial institutions such as banks to access complicated means for financing their needs. Such needs often will not be good matches for traditional financial products.

This structured finance has grown dramatically from the middle of the 1980s decade. It has evolved and expanded since then to be a significant player in the financial universe. Classic examples of such finance are CDOs collateralized debt obligations, CBOs collateralized bond obligations, synthetic financial instruments, and syndicated loans. Alongside CBOs and CDOs, there are also fairly new instruments like CMOs collateralized mortgage obligations, CDSs credit default swaps, and even hybrid forms of securities which may involve elements of both equity and debt instruments.

In fact it is most often corporations which find themselves in need of this structured finance funding. Many times they discover that a typical loan or even conventional instrument of finance (like corporate bonds) simply will not adequately meet their needs. Sometimes this is because the transaction needs to be discretionary and discreet. In order to accomplish this, creative solutions utilizing riskier instruments are employed.

The reality is that traditional types of lenders do not commonly offer such structured finance solutions and products. It is often up to investors to come up with the major cash infusions for organizations or businesses when such financing is required. Another interesting feature of these products is that they usually can not be transferred. This simply means that they can not be altered from one form of debt to another as with a standard loan.

On an increasing basis and frequency, governments, corporations, and financial intermediary organizations utilize such structured finance securitization programs. They are often deploying these to help manage risk, expand their reach of the business, develop one or more financial markets, or create new means of funding projects. In such scenarios, employing structured finance turns cash flows into lump sum payments. It also has the side effect and consequence of changing the liquidity of financial books and portfolios.

It is the process of securitization that actually creates these complex financial instruments. The magic of this process is that it creatively combines various financial instruments and assets into a single package. These repackaged instruments are rated according to a few tiers. The tiers then get sold on to investors. The advantage to this is that it encourages and fosters liquidity in markets and for businesses.

A typical example of the process of securitization is the MBS Mortgage backed security. When individual mortgages are grouped into a single pool, the issuer gains the ability to break up the large pool into various component pieces. They do this according to their risk of default. Smaller pieces can be sold off to investors, often for a better and more advantageous price by parts than the whole pool would fetch alone.

Utilizing structured finance is often appealing to a company that may lack significant physical assets which they can pledge as collateral. Yet they may possess a substantial base of clients as well as a documented, consistent history of both billing to and payments from their customers. Many times investors will loan money to these kinds of corporations. This is often true even if the companies are small. Investors will generally loan the company money on this basis for a better interest rate than a traditional bank loan would cost the firm to obtain. It also is a faster process with less administrative paper work than a typical business loan from a bank.

Subordinate Financing

Subordinate financing refers to that type of debt finance which ranks behind the primary finance. It is second in importance and position to debt that senior or secured lenders hold. This is important when a default occurs, as it determines who gets repaid first from any bankruptcy proceedings or foreclosure. The term signifies that senior lenders who are secured will be repaid before the debt holders that are subordinate.

Lenders who participate in this subordinate financing take on greater risk than the lenders considered to be senior. This is because they have a lower claim on the business or property assets. Sometimes this type of corporate finance is comprised of both equity and debt financing. A lender would be interested in this because it would offer them potential stock options or warrants that would reward them with extra yield as a means of compensating for the greater risk they take.

Where consumer borrowers and loans are concerned, subordinate financing would be a second mortgage. It takes second priority below the original first mortgage. First mortgages have the property to secure their loan and the debt. While nearly every mortgage is backed by the underlying property, first mortgages receive special seniority ahead of subordinated mortgages. This means the senior mortgage lender is repaid first in a foreclosure. With mortgages, subordinate financing could be a mortgage that is 80/20. In this case, the first mortgage would be 80 percent while the second mortgage that was subordinated represents 20 percent.

This means that only the lenders which are first mortgage holders are likely to get at least a portion of their money back if a borrower defaults in general. Should a borrower only default on the subordinate mortgage, this lender is able to foreclose on the property to regain its principal. Subordinated lenders could work to make their mortgage the senior one and then foreclose. They could do this by buying out their borrower's first mortgage. Afterwards, they could choose to subordinate the original first mortgage so that their once second mortgage became senior in the foreclosure.

Consumers should think carefully before participating in subordinate financing to obtain their houses. There are several disadvantages involved. Home owners will usually have to write two different mortgage payments each month if they do. They will also typically pay a higher interest rate on the second mortgage since these rates are usually greater than the first mortgage rates. There are also often two different loan fees, costs, and even discount points when first and second mortgages are used. Finally, this type of finance will often lead to a greater monthly payment when the two are combined than only one mortgage payment would.

The main reason that a home buyer would be interested in employing subordinated financing to purchase a home is because an 80/20 mortgage would not require them to come up with any down payment. It might also eliminate the need to pay for PMI private mortgage insurance which can be a substantial component of the monthly mortgage payment. This would depend on how the mortgage financing was originally structured.

Consumers will generally require a high credit score of minimally 700 in order to qualify for this subordinated financing. When borrowers have two mortgages, it will likely be impossible to obtain a home equity loan or line of credit at a later time.

Subordinated Debt

Subordinated Debt refers to a security or alternatively a loan which has a lower ranking to other debt securities and loans. This pertains to the claims on a corporation's earnings or assets in the event of repayment default. Analysts also call this a subordinated loan or a junior security alternatively. When the borrower defaults on the loan or security in question, those creditors who extended the loan or investment and who are only holding a subordinated security will not receive any compensation until after all of the senior most debt holders have received payment in full. In principal this means that they will get little if anything at all back in the event of an actual default. Subordinated Debt proves to be the precise opposite of unsubordinated debt.

It helps to explain why such Subordinated Debt is always riskier for creditors or investors than comparable unsubordinated debts prove to be. Those firms which borrow on a subordinated debt basis generally turn out to be huge corporations and other businesses. Their size gives them the air of likelihood to repay a less sure loan or security.

As corporations take on more debt, they will typically issue at least two types of bonds as subordinated and unsubordinated debt. Should the huge corporation later default and then file for bankruptcy, it will be the responsibility of the bankruptcy court to decide on the priority of loan repayments according to seniority of the creditors. They will order the firm to pay off its debts using the proceeds from the sale of the corporate assets according to a certain order of repayment. Lower priority repayment debt turns out to be the unlucky Subordinated Debt. Greater priority debt will be the unsubordinated debt.

As the term implies, the liquidated assets through bankruptcy sale will first pay off the unsubordinated debts. If there is any cash remaining after these creditors are made whole first, then the unsubordinated debt holders will receive a portion of their funds back according to the schedule set out by the bankruptcy court. In the unlikely event that enough cash remains, the Subordinated Debt becomes completely repaid. It is more likely that the subordinated holders will get a payment in part or nothing whatsoever.

This explains why Subordinated Debt is so very risky in practice. Potential lenders or investors always have to be aware of the solvency prospects of the company in question as well as its total assets and other more senior debt obligations when they are considering investing in a given bond issue. Yet risky or not, these less senior bond holders still have seniority over all classes of stock holders in the company, even the preferred stock holders. Subordinated Debt bondholders will receive a greater rate of interest than the unsubordinated ones in order to make up for the possible default risk, which is very real.

Like with any debt obligations, such Subordinated Debt will appear on the principal company balance sheet. First the balance sheet will actually list out the firm's current liabilities. Next comes the senior most debt, the unsubordinated issues, which will appear as longer term liabilities. Lastly, the subordinated issues appear as the longer term liabilities ranked according to their payment priority. As firms issue such subordinated bonds and then bring in the cash from the lender or investor, the cash account goes up, or alternatively the PPE property, plant, and equipment account. The firm's accountants simultaneously record a liability for the exact amount.

Swap

A Swap refers to a particular derivative contract. They allow for two opposite parties to exchange certain types of financial instruments as the name quite literally implies. While in theory the instruments involved in such an exchange could be practically anything, in reality the majority of them prove to deal with cash flows on a principal amount with which the two entities concur.

In general, the underlying principal will not be exchanged in the arrangement. The two cash flows each instead make up a single leg of the swap contract. The one will usually be variable while the other one is fixed. The variable one is generally based on an agreed upon benchmark interest rate, index price, or alternatively free-floating currency exchange rate.

These swaps never trade over exchanges. This prevents retail investors from becoming involved in them. Instead, these instruments prove to be specially traded over the counter contracts between financial institutions or firms. The most typical form of swaps is the interest rate swap. Other forms include currency, commodity, debt equity, and total return.

Interest rate swaps involve the participants changing out cash flows for the underlying rates based upon the idea of a principal amount. They do this to speculate or to hedge against the possibility of interest rates rising or falling. It is always illuminating to consider a real world example to better understand a difficult concept like this one. International British based banking giant HSBC may have recently issued out $5 million in five year maturity bonds that come with a yearly interest rate based upon the LIBOR London Interbank Offered Rate plus 1.5 percent. While the LIBOR rate remains at 1.8 percent, this would be low for the historical average range. HSBC would be nervous about the possibilities of the rates climbing.

To offset said risk, HSBC engages with Deutsche Bank in order to receive the annual LIBOR plus 1.5 percent on the principal. So Deutsche Bank will pay the interest payments on the HSBC most recent bond issue. In consideration for this, HSBC pays to Deutsche Bank a fixed yearly six percent interest rate on the same $5 million over the next five years. HSBC gains if the rates increase substantially during the next five years. Deutsche

Bank gains advantage if the rates should rise just slightly, remain flat, or decline instead over the five years period. It is important to realize that in the majority of cases, HSBC and Deutsche Bank would work through an intermediary company or other financial institution which would also participate in getting a piece of the swap deal for their trouble. Determining if such swaps make sense for two different companies comes down to the relative comparative advantage in the floating rate or fixed exchange lending markets which each enjoys.

Currency swaps involve the two participants changing principal payments and interest on debt which was originally denominated in other currencies. With these forms of swaps, the principal is not only notional. It is actually changed back and forth along with the interest payments. Entire nations can engage in these currency swaps. As a clear example, China has opened a currency swap with Argentina. This assists Argentina with stabilizing its own foreign reserves as a result. China gains the advantage of their currency being a little bit stronger and more desirable reserve currency as a result.

With commodity swaps, the pair is exchanging a predetermined floating commodity price. This could be the price of Brent Crude spot. They do this for a mutually decided on time frame. The most typically involved commodity swaps actually are for crude oil.

Debt equity swaps revolve around exchanging debt for equity. With publically traded firms, this literally means bonds in exchange for stocks. It helps corporations to effectively refinance their own debt in a far easier and less hassled way than getting approved for financing.

Finally, total return swaps are those which involve changing out a fixed interest rate in return for the total returns off of an asset. The group which will furnish the fixed rate will thus not have to spend its precious capital in order to hold the index or stock which it gets in exchange.

Syndicated Loan

Syndicated Loan refers to a special type of loan which a group of lenders provides to a borrower. It is also called a syndicated bank facility. The lending group that works in concert is known as a syndicate. Their mission is to pool their resources in order to offer funds to single individual borrowers. The borrower does not have to be a corporation in every single scenario. It could similarly be a large project, corporation, or even sovereign government. Such loans might be made up of credit lines, fixed dollar amounts in funding, or some happy combination of the two concepts.

The reason that Syndicated Loans become necessary is because sometimes projects grow too big for only one lender to underwrite them or because a particular project requires a specialized type of lender which boasts significant expertise and experience in handling a particular asset class. This permits them to spread around the considerable risk of the larger project and enables other financiers to have a part in such interesting and potentially lucrative financial opportunities which may be simply too big for the capital bases of the individual participants. The interest rates associated with this kind of loan will either be floating or fixed. This will hinge on a specific benchmark interest rate like the LIBOR London Interbank Offered Rate.

Various important components exist with a Syndicated Loan. The underwriter or lead bank is the agent, arranger, or leading lender. Such a lead lender will often put up a more significant percentage of the funding. It may also choose to handle such responsibilities as administrating the syndicate and dispersing the cash flows to the other members of the syndicate.

The primary ultimate goal in such syndicated lending lies in spreading around the default risk of the borrower over a range of lenders, including institutional investors, banks, hedge funds, and pension funds. As these Syndicated Loans are often far larger than a typical bank loan, the risks of only a single borrow defaulting could ruin only one lender. Such types of loans are also commonly employed with the leveraged buyout set in order to pay for a major corporate acquisition using both debts financing and funding.

Such Syndicated Loans will often be offered on what is called a best-effort basis. This means that when sufficient numbers of investors are not able to be brought on board, then the borrower's final amount will be less than originally forecast. Such loans might also be split into dual tranches. One group like the banks would be standard revolving funders while the institutional investors would be used to funding fixed rates varieties of term loans.

It is important to remember that Syndicated Loans are often way too big for only one lender to take on alone. It is always helpful to consider a real world example with a complex concept such as this one. Consider Tencent Holdings Limited. This just happens to be Asia's largest Internet company. They own WeChat and QQ instant messaging systems. They sought out a syndicated loan in the amount of $4.4 billion back on June 6th of 2016. Such a loan was anticipated to help fund additional company acquisitions. It was considered to be a fantastic investment for those investors who were looking out for a credit safe haven in the midst of rising default risks across China.

This loan was underwritten by five different major global financial institutions. These were HSBC Holdings PLC (Britain and Europe's largest bank), Citigroup Inc., Bank of China, Australia & New Zealand Banking Group, and Mizuho Financial Group Inc. The five mega banks combined their powers in order to fund a syndicated loan which was a five year term facility that they split between a revolver and a term loan.

Takeover

A takeover is a corporate event where a company chooses to acquire another firm in an effort to gain full control over the target firm in question. They often do this by buying a majority percentage of the firm's outstanding shares.

If such a move is successful, the company which is acquiring the target obtains control over and responsibility for its target firm's holdings, operations, and debts. If the target firm proves to be a publically traded stock company, then the company which is acquiring must place an offer to buy all of the outstanding shares of the target company.

There are several different types of takeovers in the world of business. Welcome takeovers are those like mergers and acquisitions. They typically proceed calmly as the two companies involved in the situation consider it to be a positive end scenario for all. The opposite type of takeover is known as hostile or unwelcome takeover. These often turn out to be aggressive since the receiving party does not willingly or voluntarily participate or even give its consent.

Hostile takeovers are exactly like they sound. The firm which is doing the acquiring may resort to underhanded tactics. Some of thee include a dawn raid. In this clever maneuver, a predatory firm purchases a large portion of the company's stock at the immediate opening of the market. This leads to a target firm losing control over its company before it even is aware of what is occurring. The target company's management and board of directors could choose to staunchly resist these unsolicited efforts via such defenses as taking a poison pill. Poison pills are where the shareholders of the target firm buy additional shares at a discounted price in order to dilute the holdings of the acquirer, causing the takeover to become potentially prohibitively expensive.

There are various reasons that a company would pursue a takeover. This is practically the same end result as an acquisition. Companies can perform like a bidder by attempting to build up their market share or create larger economies of scale which will aid the company in lowering its overhead so that it can boost its profits.

Firms which are the most attractive types of takeover targets are those which possess a unique advantage with a specific service or unique product. This includes smaller firms with profitable services or products but inadequate financing. Another similar company that is geographically near might decide that by combining their forces they could boost efficiency. Other examples are companies which are viable but that have to pay too high an interest on their debt which might be effectively refinanced for a better rate if a bigger and more powerful firm with superior credit ratings acquired it.

A few years ago, ConAgra tried to engage in a friendly takeover to acquire competitor Ralcorp. As the first advances were spurned, ConAgra demonstrated it would instead go the route of a hostile takeover. Ralcorp retaliated by instituting a form of poison pill strategy. ConAgra was not to be so easily outmaneuvered. They upped the ante by proffering $94 a share. This amounted to significantly more than the going rate of $65 per share for Ralcorp at the time the initial acquisition talks began.

Ralcorp declined and beat back the hostile attempts; though in the end the two companies came back to the negotiating table the next year. Eventually the deal succeeded via a friendly strategy as ConAgra paid $90 per share. At this point and time, Ralcorp had finished spinning off its division Post Cereal. This meant that the final price per share offering from ConAgra amounted to substantially more than the prior year's original offer.

Term Loans

Term loans refer to those loans a bank makes to a business or corporation for a set amount of time. These loans come with either a floating or a fixed interest rate and a pre-arranged schedule for repayment. There are numerous banks that offer such term loan programs to businesses so that they can access the funds they need for monthly operating expenses. Many times such a small business will utilize the cash they receive from this kind of a loan in order to buy equipment or other forms of fixed assets that they need for their production or manufacturing process.

Term loans are utilized for either working capital, purchases of real estate, or equipment purchases. These must be paid back in a time frame ranging from a single year on up to 25 years from issue. Payment schedules will either be quarterly or monthly. The maturity date will also be fixed on the loan. Actual interest rates could be pre-set or could vary with the floating interest rate benchmarks. Obtaining this kind of a loan will need appropriate collateral to be posted.

The approval process is exacting and extensive in order to lower the chances of default on such a loan. Small businesses which are established and that possess solid financial statements will find such loans to be appropriate for their situation. Banks will be more likely to approve them if the business is able to make a good faith down payment on the loan. This helps to lower the aggregate loan cost by reducing interest amounts and to decrease the minimum quarterly or monthly payment dollar amounts.

Funding amounts for these common commercial loans can range from $25,000 and higher. Bank loan officers usually subdivide such term loans according to one of two different categories. These are intermediate and long term loans. With intermediate loans, the loan maturity date is typically under three years. Such loans will commonly be paid back in monthly time-frame installments. There can be balloon payments due as well. Businesses expect to pay them out of their cash flow. The American Bankers Association states that repayment will typically be tied to the asset which is being financed and its useful life.

Conversely, longer term loans will last for more than three years and extend on up to ten or even 25 years long. The assets of a business will often serve as collateral for these bigger commitment loans. Usually either quarterly or monthly payments will come due. Businesses repay these installments utilizing either their cash flow or company profits.

Such longer-term commitment loans will generally come with clauses that restrict the number of other financial commitments the firm may assume in the form of debts, officers' salaries, and dividend payouts. Sometimes they will mandate that a given percentage of company profits must be put off to the side in order to pay back the loan.

While there are countless ways a business could deploy the resources from a term loan, some are more appropriate. The smartest ways to use them are through important capital improvements to the business, construction projects, large investment in capital, or buying other businesses. Working capital is another sensible use for such a loan.

The rates for these types of loans are typically competitive and not expensive relative to other forms of borrowing. They commonly cost approximately 2.5 percentage points over the prime lending rate for those loans which will be shorter than seven years. For the ones that are longer-term than this, around 3 percentage points greater than prime rates is normal. There will also be fees for such loans that usually amount to around one percent. Construction loan fees are often higher.

Trade Credit

Trade credit refers to special financing terms which are many times given to a business by a supplier. This situation arises when a business buys supplies or goods and the financial officer or owner of the vendor agrees to provide either all or half of the purchased order on credit. In the case of half on credit, the balance half would become payable on delivery of the merchandise to the business.

When businesses receive a half order trade credit, they have several possibilities for paying for the balance on delivery. If they have ample resources, they can simply pay with cash. Otherwise, they can borrow the money to pay for the other balance on the inventory. This is why such credit remains among the most critical means of lowering the amount of working capital smaller businesses especially require. It is even more common and necessary with retail operations.

Suppliers normally extend such trade credit to a purchasing business once they have been a regular client for anywhere from 30 days, to 60 days, to 90 days. This trade credit has the advantage of being interest free. An example of this concept helps to make it clearer. Perhaps a supplier ships the Great Sweater Company knitted hats. The bill might normally be due within thirty days. Since Great Sweater Company enjoys these special credit terms, they would have an additional 30 days to cover the cost of the knitted hats which the vendor supplied.

When companies first start a new business, it is difficult to obtain such credit from the suppliers and vendors. In fact they will initially require each order to be paid by either check or cash on delivery. This will be the case until the new business demonstrates that it can successfully pay its bill in a timely fashion. It is a common practice in the business world. For those startups that need to raise money to make the operations work in the early days, it is important for them to be able to negotiate some form of this credit with their suppliers. It becomes easier earlier if the business owner can provide a well-developed financial plan.

It is important for businesses to properly utilize this trade terms credit. When they become trapped in the mentality of it being a necessary means of permanently financing the operations, then the business is in trouble. Instead it should be viewed as a useful source of funding for covering shorter term and smaller needs. This credit is not really a longer term solution to the funding problem.

For businesses who do not avoid this trap, they often times become heavily committed to working with the supplier who generously extends such trade credit terms. The end result of this is that the business is not able to choose a more aggressively competitive supplier that provides better prices, more timely deliveries, and/or a higher quality product because they do not offer such generous credit terms for their buyers. There is a trade off for everything in business.

It is important to realize that trade credit is rarely free. Every supplier may have its own terms. Yet most of them will provide a significant cash discount for those businesses that pay their invoices in 10 days or less. The same as cash price may be for 30 days. By waiting for the 30 days to pay the invoice, it is costing the business the two percent discount. If a business chose to do this for 12 months a year, it would mean the merchandise was costing an additional 24 percent versus the price of paying the 10 days same as cash terms.

When a business pays after the 30 days credit expires, most vendors charge from one to two percent interest in penalties. By being late for a year, this could cost an additional from 12 to 24 percent. This is why effectively utilizing trade credit means that a business will need to plan intelligently ahead so it does not lose cash discounts consistently or pay late fee penalties needlessly. Little details like this separate successful businesses from ones which fail.

Unsecured Debt

Unsecured debt refers to a kind of loan that does not have any underlying asset which is backing it. This means that if the borrower defaults, the lender has no valuable property to seize against the loan's repayment. Such debt has a wide range of examples. These include credit card bills, utility bills, medical bills, and other forms of credit or loans which a financial institution offered without requiring any backing collateral.

These debts are extremely risky for lending institutions. The creditors will be forced to sue in an effort to collect their principal should the borrowers choose to not pay back the full amount of their obligations. It is not only personal bills which can be unsecured. Unsecured debt also includes business debts. Because the risk of default is considerable for the lenders, they usually charge higher rates of interest. This is a proverbial double edged sword. Since the higher rates make the financial burden heavier for the borrower, it can literally push them into default in an ironic self-fulfilling prophecy.

Borrowers have the ability to eliminate their unsecured debt. They can do this in the bankruptcy courts of the United States. The results will be that their debts are either discharged or restructured (in the case of businesses especially). Such an action will have consequences for the borrowers. They will find it harder to get unsecured loans in the future.

There are some important differences between unsecured debt and secured debt. Debt which is secured is backed up using a valuable asset. This could include the vehicle for which the loan is made, or the real estate for which it is provided. The official name for this is collateral. The legal terms in secured loans permit the lender to simply seize its underlying collateral which guarantees the loan if and when the borrower defaults on the payments. Secured debts cover a range of loans. These include title loans that vehicles secure and real estate or home loans that the property secures.

Naturally borrowers have far more to lose personally when they default on such secured loans than on any unsecured debts. This is because the loss of the borrower proves to be the gain of the lender in the respect of the collateral. Since this kind of debt turns out to be significantly less risky on the part of these lenders, they are happy to provide a more competitive interest rate, especially as measured against the rates on unsecured debt.

When a person does not make good on their pledge to repay on an unsecured debt, creditors will go through a number of steps. They first contact the borrower in an effort to recover payment. In the event that the creditor and borrower are unable to come to agreement on a revised repayment schedule, then the creditor moves on to the next steps in the process.

They will do one of several things. They might report the delinquent borrower to one of the big three credit reporting bureaus. They could also sell the delinquent debt on to a debt collection agency which will aggressively pursue debt collection. Finally, depending on the state in which the borrower resides, the creditor could choose to file a lawsuit in an effort to force repayment of the debt.

There are states such as Florida which do not allow legally forced collections of debt. These places protect the consumers from aggressive debt collection methods such as court ordered debt restitution. In other states, when creditors file debt collection law suits in the federal or state courts, the courts can decide to force the borrowers to pay back their unsecured debts utilizing certain available resources or assets.

Corporations also receive loans which are unsecured debt. When such debt issues are being rated by the bond ratings agencies, they will typically provide that issue with a lower rating. One example surrounds the Meta Financial Group which issued unsecured debt in 2016. The KBRA Kroll Bond Rating Agency determined that this senior unsecured debt deserved an only BBB+ bond rating because it was unsecured. This is relatively low, since junk bond ratings are BB. Highest ratings from this company were AAA ratings.

Meta Financial was fortunate to receive the BBB rating though there was no underlying asset backing the debt. This was due to the company's strong quality of assets, healthy liquidity profile, and positive capital ratios on a risk-weighted basis. Had the issue been instead secured debt, then the bond rating agency likely would have delivered an A or better rating.

US Trust

U.S. Trust today is the Bank of America Private Wealth Management division. It existed as an independent U.S. Trust Corporation from 1853 through 2000. At this time Charles Schwab and Co. acquired the bank and trust. They later sold it to Bank of America back in 2007. U.S. Trust today provides (as it has for two centuries) its clients with wealth structuring, investment management, and lending and credit facilities.

U.S. Trust has its headquarters in New York City on 114 West 47th Street in the United States. The firm counts more than 100 branch offices throughout the country across 31 different states plus Washington, D.C. They work to provide their ultra high net worth clients with specially tailored solutions and resources that help meet their needs for credit and banking, investment management, and wealth structuring. Teams of advisors serve the clientele through a wide variety of financial services. Chief among these offerings are financial and succession planning, investment management, specialty asset management, philanthropic asset management, customized credit products, family office services, family trust stewardship, and financial administration.

U.S. Trust arose in 1853 as a State of New York chartered bank. This makes it the original and also oldest such trust company within the United States. The new venture had the backing of a combination of wealthy investors who poured a million dollars into the firm which was called United States Trust Company of New York at that point.

Among the first board of trustees were thirty different influential and important New Yorkers. This included founding investor New York City Mayor Joseph Lawrence from the Bank of the State of New York who became bank trust president. Secretary of the trust went to United States Life Insurance Company of New York's John Aikman. Among the other important founders were industrialist, inventor, and philanthropist Peter Cooper; Marshall Field the department store founder; President Shepherd Knapp of Mechanics National Bank of the City of New York; and steel and iron manufacturer and railroad developer Erastus Coming.

The company became founded to serve clients of individuals and institutions as a trustee and executor of their money. This proved to be an innovative concept as trusts had not been fully conceived of at this point. It only took till 1886 for the firm to be well-established as a stable and highly regarded financial institution.

Thanks to this growing reputation, by the middle of the 1800's, the company had acquired a roster of super rich clients. It served a significant role in a number of nationally and internationally important construction projects like the Panama Canal and national American railroads. A great number of the firm's corporate clients floated securities to help finance such building project initiatives. The trust got to play the part of corporate trustee in the projects. Such a boom in enterprising and industrial projects aided the business in expanding into the management of personal trusts for the super rich as well. By the 1880's and 1890's, the firm counted such prestigious and ultra high net worth individual as William Waldorf Astor, Oliver Harriman, and Jay Gould.

The company successfully managed to survive and thrive despite a range of damaging financial crises in the last half of the 1800s and the early 1900s. In 1928, it counted over a billion dollars in trust assets. It stood well above its vastly smaller rivals. Thanks to the company's emphasis on stability, it managed to ride out the 1929 stock market crash and resulting decade long depression.

The company thrived by introducing additional specially tailored personal services in the next few decades. Among these were advising its ultra wealthy clients and families on careers, private schools, and universities for their kids. By 1958, U.S. Trust had begun its earliest ads in the newspaper society pages of The New Yorker. It was also advertising in the Metropolitan Opera and New York Philharmonic Society programs at this time.

Despite restructuring in the 1970s, 1980s, and 1990s, the company still became a takeover target by Charles Schwab and Co. in the year 2000. It ceased to be an independent prestigious outfit of nearly 150 years long at this point.

Valuation

Valuation refers to the method for ascertaining the present worth of any companies or assets. A range of techniques exist to decide this value. When analysts assign values to a firm, they consider the corporation's capital structure, the firm's management, and the potential of future earnings as well as the various assets' market values.

Securities' market values will ultimately be decided by the amount that buyers will voluntarily pay to sellers. This assumes that the two sides willingly choose to engage in the transaction. As securities become traded on exchanges, the sellers and buyers together set the true market value for the bonds or stocks in question. There is also the idea of intrinsic value. It means that the believed value for securities centers on either future earnings or another characteristic of the company that is not dependent on the going market price of the relevant security.

It is critical to understand the value of an asset in order to begin to make smart decisions for the organizations or the investors. They can not determine how much to pay or accept in takeover bids or investments, decide on which investments to include in a portfolio, determine how much and how to finance operations, or decide on dividends as part of running their operations without this foreknowledge.

The central concept behind valuation proves to be that investors, accountants, and analysts are able to engage in reasonable and realistic estimates in value on the majority of assets. This allows them to place values on financial and physical assets. It will always be the case that some kinds of assets are simpler to value than are other ones. Valuation details are not the same with every asset either. Uncertainties concerning the estimates of value will also be different with various assets. Yet in the end, what remains constant are the central principles for valuing assets.

There are basically three separate approaches for valuing any asset. The first method is using discounted cash flow valuation. Following this method of assigning value means that the asset's value must be correlated to the current value of the anticipated future cash flow for the asset in question.

The second means is relative valuation. In this method of determining asset value, The given asset value may be estimated by considering the relative pricing of like assets which have characteristics in common. Important characteristics in this consideration are cash flows, earnings, sales, and book values.

The third method analysts call claim valuation. This method works with pricing models of options in order to determine a value for the assets which have characteristics in common with such options. Each of these three attempts to provide values will often provide varying value estimates on the assets. This is why valuing models always provide their explanation for why they valued an asset in a given way at a different value from the rival other two models for valuing. It makes it easier for economists, investors, accountants, and analysts to choose the best model for valuing a particular asset.

Discounted cash flows prove to be a very popular method for assigning value to many financial or company held assets. Analysts and investors will work primarily with the outflows and inflows which the asset in question generates with this method. They must discount the cash flows with an appropriate discount rate to effectively value the assets based on future anticipated cash flows.

This discount rate adjusts for the future interest rates, inflation time value on money, and investor-required returns. When a corporation purchases a new machine, they will first contemplate the purchase price cash outflow and measure the anticipated cash inflows of the new asset. Whether they are inflows or outflows, they must all be discounted down to a current value so that the firm can come up with an NPV Net Present Value. When the NPV turns out to be positive, it makes sense for the corporation to go ahead with the investment into buying the given asset.

Venture Capital

Venture capital refers to the process of investors purchasing a portion of a start up company. Firms or individuals that engage in this are called venture capitalists. They pour money into a firm that offers a high rate of growth but that also contains high risk. The typical venture capital investment time frame generally proves to be from five years up to seven years. Such investors anticipate getting a profit back on their investment through one of two ways. Either they hope to sell their stake in an Initial Public Offering to the public, or they hope to sell the company outright.

Investors who involve themselves in venture capital investments often wish to obtain a certain percentage of the company's ownership. They might also request being given one of the director's seats. This makes it easier for the investors to ask to be given their funds back either through insisting that the company be sold or reworking the deal that they made in the first place.

Venture capitalist investments are comprised of three different kinds. One of them is early stage financing that might be broken down into seed financing, first stage financing, or start up financing. Seed financing means that a tiny dollar amount of venture capital is paid to an inventor or other entrepreneur who wants to open a business. This might be employed to come up with a business plan, do market research, or bring on a good management team.

First stage financing is the type needed as companies look to boost their capital so that they can begin full scale operations. Start up financing instead is venture capital distributed to a business that exists for under a year. In this stage, a product will not be on the market already, or will only just have been put on the market for sale.

A second type of venture capital investments is known as expansion financing. Expansion financing is comprised of both bridge financing as well as second and third stage financing. Bridge financing refers to investments that only receive interest and are short term. They are mostly employed for company restructurings. They might also be utilized to cash out early investors.

Second stage financing proves to be investment money for the purpose of growing a company already up and running. While such a company may not yet demonstrate actual profits, it is producing and selling merchandise. It also possesses inventories and accounts that are expanding.

Third stage financing is investments that venture capitalists make in companies that have at least broken even on costs or are even starting to demonstrate profits. In this case, venture capital is employed to grow the business further. For example, third stage financing could be utilized to develop more or better products, or to purchase needed real estate.

Still a different popular version of venture capital investing is known as acquisition financing. In this type of venture capital, the investment goes into gaining a stake in or the entire ownership of a different company. Management could also choose to use this venture capital to buy out yet another business or product line, whatever its development stage proves to be. They might acquire either a public or a private company in this way.

Weighted Average Cost of Capital (WACC)

Weighted average cost of capital (WACC) refers to a calculation of the cost of a capital for a company. It involves every category of the company's capital being weighed proportionately. Each source of capital for the relevant corporation will be considered by this designation. This means that preferred and common stock, bonds and all types of longer-term debt will all be included in the WACC calculation. It will go up with the rate of return on equity and beta increases. When the WACC increases, this means that the risk has increased while the valuation for a firm has decreased.

Calculating weighted average cost of capital requires taking each part of the capital components and multiplying them by their appropriate proportional weight. These individual calculations are then added together to come up with the WACC.

Companies can finance their needs through one of two main types of funding. This is either via equity issuing in the form of primarily stock shares or through debt issuance as with bonds. This measurement actually weights appropriately the two main forms of corporate financing, with each weighted according to its relevant utilization in a particular situation. It allows companies and analysts to decide how much every dollar they are financing will cost them in interest, making it imminently practical.

The reasons this is important are evident. The holders of equity and lenders of a corporation will demand specific minimal returns on their capital or lent money they have delivered. This is why WACC proves to be so useful. It shows the cost of capital for both the stake holders (as equity owners) and the lenders (as the debt holders). This means that both groups will be able to understand the levels and amounts in returns they can anticipate receiving. Another way of looking at the weighted average cost of capital is that this is the opportunity cost of any investor for assuming the risk which investing in the corporation entails.

A firm's WACC represents the all around return on capital for the company. This means that the directors of the corporation will commonly utilize the numbers internally to make appropriate decisions for the organization. Such decisions might include evaluating opportunities for expanding the business or the financial practicality of engaging in an acquisition or a merger.

It is helpful to consider examples to best understand this complex concept of weighted average cost of capital. Assume that a corporation is a money pond. Money comes into this pond out of two separate streams which are the sources. These streams represent the equity and the debt of the company. Money which the daily business operations bring in does not count as another source. The reason for this logic is that once a firm pays down its debt, any remaining money that they do not pay out as dividends or for share buybacks becomes what analysts call retained earnings held in trust for the shareholders.

Consider lenders that want eight percent return for their funds they loaned to a given company. At the same time, the stakeholders possessing the stock share may want a minimum 16 percent return on their investments or they will not hold onto the shares of the company. This means that the projects which the corporation funds using its money pond will need to provide an annual recurring return of 12 percent so that both their lenders and equity holders will remain happy. This 12 percent represents the weighted average cost of capital.

Going back to our original example of the money pond, if it contained $100 in debt holder money and $100 in investments from shareholders, the company might invest $200 in one of its projects. They would then require an annual return of 12 percent total, or $24 from the project funded by the pond. This would mean that $16 of this return was for the share holders while $8 of the total return was for the debt holders.

Wholesale Banking

The concept of wholesale banking pertains to those banking services which are done between merchant banks or commercial banks and various other financial institutions. This form of banking services has to do with bigger bank clients like enormous corporations or other financial institutions. In contrast, retail banking concentrates on individual clients and small businesses. Such particular banking services cover financing of working capital needs, currency conversions, large trade transactions, and a range of alternative and specialized banking services.

There are so many different avenues which wholesale banking covers. This specialized department within the mega banks handles capital markets products, integrated credit, and a range of different advice and guiding for risk management, funding needs, and investment products and services for international and domestic major corporate clients. Such products and services run the gamut of structured transactions, specialized finance, credit structuring, loan syndications, project finance and securitization, merchant banking, wholesale equities, and public sector financing of infrastructure projects.

Among the many different types of wholesale banking clients are corporations which are medium sized to large, institutional investors and clients, pension funds, governmental departments and agencies, and other global banks and financial institutions both domestic and abroad. The services which they often need in day to day operations include equipment financing, cash flow management, large loans, trust services, and international merchant banking.

The concept also relates to lending and borrowing between larger institutional banks and other financial organizations. Such lending mostly goes on in the interbank market and revolves around huge sums of money in practice.

The majority of commercial banks function as such merchant bank operations, providing wholesale banking services besides the more usual retail customer banking services. It makes it more convenient for those customers who require wholesale banking services, as they will not be required to track down and go visit a specialized financial institution. Rather they are able to deal with the same bank which handles the customer's individual retail banking needs.

The most understandable means of comprehending this wholesale banking phenomenon is to draw parallels with a discount superstore chain such as Sam's Club or Costco. These outfits trade in such enormous quantities that they are able to feature special deals and lower fees per dollar of sales. For bigger institutions or organizations, this makes it advantageous for them who possess high dollars of assets and business banking transactions to participate in this banking wholesale instead of going the more traditional retail banking customer services route.

As an example, many businesses possess numerous locations throughout the country. They often times require a solution for their cash management, which wholesale banking can easily provide. Technology companies are an especially relevant business line for this type of banking. Perhaps an SaaS firm owns 10 sales offices throughout the U.S. It might be that every one of its 50 sales department members needs their own access to the company's corporate credit card. The company owners also insist on every one of the regional sales operations maintaining at least $1 million in cash reserves on hand. This amounts to $10 million worth throughout the various offices combined. Companies with these type of needs will be too big for the traditional format of ordinary retail banking.

The owners of this company might instead contact a significant sized bank and ask for a corporate account which will handle each of the company's financial accounts. These services function as a facility which will provide discounts to the company in exchange for meeting a minimum dollar level cash reserve requirements as well as a minimum level of monthly bank transaction requirements. It is in fact easy for the SaaS company to hit such targets each and every month. This is why the company will seek out such a corporate facility in order to properly consolidate together each of its financial bank accounts so that it may effectively reduce its total fees. This makes so much more sense for a larger company than instead having 10 different regional bank checking account and 50 separate retail bank corporate credit card accounts.

Working Capital

Working Capital is a company metric. This proves to be a useful corporate measurement for two significant purposes. On the one hand it is a metric for discerning shorter-term financial health. On the other hand, it is also a means of ascertaining the firm's efficiency. The equation for working capital is current assets minus current liabilities. The working capital ratio is defined as current assets divided by current liabilities. This reveals if a corporation possesses sufficient shorter term assets to cover its shorter term time frame debt liabilities. Sometimes this concept is also referred to as net working capital.

When the number comes in at less than one, this reveals a negative working capital (also known sometimes as W/C). Any number which proves to be higher than two means that the company does not sufficiently invest its excessive assets. The most highly desired ratio proves to be a figure between 1.2 and 2.0.

The sobering facts are that when the firm's current assets are not greater than its current liabilities, it can run afoul of its creditors and the ability to repay them over the shorter term. In the worst case, bankruptcy can ultimately result. Decreasing working capital ratios throughout an extended time frame serve as a prescient warning that should be carefully and thoroughly investigated by analysts and would-be investors alike. It might be that the critical company metrics of sales volumes are steadily declining over time. This would mean that the account receivables amounts would go down and continuously deteriorate little by little.

This figure also reveals to investors and analysts alike the underlying operational efficiency of the firm. Money which is tied down in the form of inventory or which other clients still have not paid to the firm in due receivables will not be available to pay down company bills and other obligations. This means that if a company has consistently slow collections, it will be revealed as a rising number in the working capital figure. The best way to understand this is through contrasting the figure from one time period through to another one or even several like time periods. Slower collections can mean that the company and its operations have potentially fatal flaws.

It is important for investors to remember that high working capital ratios do not signal good things for the company in question. Instead, it means either that they are not sufficiently investing their excess reserves, or that they possess too large an inventory. Investors know all too well that they can quickly ascertain the company balance sheet strength by considering three important categories of quality. These include asset performance, working capital adequacy, and capitalization structure.

This means that analysts can discern the real liquidity of the firm and its efficiency with regards to the current position of the firm. Companies utilize an analytical tool to successfully accomplish this. It is called the firm's cash conversion cycle. Still, while companies like to bandy about this number in such important arenas as their annual reports, the quantity of working capital does not provide much insight on the quality of the liquidity position of the firm in question.

The cash conversion cycle proves to be the gold standard analytical tool for assessing the investment grade quality for the two crucial assets of the firm, the accounts receivable and the inventory. This CCC cycle is made up of three standards. These include the trade receivables category, the trade payables category, and the associated ratios pertaining to the inventory turnover. The three parts may be detailed in a number of days or a number of times each year.

Yield

In business and finance, yield is the word that states the quantity of cash that comes back to a security's owners. It is measured independently of variations in price. It proves to be a percentage of total return. It is used for measuring the return rates of fixed income investments, such as bonds, bills, strips, notes, and zero coupons; stocks, including common, convertible, and preferred; and various other insurance and investment hybrid products like annuities.

Yield can mean different things in varying situations. It is sometimes figured up as an IRR, or Internal Rate of Return, or alternatively as a ratio. Yield describes an investment owner's entire return or a part of the income.

The end result of the many differences in yield is that they can not be compared one against the other. This is because they are not all the same from one branch of finance and investments to another. You could see numerous different formulas for figuring up yield used by different investments and groups.

Bonds are a classic example of this. Nominal yield is also known as coupon yield. This proves to be the face value of a bond divided into the annual interest total. Current yield instead is those interest payments over the bond's price on the spot market.

A yield to maturity is the internal rate of return on the bond cash flow, including the bond principal when maturity arrives plus the interest received, and the purchase price. Finally, a bond's yield to call is the bond's cash flow internal rate of return if it is called in by the company at their earliest opportunity.

Bonds yields are unusual in that they vary inversely to the price of the bond. Should a bond price decline, then the yield will rise. If instead the rates of interest drop, then the bond's price will go up in general.

Some securities come with real yields. TIPS are a primary example of this. A real yield means that the face value of the instrument will be adjusted upwards compared to the CPI inflation index. It would then be set against this principal that is adjusted to make certain that an investor makes a better return than the rate of inflation.

This ensures that his or her purchasing power is protected. TIPS are one rare investment that will not allow investors to lose money if they purchased them in the auction and keep them until they mature, either as a result of deflation, meaning falling prices, or inflation, signifying rising prices over time.

Yield to Maturity (YTM)

Yield to Maturity is also widely known in investment and analyst circles by its acronym YTM, as well as by the phrases book yield and redemption yield. This represents the aggregate return which investors can expect to receive for a bond if they keep the security until the end of its actual life. This is why YTM is generally called a longer term bond yield even though it is still expressed as a rate per year. Another way of saying this is that this proves to be the investment's internal rate of return for the bond if the owner keeps it all the way through maturity. This assumes of course that the bond issuer makes all of its payments both on time and in the full amounts contracted.

In order to understand the Yield to Maturity calculations, it is critical to realize that the formula assumes all coupon payments the issuer makes will be exactly reinvested for the rate of the current yield of the bond. The formula similarly considers the bond's par value, current price on the market, term to maturity, and coupon interest rate. All of this makes the YTM a complicated yet good formula for determining the return of a bond. It allows investors to effectively compare and contrast those bonds which possess varying coupon rates and maturity dates.

There are several different ways to figure out the Yield to Maturity. It is a complicated formula so many investors simply fall back on pre-printed and -figured bond yield tables. Determining the exact YTM requires either a software program or the use of a financial or business calculator. This is because the value for a basis point drops as the price for a bond increases in an inverse manner. Many firms actually calculate YTM for six month time frames as well as on an annual basis. They do this because most coupon payments take place twice per year.

A significant difference between Yield to Maturity and the current yield lies in the fact that the YTM takes into account money's time value, while the simplified current yield computations will not. This is why investors often prefer to utilize the YTM instead of the current yield when they are crunching number on bond returns to compare and contrast with other bond issues and different types of investments.

There are a number of similar yet still variations on the classical Yield to Maturity figure. These should never be confused with the true YTM. Among these are the Yield to call (YTC), Yield to put (YTP), and the Yield to worst (YTW). Yields to call go with the assumption that the bond issuer will recall the bond by repurchasing it in advance of it reaching maturity. This assumes that the resulting cash flow period will be shortened. Yield to put is much like the YTC, only the seller is allowed to and may sell the bond back to its issuer on a specific date for a pre-determined price. Finally, Yield to worst means that the bonds in question can be put, called, or even exchanged. This is why YTW bonds usually have the smallest yields from the three variations on YTM and the YTM rate itself.

There are some important limitations to the utility of Yield to Maturity as a measurement for comparing and contrasting various bonds against other bonds and other forms of investment classes as well. With YTM, these calculations never take into account the actual taxes which investors will have to pay on the bonds. This is why YTM is sometimes called the gross redemption yield. These calculations for yield also do not factor in either selling or buying costs for the bonds themselves.

It is also important to keep in mind that YTM is limited by the fact that both it and current yields are estimate calculations. They can not ever be 100 percent accurate or reliable. The true returns will vary with the realized price of a bond when a holder sells it. The prices of such bonds can vary significantly as the market actually determines them (and not the issuer). Such variations in the value of a bond and the price for which it is sold may impact the YTM substantially. They more drastically impact the current yield calculations and measurement in the end.

Zero Balance Account (ZBA)

The zero balance account, also known by its acronym ZBA, refers to the type of checking account which maintains a permanent balance of zero. The account does this through an automatic transfer of funds out of a master account. The amount which transfers over only proves to be sufficient enough to cover any and all checks which other financial institutions present to the bank where the holder's account resides.

Corporations utilize these zero balance accounts in order to draw down excessive balances from separate accounts. It also helps them to keep better and stricter control over amounts they disburse in the ordinary everyday course of business operations.

These accounts will therefore only have a zero balance within them. The only exception to this zero balance account status is when checks are written against them and presented to the bank in question. In this way, companies are able to keep the balances as close to zero for accounts that do not have any reason to hold excessive reserves. The activity in these ZBA's is restricted to only processing payments. This is why they do not maintain any ongoing balances.

Because of this, a larger sum of funds will remain available for the company to deploy. They can instead put them to work in investments and company cash flow purposes rather than keeping low dollar amounts lying idly by in a number of sub-accounts. It does not present a problem when checks must be paid off from these special zero balance accounts, since the electronic clearing system recognizes that these accounts are in fact ZBA's and they will move the necessary funds over from the master account at the financial institution in the precise dollar amount needed to clear the check.

Companies and other organizations can also rely on a zero balance account to fund purchases which employees make with their debit cards. This allows them to carefully monitor all of the financial transactions and any activities which take place on the cards, since the debits must be pre-authorized. This works well for companies and charitable not for profit organizations which are protected by not maintaining any idle funds within the ZBA's.

The debit card transaction will not be approved by the bank which backs them until and unless the requisite funds become available to the account by a transfer from the authorized account representative at the firm or NGO. This means that debit card transactions simply can not be run without prior authorization by the appropriate superior in the organization. Businesses are able to reduce their risks of activities which are not approved of occurring.

This is critically important to especially larger organizations with many employees and numerous sub accounts and associated corporate debit cards. There is no better spending control oversight for these types of situations than the zero balance account. Incidental charges can be monitored throughout the sizeable operations.

Since incidental expenditures are variable in nature, it is harder to fund and control them without such an account. Large companies and not for profits effectively reduce rapid access to the company or charitable funds with these debit cards. In this way, they have put into place the best practices for approval procedures. It ensures that such procedures will be adhered to in advance of a purchase being made by an employee.

As budget monitoring tools, these ZBA's are also ideal. They may be established as one account per department or business operation. This allows the accountants at the company an easy and fast means of monitoring annual, monthly, and even weekly to daily purchases. The company book keepers are also able to effectively track particular shorter term projects and their financial expenditures by utilizing such a ZBA. Projects which are in jeopardy of running significantly and rapidly over budget also benefit from such accounts. The overseers can maintain control of all purchases by requiring proper approval and notification before the charges take place.

The master account of such zero balance accounts is the critical component of this entire concept. As the central operational center for all fund management in the organization, the account will be employed to disperse funds to all ZBA subaccounts as needed. These master accounts typically include other benefits like better interest rates for balances which they hold.

Other Financial Books by Thomas Herold

The Money Deception - What Banks & Governments Don't Want You to Know

High Credit Score Secrets - The Smart Raise And Repair Guide to Excellent Credit

Other Books in the Herold Financial IQ Series

99 Financial Terms Every Beginner, Entrepreneur & Business Should Know

Personal Finance Terms

Real Estate Terms

Bank & Banking Terms

Corporate Finance Terms

Investment Terms

Economics Terms

Retirement Terms

Stock Trading Terms

Accounting Terms

Debt & Bankruptcy Terms

Mortgage Terms

Small Business Terms

Wall Street Terms

Laws & Regulations

Financial Acronyms

www.ingramcontent.com/pod-product-compliance
Lightning Source LLC
Chambersburg PA
CBHW071544210326

41597CB00019B/3111